About the Author

Michael Keating is a journalist and photographer who has been active as both an alpine and cross-country skier since childhood. His columns on skiing have appeared regularly in several newspapers. Keating has recently travelled to a wide range of ski areas across Canada to write feature articles for *The Globe & Mail.*

Michael Keating's
Cross-Country Canada

Handbook and Trail Guide
for Cross-Country Skiers

Foreword by Jack Rabbit Johannsen

Van Nostrand Reinhold Ltd., Toronto
New York, Cincinnati, London, Melbourne

To my wife, Nicole, whose encouragement and help made this book possible.

Cover Photograph: Simon Hoyle
Design: John Grant/Grant Design
Printed and bound in Canada by The
Alger Press Limited

Photo credits will be found on page 212

ISBN 0-442-29868-4
Library of Congress Number
76 29501

76 77 78 79 80 81 82 83 8 7 6 5 4 3 2 1

Foreword

This book will be welcomed by every cross-country skier who seeks health and recreation through this greatest of all outdoor sports. It will help both expert and beginner to strike out with confidence into our wonderful Canadian wilderness, using equipment adapted to comfortable travel in rough or easy country and on any kind of snow.

When I was an active competitor in Norway during the early 1890's, we used the same pair of skis for slalom, downhill, jumping and cross-country, and our crowning achievement was the 50-kilometre race. An entirely new course was laid out for each competition, over deliberately difficult terrain and often under varying snow conditions. Since no competitor was allowed to run the course before the official start, each participant had to draw upon the agility he had learned in slalom, the courage he had acquired in straight downhill running, and the balance necessary for jumping. The 50-kilometre race was much more than proof of prolonged endurance. It was a real test of all-round skiing ability.

Since that time I have retained a keen interest in skiing, and have had a good deal to do with the development of the sport in a number of countries.

It is a sad fact that whenever any sport comes into vogue, it is not long before it is commercially exploited. It is no surprise, therefore, that when slalom and downhill became increasingly popular in the 1940's, both disciplines fell easy prey to big business. Enormous sums of money were spent on costly facilities which included chair lifts, artificial snow, and the usual complement of bars, restaurants and satellite industries. At the same time, individual equipment became highly specialized. Exaggerated boots, heavy skis and safety bindings made their appearance. These were designed for faster and faster speeds on mechanically groomed slalom and downhill slopes, but were impossible to manoeuvre independently on the level or for uphill climbing. The skier became a virtual slave of his equipment, and what had been a simple sport soon became an expensive racket.

But the pendulum is now swinging back. Today, some 30 years later, many skiers are tiring of the crowded slopes. They long for the wide open spaces away from the herd. And what do they find? The exploiters are already lying in wait for them with more specialized equipment and with artificially scored tracks, this time to accommodate extra light-weight skis, which are totally useless if the skier is forced off the path into deep snow. The developers are, in fact, trying to turn cross-country skiing (which has been a normal means of winter transportation in Norway for 4,000 years) into yet another kind of money-making rat race. They are marketing skis in proliferating styles, many of them quite unadaptable to varying conditions. In eliminating weight, they often sacrifice strength. They ignore the fact that the key to the real joy of ski-touring lies in dependable, durable, simple equipment with which one can leave the beaten trail and skim the fresh snow, penetrating with minimum effort into new and untrampled territory.

That is why I like this book. It takes the mystery out of cross-country skiing. It opens up untold possibilities for healthy winter enjoyment. It stimulates independence, resourcefulness and initiative in the individual, and it stresses our collective responsibility towards the snowy environment on which our sport depends.

Read this book. Digest it. And then get out on your skis. The hills are waiting! Good luck.

"Chief Jack Rabbit"
H. Smith-Johannsen

Preface

Cross-country ski touring is one of the most explosively popular sports in Canada. By 1976 the Canadian Ski Association estimated there were about one million of us on "skinny skis" and hundreds of thousands of people joining the ranks each year. That means there are hundreds of thousands of people seeking instruction and looking for places to try out their new skills and equipment. The aim of this book is to serve all these needs. It is the first book to compile a nation-wide list of trails and provides information on over 400 routes with more than 11,000 km of skiing from St. John's, Newfoundland, to Victoria, British Columbia and from the heart of Toronto to the high Arctic.

The first section gives general information about cross-country skiing. It illustrates basic technique, outlines equipment and describes such aspects of outdoor winter life as navigation, ski touring, winter camping, survival, winter photography and car tips for skiers. This is a survey of the subjects which should be of considerable help to newcomers to the sport but which will also provide information of use to intermediates and experts. It will help you join the many other Canadians who have discovered the pleasures of this sport.

In the trails directory there is something for all types of skier: small but convenient trails tucked away in city ravines, ski resorts in the country, and remote wilderness trails for the expert. They are organized by province and where there are large numbers of trails within a province there are regional subdivisions. In addition to listing trails, the book gives where possible a description of the type of skiing and such features as food, shelter, instruction and rental equipment. It tells where to write for lodging and general tourist information and describes some of the more popular ski events such as marathon races.

Cross-Country Canada will help you discover the skiing possibilities not only in your own region but in other parts of the country as well. It is a book to be read at home while planning winter weekends and longer vacations, and a book to be slipped in a suitcase, packsack or jacket pocket during the trip.

I would like to thank the many people across Canada who took time to answer my queries for ski trail information and who often included encouraging notes showing a desire for this kind of book. In particular I wish to thank Mike Exall and John Ardill of Seneca College, Robert Rick of the Alpine Club of Canada, Mike Naughton of the Federation of Ontario Cross-Country Skiers, and the cross-country division, national office, Canadian Ski Association for special help. And, I want especially to thank Doretta Keating, who encouraged my endeavours in skiing from the start.

M.K.

Contents

Introduction

Cross-country skiing is one of the sports most suited to the Canadian climate and terrain. In a country that is snowbound anywhere from three to six months each year, these light skis are an ideal method of transportation and recreation. Canadians began to discover the pleasures of winter vacations with the boom in downhill skiing which started in the late 1950's. The physical and financial demands of downhill skiing however, limited its popularity to some degree. Now, cross-country skiing opens up possibilities of a winter holiday almost anyone can enjoy.

The equipment is not very expensive and many trails are free. Even the cost of lodging is usually lower in the winter. Beyond the range of permanent shelter, the even more exciting world of winter camping awaits the hardy and adventurous. It holds no fears for those who feel at home in the out-of-doors, those who would meet nature on her own terms and enjoy the experience.

Cross-country skiing can be either a solitary or a convivial sport. On the one hand, there is the lone skier making his way through the silent woods, enjoying the feel of fresh snowflakes on his face and the natural rhythms of an easily moving body; on the other hand, a group of friends around a campfire sharing a thermos of coffee and a hunk of sausage. The sport has brought back ''the good old days'' of skiing, the atmosphere of an era when there was just one type of skiing. Much of that cameraderie was lost in recent years when the downhill version of the sport became a highly developed industry.

The earliest days really go back thousands of years, to the early inhabitants of Northern Europe. Archeologists have unearthed pieces of skis which have been buried in peat bogs for about 4,500 years. Runestone carvings found in Finland and dated to 2,000 B.C. show people on one short and one long ski. Since it has been established that Nordic settlers landed on the tip of Newfoundland 1,000 years ago, we might claim Canadian ski history goes back that far, but it is safer to refer to the records indicating that skis were seen at an ice carnival in Quebec City in 1759.

Until this century, skiers walked and slid as best they could on wide boards with no special ski waxes to help them grip the snow. Then two things happened: the development of waxes which would both grip and slide on snow and the building of mechanical ski lifts. The former discovery led to the system of waxes which now enables us to climb up hills without sliding backward, then glide down the other side. The latter led to the splitting of the sport into two distinct branches. Now there is cross-country, sometimes known as nordic skiing because of its origins, and there is downhill, often referred to as alpine skiing because of its development in the Alpine regions of Europe.

While the downhill skier is garbed in heavy clothing, slides on wide, stiff skis and is locked in high, plastic boots, the cross-country skier is lightly clad and slips along on skis made of flexible strips of wood or synthetics. It is this sense of lightness and freedom that has attracted many people to the sport, but there are other factors. Two of them are health and the environment.

Medical-scientific studies prove what cross-country skiers have long suspected: the sport is one of the most complete and effective methods of exercise one can find. It is frequently compared to marathon running with the added factor that skiers, using their arms to pole, do about 18 per cent more work than the runner. In addition to the simple muscular exercise, the skier burns hundreds, even thousands of calories in an outing and develops the heart and lung capacities. Living proof of the benefits of the sport are found in the meeting rooms of cross-country ski clubs around the world. There are very few overweight, out of shape serious cross-country skiers.

At a time when more and more people are seeking relief from the mechanized world, cross-country skiing is a refreshing change. It is a sport of varnished wood, waxed leather and figures moving across a white surface in a silence broken only by the occasional shout or laugh. The skis carve a thin line in the snow that will shortly disappear into the wind or under a fresh snowfall. However, even this brief passage has some effect on the environment by compacting the snow on top of plant life and the burrows of tiny animals. For this reason, skiers who seek each other's company should know when it is time to move to another route rather than crowd a trail that has already been over-used.

This book should offer some of those alternatives.

Basic Equipment

One of the great pleasures of cross-country skiing is the light, graceful equipment. Particularly for people used to the heavy, sometimes cumbersome gear developed for downhill runs, the slender skis and low-cut boots developed for gliding over the snow can be a revelation. And cross-country outfits are delightfully simple.

The delicate lines of the skis are broken only by small, metal bindings which clamp the toes of the low, leather boots in a firm grip but leave the heels free to rise and fall in a natural stride. Poles are long, slender wands to be rhythmically swung and leaned upon as the skier slips across the frozen countryside. Suitable clothing means something loose and relatively light in weight, since the constantly moving skier generates a steady flow of body heat.

Another pleasure of cross-country outfits is the relatively low cost — especially in comparison to the expensive downhill material. As a rough minimum you should count on spending about seventy-five dollars for a cross-country package: decent wood skis with aluminium bindings, leather boots and bamboo poles. A comfortable outfit can be made from long johns, jeans, sweaters and a nylon jacket, but as time goes on you will most likely want a pair of the comfortable knicker pants and possibly a matching jacket with such features as a windproof front, stretch inserts and zippered pockets.

There are a few rules to remember when buying equipment, especially a whole outfit. The first is to take time to find out what you need and to get it properly fitted. In other words, don't hit the first ski shop on the street after five on Friday and expect to walk out of the place properly outfitted by closing time. You'll probably need at least an hour to choose a pair of skis. If ski fever hits you overnight, go to a nearby resort on Saturday morning — early Saturday morning — rent equipment and take a lesson. In any case, renting is not a bad idea since it lets you try the sport for a few dollars.

Even if you feel ready for the salesman take a bit more time to ask some other skiers and several ski shop people for advice on what equipment sold in your area would suit your needs. Shop around as long as you're at it. Many stores will offer a discount if you buy a package and most have sales before and after the peak season. These days competition is so fierce that there seem to be ski sales at every time except Christmas. If you know what you want, keep an eye out for ski swaps run by local clubs. Sometimes there are genuine bargains among the battle-scarred relics.

A word about discount and mail-order houses. Know what you are after and what size you need. In the case of the mails there will be a long wait if you make a mistake and some discount houses economize so much on staff that you practically have to serve yourself. The advantage of a specialty ski shop is that it usually houses some expertise, but again make sure your salesman is not just a downhill specialist or a tennis bum sitting out the winter. Ask some pointed questions; for example, what kind of skis does he use and why does he think Brand X is best for you?

Once you latch onto a good salesman, give him a good idea of your ability and ambitions so he can advise you well.

Skis

Believe it or not, the wide, stubby skis used by many downhill skiers and the long, narrow skis for cross-country trips have a common origin. Skis seem to have first evolved in the northern parts of Scandinavia and Siberia in various combinations, including pairs in which a short ski was used for pushing and a long one for gliding. During the last century, the skis brought to North America by Scandinavian immigrants were each the same length and two or three feet longer than the skier was tall. This type of ski, a board planed, sanded and then steamed so the tip could be bent up, was used as late as the 1950s. About the only place you see them now is over the mantels of fireplaces in ski lodges.

Over the past several centuries downhill skiing as a specialty evolved slowly — perhaps because until ski lifts were developed in the 1930s, the equipment still had to allow for skiers to walk and climb back up hills. With the advent of lifts and crowds, ski slopes became hard packed and strong, heavy skis with steel edges were introduced for the downhill runs. On the other hand, cross-country skis were being made even slimmer and lighter for speeding along tracks in the snow. Now a pair of light touring skis weighs and costs about half as much as its downhill equivalent.

In this century manufacturers started gluing different types of wood together to get the best combination of strength, springiness and durability from a wood ski. Good laminated skis can have as many as thirty-five strips of wood sandwiched together. Despite the arrival of metal and fiberglass materials, wood skis are still a good investment and offer a few advantages.

In addition to the beauty of well-varnished wood, you can count a price advantage and the fact that wood is still the best base material for cross-country skiing. No synthetic will directly take wax as well as a wood base or continue to grip the snow as well once the wax wears thin. Some people take satisfaction in caring for wood and develop a rapport with the skis as they carefully soften pine tar with a torch and rub it into the bases each year to waterproof the wood.

But in cross-country as in downhill equipment, fiberglass is likely to take over in the next few years. Synthetics are generally stronger and they are virtually immune to warping if carelessly stored. You can get a quite decent pair of wood skis for about forty dollars, and seventy dollars or so should buy the best of that type. Fiberglass skis start at about that range and can cost more than one hundred dollars.

Ski sole or base design is still in a state of flux. On the one hand there is the classic wood surface which must be waterproofed periodically with pine tar but which holds wax well. Then there are the various types of smooth plastic bases found on all synthetic and some wood skis. They don't need tarring against wetness, but they do need more careful waxing than wood to achieve the proper grip.

There is some experimentation with slippery plastics such as P-Tex used on downhill skis. The theory is that the plastic will provide all the glide necessary and a small amount of sticky wax will give the grip needed to get moving.

For several years there have been moderately successful attempts to eliminate waxing completely by designing a sole which will both grip the snow and allow gliding. The major designs are either a step or fish scale-like pattern in the plastic or strips of short bristles, often referred to as Fiber-Tran or Mohair. However, these designs are not as effective in all types of snow as waxes and they are usually recommended for casual skiers.

No matter what the color, construction or base design, the key factor in choosing the right type of cross-country ski is width. Basically there are four types: mountain, touring, light touring and racing. Any ski wider than 60 mm (about 2 ½ inches) at the centre is considered a mountain-type ski and is best suited for people who climb high hills and make long runs in all types of snow conditions. These are virtually downhill skis and are unsuited for the kick and glide motions which propel cross-country skiers over flat ground.

Next in size is the touring ski, the widest true cross-country ski. With a width of about 55 mm under the bindings, touring skis are big enough to float over unbroken snow and strong enough to handle the sometimes abrupt changes of terrain one finds while bushwhacking off the beaten track. This is a good ski for someone who will be skiing both on and off prepared trails and might carry the occasional pack or wander into hilly terrain where the descents won't be too steep for wide, gentle turns.

Slimmest of the general purpose skis are the light touring models, which are about 50 mm wide at the waist. Though not as strong, stable or good at floating over soft snow, the light touring models are livelier and faster. Many recreational skiers, especially those who will usually be skiing tracks made by other skiers, choose them for lightness and speed, and some professionals even use them in the bush and mountainous terrain.

The narrowest skis– 40 to 50 mm– are the racing models. These slender boards are meant specifically for flashing along prepared tracks and are not suitable for all-round use. Choosing the right width of ski is simply a matter of deciding what type of skiing you want to do.

Choosing the right length is also fairly easy. There is the classic method of raising your arm straight up and picking a ski that comes to about your wrist or palm. Then there is the more recent paper test in which you stand on a ski on a flat surface and should just be able to pull a sheet of paper from under the mid-point. Many ski shops have simple charts which correlate height and weight of purchasers to the correct ski length.

Boots

Just as there are four general types of skis there are four boot types to give the right degree of flexibility and control. You need something like a hiking boot to muscle around a mountain ski, while the racing boot is like a lightweight track shoe. The touring and light touring boots are also quite light and flexible to allow a good stride.

In cross-country boots, more than anywhere else in the sport, tradition is hanging on. Though synthetic soles have almost completely replaced leather, natural material is still the best for the uppers. Its unique advantages are that it remains supple at all temperatures and it breathes– allowing perspiration to escape from around your feet. Until a synthetic with these properties is discovered and produced at a reasonable price, we will continue to be best shod in leather.

Leather, like wood, is sensitive to moisture over a period of time and needs some protection. Boots should be regularly treated with wax or shoe polish and should be waterproofed with silicone or a paste called Sno-Seal. If you are skiing in very wet conditions, such as in the spring, consider a pair of neoprene overboots sold in ski shops.

When you are buying boots you should expect to pay thirty dollars and up for adult models. High quality boots can hit double that base figure. Look for good, even, heavy stitching, a solid bond between upper and sole, and resistance to twisting motions such as you exert when turning skis.

If you are going to be skiing off the beaten track at all, you will also want a snow cuff. This is a padded area around the opening in the boot and will fit snugly against your ankle to keep snow from getting into the boot. All cross-country ski boots have three small holes drilled into the bottom to mate with the three pegs in cross-country ski bindings. Almost all manufacturers have adopted the Nordic norm to standardize the fit of boots to bindings, but it is still wise to actually try out your equipment for fit in the ski shop.

You may be surprised to see that many cross-country boots are lined only with a thin layer of leather-like street shoes. While your feet would freeze solid if you just stood around in them, the constant motion of skiing sends a steady flow of heat to the extremities. If you plan to tour during very cold weather and to stop for lunches, or if you suffer from cold feet, consider a pair of fleece-lined boots with room for a heavy pair of socks. You can beef up this insulation on very cold days by slipping another pair of heavy, wool socks right over your boots and lower legs.

Bindings

For most cross-country skiers there is only one type of binding, the toe clamp, sometimes called the rat-trap because of its shape. This light, inexpensive (about ten dollars) combination of aluminum plate and wire holds the sturdily built toe of a boot to the ski while leaving the heel completely free to rise and fall. This allows the skier to lunge forward over one ski at a time, thus shooting the ski across the snow.

The traditional toe clamp binding has a wire bail which snaps over the welt of the boot, but some new models are using variations on the design to allow pole-tip opening of the bindings and even step-in, self-locking catches. The heel plate is a simple metal and plastic affair with sawteeth to grip the boot heel. This gives some stability while making turns.

Persons bent on skiing in heavy bush and deep snow most of the time might consider the more constraining, but more stable heel clamp binding. This type of attachment was commonly used for skiing earlier in the century. Another type of cable binding has the locking clamp mounted in front of the toe piece.

By their nature, cable bindings restrict the lift of a skier's heel and do not allow the long, free strides which characterize true cross-country skiing. However, the moderately stiff cables give a skier far more control in turning skis and this is more important in mountain skiing and some deep snow situations in heavy bush.

Poles

While changes in technique in recent years dictated that downhill ski poles become shorter and relatively stiff, cross-country poles remain as long, flexible wands. They must have some spring to help catapult you forward with every stride, but also be strong enough to resist breaking when you lean on them for stability or even fall on them. The tips are curved rather than straight to make it easier to pull them from the snow as you move forward and the grips are slim and smooth to allow movement of your hand as you reach forward, then let the pole trail behind for a second. When buying poles make certain the straps are adjustable, since you will want to fit them snugly to whatever type of glove or mitt you are wearing.

For many years Tonkin bamboo was the standard material and it is still used for the cheapest poles. However, it has one serious disadvantage for the skier who will be making wilderness or downhill trips: it can break if you fall on it. Not only that, it can shatter into sharp splinters. At prices under ten dollars, a pair of Tonkin poles are good for beginners or skiers on a tight budget. But many consider it a good investment to double that outlay for the security of fiberglass or aluminium. If these are made of high-quality material, they are almost unbreakable.

Clothing

If three words can describe the right type of clothing for cross-country skiing they are, *light, loose and warm.* It is amazing how much heat the body can generate during the steady movements of skiing and how little clothing one can support even during cold weather. However, once you stop moving (for example, during a lunch break) the body quickly cools and will chill unless you have extra clothing at hand.

A basic outfit should include:

– A set of long underwear. Thermal designs, with a layer of cotton sewn to one of wool, have made the reputation of Duofold with both cross-country and downhill skiers. Be aware that this type of underwear is available in different weights for different climates. An alternative used by many is the fishnet-style underwear associated with Nordic countries. It allows for evaporation of sweat but does not give the wind protection of Duofold under severe conditions.

– A cotton turtleneck is next. There are many brands on the market but one of the most reliable over the years is the Medico. The turtleneck keeps your neck warm and allows evaporation of perspiration.

– Now slide on a pair of knee-length knicker socks. They should have some elasticity and should be long enough to prevent any cold gaps where the pants end. Some skiers like two pair of socks during cold conditions or like to use fleeced cotton ''thermal'' socks. However, wool is the best material for retaining warmth while wet.

– The knicker pants come next. Here the choice is wide, with everything from the once-popular corduroys, the poplin, cotton and nylon combinations, to the stretch knickers which cling to the body. Basically a hard, smooth, windproof but not waterproof material is best. Look for snug fitting cuffs and strong zippers in the pockets.

– On top goes a wool sweater, preferably of the flat knit type. This heavy material is quite wind-resistant and will shed snow better than the open knit styles. Hundreds of styles are available since this is the type of sweater used for years by downhill skiers. This sweater will run in the thirty dollars and over category, but it will keep you warm for years, probably decades.

– Last of the basic layers is the jacket, possibly part of a suit bought with the knickers. For light and general touring most skiers are using jackets made of the cotton, poplin or stretch nylon materials. They should have good ventilation but may feature a windproof panel in the front to keep your chest warm while allowing sweat to evaporate from behind.

– If you are not easily chilled you will enjoy the freedom of movement provided by ski gloves. During warm weather you can get by with a pair so light they look like driving or dress gloves. When the temperatures dip, you will need one of the thermal styles used by downhill skiers. If you suffer from cold hands most of the time, buy a pair of lined mitts, even down-filled ones if you really feel the cold.

– To cap it off you need a toque of the same type of wool as your sweater. Again those who suffer from the cold should look for the balaclava types which unfold to make a complete face mask. Some persons are very sensitive to cold wind in their ears. They should look for the windproof bonnets which will completely protect their heads or wear a jacket with a comfortable hood.

This basic outfit is all you need for an outing in all but severe weather, and during the spring you may well shed the jacket while in the sun. From here on you get into the extras that are useful and sometimes necessary. An insulated ski jacket is a handy piece of clothing for anyone, even a non-skier, and most people have one around the house. The most useful though no longer the most fashionable type is the ''instructor'' model which covers the hips and snugs against drafts with a belt.

Two types of linings are popular and both have their strong and weak points. Down is the classic for minimum weight and maximum insulation. It is expensive but in high demand for cold weather clothing and sleeping bags. There is one major disadvantage, however: when wet it compacts into a sodden mass with the insulation power of a used Kleenex. Wetness is not a common problem during the winter, but can occur during long expeditions or in spring conditions.

Synthetics, on the other hand, do not have quite the warmth of down but are generally cheaper and more resistant to compacting while wet. Mountaineers use both. If you are on a budget the choice is simple: synthetic. With a bit more money you should consider both carefully and ask the opinion of qualified people familiar with skiing conditions in your area.

A ski jacket may be a necessity if you are out on bitterly cold days and will almost certainly be one if you are planning overnight trips or even lunch breaks during cold weather. Lightweight down jackets, known as down sweaters, are useful for short trips when the weather looks as if it might turn cold and they are handy for lunch stops. Down is easily compacted, so these sweaters can be stuffed into a waterproof bag and will take up no more room than a loaf of bread.

Gaiters are a relatively new item in North America, but many skiers consider them essential for trips through deep snow. They are tubes of nylon or cotton which snug around your boot tops and reach to your calves. Gaiters keep snow from getting into your boots or sticking to your socks when you are travelling off the beaten track. During wet, spring conditions many skiers also use soft, neoprene boot covers which slip over their footwear like loose rubbers and prevent water from soaking the leather.

Wind or warm-up pants, which zipper completely open down the sides, became popular with downhill skiers during the mid-1960s. Though they are not necessary for most cross-country skiing, they can give needed insulation for someone spending a night camping out or travelling over exposed terrain during cold, windy weather.

When buying ski clothing there are a couple of points to watch. Cross-country skiing generates considerable perspiration, so you don't want clothing which is waterproofed because it will turn you into a perambulating sauna. When you stop moving, you will then become an ice cube. This rules out coated nylon except for specific cases where you expect to hit wet weather and need to keep clothing, especially down jackets, from getting wet.

There is a great range of styles and prices in ski clothing these days. Take your time to find something suited to your real needs and check for at least reasonable quality of construction. These days a lot of the European name brand manufacturers are having second line clothing made in the Far East from their last year's designs. This can provide well-styled gear with quite good quality at respectable savings.

In all cases, check the clothing for well-stitched seams and strong zippers and reject anything which does not look and feel sturdy.

Accessories

A skier in a big hurry, racing perhaps, might start out with no more than the skis beneath him and the skimpy racing suit on his back. However, most people out for a relaxed tour find they are in need of such odds and ends as fresh or different wax, a Kleenex, some suntan lotion or a snack on the last leg home. Over the years most people build up some sort of casual checklist of things to stuff in pockets or pouch before each trip.

The essentials for most skiers start with a pack of at least two or three waxes, a scraper to remove old wax and a cork to smooth on a new coat. Even if you are just wandering through a woodlot, it can be useful to refer to a compass for the quickest route back to the car and in wilderness skiing a compass is *essential*. Under the sun, dark glasses are useful to prevent eyestrain and during cloudy, windy or snowy conditions, yellow goggles make the going a lot easier. Both types

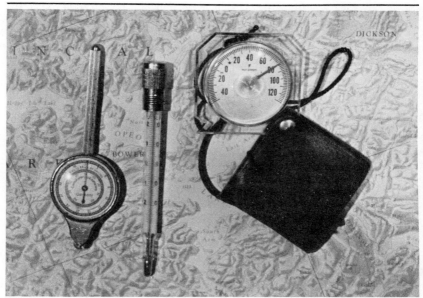

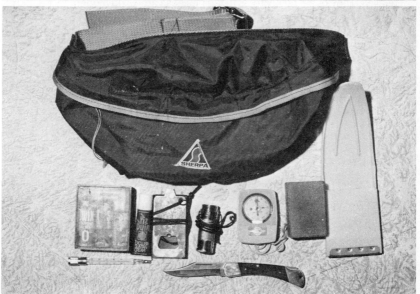

Three useful little items for the touring skier: a measuring instrument for maps, snow thermometer to help in choosing wax and a pocket thermometer.

Fanny pack with some equipment for a short trip. Included are: wax kit, cork and scraper, spare ski tip, snow thermometer, waterproof match case, knife, compass and suntan lotion.

of eye protection keep those eye pokers, twigs, from jabbing you while you are in bush country.

By now you have probably filled your pockets with the little essentials for any outing on skis. But if you are roaming off the beaten track or on a long trail in a resort, you may want a few more extras. It is probably easiest to get a pouch belt commonly called a fanny pack and stow in it the most regularly used items along with a bit of emergency gear.

This would include a spare ski tip (preferably the metal kind) for any lengthy trips, matches in a waterproof metal container sold in sporting goods stores, a stout folding knife or a hunting knife in a solid sheath, a hank of orange parachute cord also sold in sporting goods stores and a couple of chocolate bars and some Dextrose tablets. In addition, it is wise to carry a map of the area if possible or even sketch one out on a piece of paper if you can get details of the trail before starting out.

The list can keep growing if you are planning a trip in real wilderness, where an emergency could force you to make an emergency camp. In this case you should carry a small packsack with suitable equipment. This will be discussed in detail in the chapter on touring and winter camping.

Quality

Everybody loves a bargain and with a sport as popular as cross-country skiing, there is lots of competition and considerable choice. Many of the Nordic manufacturers have been in the business for generations and their names are a guarantee of quality. Many of the newcomers to the business are using modern technology to produce equipment even stronger than the best handmade product. However, the old saying that you get what you pay for applies to some degree even in this sport.

Under the forty dollar range, the skis tend to lack the sophistication and sturdy construction of more expensive equipment. Cheaper boots may start off well, but they tend to split and rot at the seams before their more expensive counterparts do. Poles that are too cheap won't last as long. Bindings that are too fragile will bend or break, clothing ill-woven and poorly sewn will rip and tear at awkward times.

All this is relative of course. Cheap equipment will function very well for the casual skier who wants only the occasional tour around a nearby trail, but it might fail under the heavy stress of a long trip through the heavy snows of wilderness skiing. The rule is to match quality to the type of skiing you expect to do and never to buy something that looks in the shop as if it will jam, bend or break, because on the trail it surely will. Hans Gmoser, the Austrian mountaineer who founded helicopter skiing in Western Canada and made it world famous, writes to all skiers planning to tackle the difficult mountain conditions: ''In the mountains, the best is only just good enough and repairs are difficult to make in remote places such as these.''

Basic Technique

One of the commonest phrases used to describe the simplicity of this sport is: "If you can walk, you can cross-country ski." Some skiing parents find that their children are able to slide around on skis even before they can walk across the living room floor. This is not surprising considering the extra stability of a pair of skis. Once you get used to the feel of the boards under your feet and make the mandatory few falls which await any beginner, you will find the skis stable on level ground and quite manageable on gentle slopes.

Over the past 4,000 or so years people have tried skis ranging from a few feet to more than nine feet in length and have even used two skis of different lengths. For most of that period they resorted to a single pole, usually about six feet long and sharpened at one end. This produced a technique not unlike that of a canoeist or rafter poling his way down a stream. In the past century things have been sorted out into a simple, natural form which is basically a step and glide using a pair of matched poles for stability, rhythm and propulsion.

While downhill skiing involves complicated manoeuvres of weight shifting, body twisting and knee bending to accomplish competent (let alone graceful) descents, cross-country skiing is relatively simple. A skier usually needs several years to become reasonably proficient in downhill technique but only a single season, with lessons, to be fully at ease on cross-country equipment.

Lessons are highly recommended, especially by those skiers who have learned the hard way trying to teach themselves. A few dollars invested in professional instruction saves many hours of trial and error. To begin with, there is a trained skier calling out the learning steps as you need them and setting a proper pace in a good learning area. Just as important, the instructor can detect errors in technique that you can't see in yourself at an early stage and that can be eliminated before they become ingrained as bad habits.

This series of photographs illustrates the basic learning sequence for someone starting the sport. It shows the progression from walking on skis to the diagonal stride, the name given to the technique used for cross-country motion. Next displayed are simple methods of climbing and skiing down hills under control. The demonstration is provided by John Ardill, director of cross-country skiing at Seneca College of Applied Arts and Technology, just north of Toronto. This is the technique generally used by cross-country ski instructors across Canada.

Starting Off

Two of the first things a beginner should learn before setting out on his first trip are how to set a proper track and a proper pace. Though it may seem too simple to discuss, the laying of a good track in fresh snow is obviously not understood by many skiers. Witness the wandering ruts that result when someone leading the way doesn't keep their skis evenly apart. Once such a track has been used a couple of times, the compacted snow freezes and everyone who follows is stuck with a trail on which they cannot get a smooth, even glide. The lead skier should keep his skis consistently about a handsbreadth apart and keep a sharp eye peeled ahead for obstacles so he can make gentle, even curves in the track, which will not slow following skiers.

Pace is important for any skier, very important when there is a group and crucial in wilderness or mountain skiing. A person in even moderately good physical condition can easily ski a half day on flat land if he follows a steady pace which will not wear him out in the first hour or so. Even racers who are moving fast are actually keeping themselves in control to save some energy for the last leg of the trail.

On a group trip of more than a couple of hours duration, the leader should keep a sharp eye on the party to make sure the pace is not too fast for the weakest member. He should set a pace which will allow a good, smooth diagonal stride but which will not tire anyone too quickly. If the party is breaking trail through new snow it is a good idea to rotate the leadership so that one person will not become exhausted with this chore.

As in any sport there are some simple rules of etiquette. It is the responsibility of the skier coming from behind, be it on a flat track or going downhill, to avoid persons in front and to warn them of his approach with the shout: "track," and more usefully, "track on your right" or "track on your left." The skier ahead on a trail should avoid any sudden moves and should step aside as much as possible so the person behind can pass.

When you fall in soft snow you will create a hole known among skiers as a *sitzmark* Particularly on a trail or well-used slope, it is important to fill in such a crater so it won't trip the next skier. If you are climbing a slope, avoid hacking up the track used by skiers coming down the hill.

Advanced Skiing

After you have a good grasp of the fundamentals and feel at ease gliding along a smooth track or snowplowing down gentle hills, you may be interested in developing a more professional style. For the diagonal stride, that means perfecting all the little movements which go into the technique. These include working on the evenness of your stride, eliminating any tendency to rock from side to side, planting your poles at the right angle, relaxing your grip on them as you finish the push and getting the most from each glide. The best person to help you polish your technique and get the most from each movement is a good instructor. In addition, you can learn a lot from watching racers and other professional skiers who have worked for years to develop an almost serpentine smoothness and power in their movements. Avoid paying too much attention to other skiers learning the sport, since you can easily pick up bad habits as well as good ones from them.

Skiing downhill, whether on the heavy equipment specifically designed for that sport or on the light, cross-country equipment, is where the techniques of skiing finally meet again. This is not to suggest that you should tackle the steep, hard packed slopes of Mt. Tremblant or Mt. Norquay on cross-country equipment. With the soft boots and flexible bindings which allow an easy stride, you lack the turning power which comes with heavy equipment and without steel edges, you would probably slide half way down the hill before grinding to a halt.

But a snowplow is a snowplow on any pair of skis and this applies even for christies, in which the skis are kept parallel throughout the turn. Most people can make snowplow turns on cross-country skis on snow that is not too hard packed and good skiers can make linked christies down mountain slopes which are not too steep and have soft, fluffy snow. In fact, out on the trail anything goes if it helps you get down the hill more efficiently. The famous Herman "Jack Rabbit" Smith-Johannsen once astounded a companion when they were skiing a steep slope through the trees by lowering himself through the brush by hanging onto branches and letting them slide through his grasp.

Walking

Ignoring your ski poles at first, you can get the feeling of the skis by simply walking forward in a straight line on smooth, level snow, letting your arms swing freely. The aim is to develop a relaxed stride and there is no attempt to slide the skis at this stage.

Forward Shuffle

Here you begin to get the feel of sliding. You flex your knees and, using the same track in the snow as before, literally shuffle along, taking short glides as you step briskly forward onto one ski after the other.

Kick and Glide

This movement is the basis of good cross-country ski technique. Starting on your track in the snow, bend your knees, advance one ski slightly and put most of your weight on it. Then slide the rear ski forward, stepping onto this ski as it moves in front of you. As you step forward, push yourself ahead by kicking backward with the other foot. For a moment, the trailing ski will have no weight on it, as shown in the photo above. This kicking motion will propel you into a glide along the track, giving the first sensation of cross-country skiing.

Double Poling: Push

Now leave the kicking for a time and take up your poles to learn the second half of your propulsion technique. Plant the tips of the poles a few inches in front of and to each side of the bindings. The poles should be slightly angled to the rear. Bend your knees and pull yourself forward. As your hands pass your hips, bend forward at the waist and push as you slide past the poles.

Double Poling: Finish
Keep bending forward at the waist to get the last ounce of push into a glide, then let the poles trail out behind you, relaxing your grip on the handles a bit. On a hard, fast track or while going down a gentle hill, double poling alone will increase your speed.

Diagonal Stride
This is what cross-country skiing really looks like. It is the motion which can propel a skier over fifty miles or more of terrain in a day. The diagonal stride combines all the techniques previously learned, using the swinging arm you began with – except that now you are pulling, then pushing on a pole with each swing. In fact, the rhythm of the arms sets the pace for the legs and determines how fast or slow you will ski at any given time.

Uphill Diagonal Stride
As the steepness of the slope increases, the stride becomes shorter, the knees are bent more and there is more of a springing motion. There has to be a definite weight shift to plant each ski and make the waxed base adhere to the snow. At times you will literally stamp your skis into the snow to make them stick on a steep climb. Also, you will lean harder on your poles and they will serve as brakes if you start to slide backward.

Double Poling with Kick
This is a combination of the kick and glide, and double poling techniques. In addition to a push with both poles, you give a kick with first one leg, then the other; but instead of gliding on one ski, as in the diagonal stride, you glide on both as in the original double pole method. This is useful for increasing your speed on flat ground or on a gentle downgrade, and gives you a bit more speed than the simple double poling.

Herringbone
When the slope gets too steep for a straight climb and your skis are constantly slipping, spread the tips apart as much as necessary to regain traction. You will be taking short steps and planting the poles behind the skis but will keep moving at a reasonable speed.

Sidestepping
This is the slow but sure method to make your way up or down virtually any slope. Simply turn your skis at right angles to the hill, bend your hips, knees and ankles into the hill if necessary to get more bite into the snow from the edges of your skis and begin stepping your way up the hill.

Downhill Traverse
As the old saying has it, what goes up must come down. You could sidestep back down the hill or if things get desperate take off your skis and walk down. There's no shame in that. However, it's much more exhilarating to start running straight down small hills, if there's lots of room at the bottom and then to tackle bigger hills. Here the skier is traversing across the slope at an angle to keep his speed down. He is bent slightly at the waist, knees and ankles, has more than half his weight on his downhill ski, has advanced the tip of his uphill ski and has angled his hips slightly into the hill.

Snowplow
This is the basic method for slowing, stopping or turning on skis. Coming down the hill you keep the ski tips together, tails apart (opposite of the herringbone climb) and press your knees toward the ski tips to increase the bite of your ski edges. It is a simple and very useful manoeuvre.

Snowplow Turn

This fundamental turn begins with the snowplow. Plant your heels firmly on the serrated plates to get a good grip, press forward with your knees and twist your feet to apply steering action. As you turn you will place more weight on the downhill ski. By alternating the movements you can make a series of linked turns down a long hill, keeping your speed under control and avoiding obstacles.

Waxing

Waxing is one of those subjects which looks terribly complicated on paper but is not very hard once you have the stuff in your hands. The making of ski wax has been compared to a black art and the bubbling concoctions in some mixing pots furthers that impression. Nineteenth century residents of the United States west used to amuse themselves during the winter by racing on skis they had dubbed "Norwegian snowshoes". The racers would "dope" the bases of their seven to twelve-foot long skis with imaginative mixtures of pitch, tar, tallow, castor oil, rosin and other ingredients. The results were impressive: these human missiles could hit speeds up to 90 mph.

Modern ski waxes may still contain a few trade secrets and they are also intended to be as easy as possible to apply. Many manufacturers are producing two-wax kits: one for dry snow and the other for wet conditions. In Canada one of the best known of these is the Jack Rabbit wax kit.

First a bit of theory to explain why waxing is needed. For many years skiers relied on the natural friction of wood on snow for the grip needed to get moving. In deep snow this worked not too badly, but on any smooth surface there was obviously a lot of backsliding. Then one day an anonymous but inspired skier discovered that wax has a natural propensity to stick to snow along with a lot of other things. From there on it was just a matter of time to find a series of waxes of different hardness which would not only stick to snow when skis were stationary and weighted, but that would slide easily once they got moving.

There is a lot of chemistry and physics involved, but essentially tiny snow crystals will grip a waxed surface much as sand would. When a skier lifts a waxed ski and slides it forward, this grip is broken and the friction of the moving ski will momentarily melt the snow beneath and the ski will be riding on a minute layer of water. As soon as the ski stops, the snow crystallizes and the tiny bits of ice grip the wax. This is why a well-used ski trail or slope becomes icy with continued use.

The secret in getting both a good grip and glide is in matching the hardness of the wax to the hardness of the snow. This can be done by squeezing a handful of snow to see if it stays dry and fluffy, indicating considerable cold and a hard wax; if it compacts, indicating a medium wax; or drips water, indicating a soft wax. For greater precision, measure snow temperature with a thermometer and refer to the instructions on wax packages.

The easiest way to begin is with a package of two or three waxes, which will handle most snow conditions. With experience you will probably add a few more waxes and one or two of the sticky klister waxes used for very icy or very wet runs. Most skiers like to pick up a rectangular waxing cork to get the thin, smooth, hard layer of wax suitable for dry snow conditions. However wax can be easily applied

In a pinch you can use the palm of your hand to rub wax onto a ski. Note how dabs of klister have been applied, ready to be rubbed smooth along the ski base.

and rubbed in with the palm of your hand. A scraper is a handy item for removing old wax or the wrong kind of wax.

When you are starting out it is best to put on a wax which is too hard rather than too soft. A softer wax can always be rubbed on over a harder wax but the reverse is not true. As well, a harder wax will give you greater speed and if you are slipping a bit you might get by just rubbing a rough ''kicker strip'' of the next softest wax on the centre one-third of your ski bases. If there are at least two skiers you don't even need to take off your skis for this.

A few more tips in what is really a brief survey of the subject: wax your skis indoors, then set them outside to cool for at least a half hour if possible and ''run-in'' the wax for a couple of minutes before deciding to try another hardness if you are not moving smoothly. If you have just bought a new pair of wood skis, the salesman should have explained the necessity for pine-tarring the bases to seal them against water and therefore warping. Many shops will do the job for a nominal charge, but if you enjoy messing around a bit, tarring your own skis can give you a better feeling for the sport.

There are two methods: cold tar and hot tar. The cold tar is simply brushed on from the can and then rubbed in with a cloth. It is a relatively simple procedure but does not penetrate the wood as well as the hot tar, which is brushed on and then gently heated with a blowtorch until it bubbles a bit. In either case, only apply a thin coat of tar and the bases should be slightly tacky when they have cooled. Of course with the synthetic bases tarring is unnecessary, but you usually need to apply a special coat of binding wax to provide a good grip for the various waxes you will use on the trail.

This is an outline of the subject of waxing. More detailed information is available in other books or magazines and in brochures distributed free by many wax companies.

Conditioning

Cross-country skiing can be one of the most physically demanding sports in the world. Studies of racers have shown they burn as many as 2,500 calories per hour– more than competition swimmers or marathon runners. Most of the skier's body is in almost constant motion: the arms are pulling, then pushing on the poles, the legs are flexing, the torso is twisting and the feet are springing. After about one-half hour of fast skiing the body will have exhausted its ready supply of carbohydrates, in the form of glycogen, and will begin to burn its reserves of fat. This is why serious cross-country skiers are slim and wiry.

Cross-country skiing is undoubtedly one of the best physical conditioners, especially since it can be pursued at your own pace. As with any sport, you should already be at least in reasonable physical shape before starting serious activity. This is particularly important for anyone who knows or suspects they may be prone to a heart problem. But even the young, apparently healthy person who drives to work and to the corner store for a pack of cigarettes and considers a dip in the pool his exercise should make some preparation for skiing.

One of the best ways to get in good physical shape and stay that way is to find several sports or activities which will carry you through the changing seasons. For example, you may swim and play tennis during the summer, cycle whenever the roads are free from snow, canoe, hike, climb mountains, play squash or soccer to name just a few of the many sports. Even walking and especially jogging and running are good conditioners which will help get your legs and lungs in shape for skiing.

If this is your first time on skis remember the old saying: easy does it at first. There is a good, medical reason for this. If you push your muscles well beyond their normal levels of activity, you will trigger several chemical processes including the buildup of lactate, a combustion product of overexertion. The result, in simple terms, is muscle stiffness, which can leave you with all the suppleness of a mannequin for the next couple of days.

If you feel "out of shape" before you take to the trails, try to work in at least a few brisk walks and some light calisthenics for at least a week or two before putting on the skis. Then start with a lesson and a half day of skiing and take the rest of the day to relax and enjoy the scenery. You'll feel a lot better for it and be in better shape for the next day.

Touring and Winter Camping

Touring

If you have learned the basic technique of cross-country skiing, have skied a few trails at resorts and are enthusiastic for new adventures, you are ready for touring. Touring takes you beyond the simple outing on a short trail. There is no hard and fast line between the two, but basically the touring skier is heading out for at least a day on the trails and often plans a trip of several days duration. If one thing physically separates him from the non-touring skier, it is the pack on his back—in which he carries food and drink, plus other equipment to meet any emergencies encountered on the trip.

In Europe, especially in Scandinavia and around the Alps, ski touring has been popular for decades and there are many well established trails leading from one cabin or hotel to another, allowing days of potential travel on one trip. There you find people of all ages. Youth groups, school classes, friends and families take winter holidays to seek out fresh snow and sunshine and escape the gloom of winter in the cities.

North Americans are just starting to catch up with the Europeans. In the New England states it is possible to ski from one hotel to another for several days and have a room and hot bath waiting each night. During the 1930s Jack Rabbit Johannsen laid out the Maple Leaf Trail in the Laurentians, north of Montreal. It ran from Labelle for 80 miles south to Shawbridge and Johannsen was canny enough to lay it between hotels so he could always find a place to stay at night. In the Rockies, alpine clubs have used well established cabins as way stations on ski tours, but these were placed for trips in which climbing mountains to ski down untracked snow was the aim.

Where should one look for touring trails?

Most of Canada can be toured during the winter, but it is wise to start out at least on terrain that is not too rugged or bushy. You don't want an expedition to lay new trails; you want to enjoy skiing paths that already exist. Obviously you will avoid rocky terrain at the start of the season when the snow cover is light and will keep away from marshes and watercourses during thaws. Flatland is ideal for keeping up your speed, but it can get boring so that you will soon be looking for rolling countryside. If it is a windy day, you will seek trails through the woods rather than in open fields and if you are competent on the downhill pitches, you will seek out and enjoy a few runs down gentle hills. Just make sure everyone in your party is as capable as the leader.

There are three main sources of prepared trails and the condition of their routes will range from barely cleared and marked to carefully mapped and groomed each day. First is the commercial operation– a ski resort, lodge or hotel. This is a profit-making venture, so there will be a fee, usually a dollar or two for a day of skiing, or it may be included in the cost of your accommodation. Commercial trails tend to be loops of a few miles in length, though some have pushed out wilderness trails allowing scope for even the winter camper who wants at least a two-day run. Commercial trails are usually well marked and are often groomed.

Then there are ski club trails, usually laid across public or private land with the consent of the owner. These are generally ''free'' in the sense that there is no one sitting at the entrance to charge you a fee, but the clubs try to finance the operation by selling memberships and possibly trail maps. Since the marking and maintenance of the trails is a voluntary operation, it is often wise to invest in a map and possibly key it to a topographic map for the area to aid you in navigation. Club trails may wander for a mile or two through some farm fields or they may penetrate mountain valleys and northern forests for many miles. There are even efforts to link up trails as in the North Shore area of Quebec. In addition to trail information, club membership introduces one to people with similar interests and often provides free or discounted lessons, equipment clinics, travel and expertise on the sport.

The third type of organized ski trail is found on parkland: federal, provincial and municipal. Many governments are just starting to respond to the demand for more ski trails, so the availability of such routes tends to be spotty. Some are professionally maintained and there is even a service charge. Others, including some done under such auspices as the now defunct Local Initiatives Program, have been blazed but are no longer maintained.

Many of the national parks, especially those in the west, have developed trails; a large number of provincial parks are creating trails and some cities have even laid out trails within their boundaries. Beyond these organized routes there is an endless expanse of countryside, much of it laced with paths of one form or another which can be skied. Hiking trails are an obvious choice, but you should check them out before planning a day trip along one of these. Remember that hikers don't have to manoeuvre on skis, so the trail may twist through heavy brush or include a number of steep sections on rocky hillsides. Most trail clubs can supply you with maps and information about the suitability of various sections of their footpaths for skiing.

Canoe routes are another definite possibility, especially for canoeists who enjoyed the countryside during the summer and would like to see it again during the winter. Again a couple of things to watch out for. Portage trails are cleared for use during the summer and if there is several feet of snow on the ground you may find your head in the branches, slowing your pace in some sections. Also, a well-worn footpath is easy to follow in the summer but may not be so obvious in the winter when everything is beneath a smooth blanket of snow. Of course, the route is largely over water, so you must be on the lookout for any potential hazards.

Then there are unplowed rural roads and bush tracks such as fire roads and logging roads where you can lay your own track. You are limited only by your imagination and the stock of maps you lay in.

About the only type of track to avoid if possible is the well-used snowmobile trail, and this may not always be easy. One or two passes of a snowmobile are fine for compacting fresh snow and making it a lot easier to ski, but a regularly used machine trail quickly becomes full of undulations. In addition, you will be bothered by their noise and the fact you will have to get off the track frequently.

Even as this book is being written, resort operators are expanding their ski trails, hoteliers are realizing the scope of the ski boom and are laying out trail networks from their front doors and ski club members, armed with saws and surveyor's tape, are marking new routes through the countryside. All this augurs well for the touring skier; there are ever more trails for trips of a day, a week or a month.

Many Canadians are starting to realize this and are quietly booking their vacations during the winter, when it is easy to get time off from most jobs, and are heading away to a favorite lodge in the north country. There, they and their families spend day after day exploring the silent countryside as they never could in summer. Evenings are spent in camaraderie around a roaring fireplace or in a quiet corner with a book or some topographical maps. At night, the tired skiers crawl under heavy, wool blankets, down sleeping bags for a well-earned rest.

The step into touring should be a natural one from short trips. If you are leaving well-travelled terrain it should be in a party of three or more skiers. Travelling alone in wild country can be exhilarating but it also brings risks which you should regard seriously. If you have an accident, even a simple one, you must be prepared to make your way back out alone through deep snow and cold and without any help. This is exhilarating only if you succeed.

Better to have at least one skier to stay with you while another goes for help. No matter how large the party, you should leave word with some responsible person just where you are going and when you expect to return. If you don't show up after a reasonable length of time, there will be someone near a phone to call for help. As a minimum measure, you should leave a note inside the windshield of your car indicating where you are going and when you expect to return. In the national parks of western Canada, where conditions can be hazardous at times, touring skiers are required to register when they leave for a trip and to check back in when they return.

For even a half day on a little used trail, you should carry a fanny pack with a few emergency items as listed in the accessories section. If you are heading out for a day in the wilderness, you should carry more.

What is wilderness skiing? Mike Exall, the outdoor recreation co-ordinator for Seneca College, provides this definition: "You are in wilderness when you get into areas no longer bounded by concession roads." In such an area it is possible to become lost and get into serious trouble if you are not prepared to navigate and, if necessary, make an emergency camp.

For many years mountain guides, many of them from European alpine centres, have been leading climbers and skiers into the mountains of Western Canada. These guides must be expert at coping with the terrain, making regular or emergency camps, finding their way through adverse conditions and coping with emergencies such as avalanches, rockfalls or injuries in a party.

The Canadian Ski Association (CSA) recognized that the boom in cross-country skiing was creating a similar need for guides who could lead skiers across non-mountainous terrain. Exall, a mountaineer, skier and outdoor instructor with experience in Europe, New Zealand and Canada, prepared the manual for training such leaders. He feels anyone who takes a tour of any size into the back country should be trained in such things as tour preparation, the psychology of leading a group, navigation, survival, first aid, rescue and evacuation. Graduates of the CSA courses can be identified by oblong pins bearing the title "Cross-country Tour Leader" over a maple leaf. This pin is an assurance that the wearer has been trained to safely guide parties through wilderness conditions in everything but the high country.

There are three levels of certification. The lowest level, indicated by a bronze pin, denotes a leader qualified to take skiers on day tours or overnight tours if the party is making its way to some permanent shelter such as a cabin. The silver pin goes to leaders qualified to handle any type of winter tour, including winter camping trips which will involve tenting out. A gold pin is worn by leaders who are also qualified to examine candidates for the other two levels.

Ski parties have been heading into the wilderness for many years without the benefit of certified leaders and will obviously continue to do so for many more years. However, in the past, the kind of person adventurous enough to tackle the winter wilderness was usually someone already oriented to and experienced in outdoors living. Over the years he had picked up some expertise by reading and being with other outdoorsmen and had earned a healthy respect for the wild country.

Now tens of thousands of people, many of them permanent city dwellers, are taking up the sport of cross-country skiing and after learning the basics, will be looking for new fields and forests to conquer. Naturally many of them will want to try some of the trails of our provincial and national parks, logging roads through forest land, wilderness hiking and even animal trails.

Anyone who wants to tour off the beaten track would be well advised to start this kind of tripping with other skiers experienced in such travel. If you don't know any personally, you can probably find them in one of the many ski clubs. There is no better way to learn than by watching someone who already knows how it is done.

Before setting out on day-long tours, you should try a few half-day trips to get the feel of breaking trail through fresh snow and to gauge your own ability to handle the rigors of such travel. This will also give you some experience in simple navigation; for example, learning how to decide which fork of a trail takes you in the direction you want to go.

You should have three things prepared in advance of any tour. First, you need to know where you are going and how you are going to find your way—in precise terms. This means a knowledge of the trail marking system if there is one, a map of the area if it is not very well marked or you suspect it may not be clear at points, a compass and the ability to use it. Secondly, you need the knowledge and preferably some training on how to cope with possible emergencies ranging from a broken ski tip to a broken leg. Thirdly, you need the proper equipment.

The ski tourer is easily distinguished by a packsack carrying food, extra clothing and equipment to cope with any problems which might arise. A good packsack is a small mountaineer's type bag made of waterproof nylon and having well padded and easily adjustable shoulder straps and a waist strap to keep it from flopping from side to side and throwing you off balance. Make sure you get a decent sized bag so you can stuff in adequate supplies of food, drink and bulky, but warm clothing to wear during lunch breaks or if the weather turns foul. Look for such features as side pockets to carry small items you may want in a hurry, such as wax, a map pocket in the flap and loops or other means of attaching your skis if you want to carry them a short distance. There are many good sacks on the market, starting at about twenty-five dollars, and the best way to find a good one is to ask other skiers what they like and check out a couple of good outdoor stores.

Here is a suggested list of what you might put in the bag for a day tour:
wax kit, including cork and scraper
spare ski tip
sunglasses and yellow goggles
nylon cord
map and compass
sheath knife or heavy folding knife
hatchet (unless you will be above the timberline)
repair kit with tape, wire, binding screws, screwdriver and tool to make holes in skis
matches in waterproof container
plastic garbage bags
first aid kit
food and drink for a hearty lunch plus emergency rations
warm jacket plus waterproof clothing if rain is a possibility
flashlight
tarpaulin: heavy plastic, coated nylon or a "space blanket"
a metal cup or can for melting snow into drinking water
heavy mitts and extra socks
gaiters
wind pants (if you could hit severe weather)
fire starter– a heavy candle stub is useful.
Kleenex

Winter Camping

This is a sport which has developed across Canada along with cross-country skiing. Until recent years it was the domain of the hardy trapper, the Eskimo, the lonely Mountie on patrol, the mountaineer or the adventurer. It is still a sport for the hardy and vigorous and one area where there will never be crowded campsites.

There is a satisfaction in being very close to nature when she is in a tough mood. You down a meal before it can freeze on your plate, bed down with just a thin layer of material between you and the frigid elements and turn through the night to avoid freezing the part of your body in contact with the ground. There is a great satisfaction in awakening the next morning to make a hot cup of tea laced with honey and to stagger out of the tent to watch a sunrise over the frozen landscape.

Relatively few Canadians can say they have pitched a tent in the middle of winter, taken a last run across moonlit snow and listened to the cry of coyotes or the howl of a distant timberwolf as they dozed off. Obviously it is not the sort of adventure to be taken lightly. Everything must be organized and functioning properly or you will be in for a long, very cold night. Novices should not try such a trip unless they are with a seasoned winter camper who can check out their equipment, pitch camp and make meals. The best way to learn the skills, of course, is to start camping with someone who has done it many times. It is also possible to get training with a number of ski clubs and organizations such as community colleges. Naturally a person planning winter camping would be well advised to have summer camping experience to provide a grounding in the methods of tenting.

In addition to experience, good equipment is essential. If necessary, you can spend a night of reasonable comfort in a lean-to shelter with a roaring campfire in front—provided you have warm clothing and a thick sleeping bag. Once you stop moving and especially after the sun sets, you will need lots of insulation. A good combination is a heavy ski parka and insulated warm-up pants of the type worn by downhill skiers. Ski gloves will no longer be warm enough and you should opt for down-lined mitts or possibly the heavy wool mitts from Europe. A good combination is a pair of light gloves inside the mitts so you can tackle finicky jobs without exposing your hands.

The light ski boots are little insulation, even if you follow the standard advice and put on a fresh, dry pair of socks. Better to throw in a pair of insulated mukluks or lined snowmobile boots for knocking around camp. That way you'll be well covered from head to toe. If you start getting chilled you not only start fumbling simple tasks, your body and mind slow down.

You will need a good-sized pack to carry all the gear for a night out. While the frame packs so favored in the summer will carry the freight very nicely, they do not have a good balance for cross-country skiing, especially on downhill pitches. These high-riding packs tend to overbalance a skier and many a person has found himself buried face first in the snow as a result. A better choice, if you can afford it, is a mountain climber's sack designed to hug the body. However, these packs tend to run in the fifty dollar and over range.

In addition to the equipment already prepared for a day pack, you will need to add more food and clothing, more eating utensils and some specialized equipment. Most important is the sleeping bag. Here you can get into great discussions about material and design, but essentially you will need what is called a ''winter'' bag rated by the manufacturer for the lowest temperature you expect to encounter. This way you still have a safety margin in your ski jacket and overpants, which you can wear at night for extra insulation.

Every year more models of sleeping bags are coming on the market, so you will face a wide choice. It is virtually impossible to rent or try out new bags, so the best

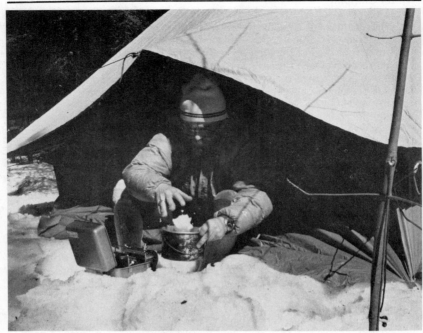

The first job of any winter chef is melting snow for drinking water and cooking. This is a time and fuel consuming task.

way to shop is to talk first with experienced winter campers and see how the insulating loft of their bags stood up to usage. Loft is the term used to describe how much the insulating material will fluff up once the bag is unpacked. This creation of airspace between the feathers or synthetic fibres is what provides insulation. Unfortunately for your pocketbook, high quality materials and workmanship needed to design, fill and finish a good bag lead to price tags over $100. However, it is an investment which will last for a long time.

Fire for warmth and cooking is another major requirement. You can make a campfire if you have the time and energy to find and cut dry wood and haul it through the snow, but even then you may face the prospect of trying to keep a fire going and cook outside during a snowstorm. Most winter campers rely on a portable stove which can be used outside the tent, at the entrance or (with great caution and adequate ventilation) inside the tent if a storm is blowing. The use of such stoves is something which should be learned from experts since a wrong move can create a severe fire hazard and the loss of your shelter is a serious matter during the winter.

The Optimus 111B has been the standard stove for many years. It burns readily available white gas and has a pressure pump. Similar stoves without a pump or the bottled gas stoves so handy and so popular in the summer are not suitable for cold weather usage, since low temperatures drastically reduce the pressure inside the fuel tanks.

Shelter can take many forms. Eskimos have lived for millenia in igloos, Indians made do with simple wooden shelters and wilderness travellers have survived if not flourished, huddled under the thick, low branches of evergreens. Some winter

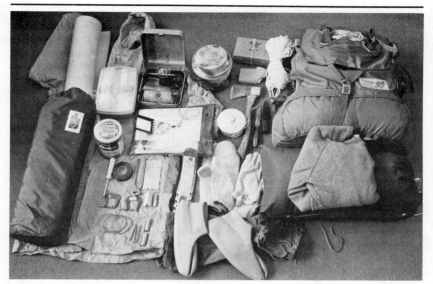

Full kit for winter camping. Included are mountain-style pack, winter tent, gas stove, cooking, first aid and repair equipment. In front are waterproof boot covers for wet travel conditions.

adventurers who are making a base camp on a long trip actually prefer to build a snow cave or igloo, especially if they have to wait out a severe storm.

Most winter campers who don't have a cabin at the end of the trail rely on tents. You can get by decently with many of the summer tents, especially if you are camping in forested areas sheltered from high winds. Some designs are more suitable than others for the rigors and problems of winter camping. For example, many of the new tents are self-supporting thanks to fiberglass rods which eliminate the need for burying guy ropes in the snow. Usually these models are highly wind resistant and with half-tunnel shapes provide a large amount of useable room inside. So-called mountain tents have such special features as poles which are braced on the tents themselves rather than on the ground, flaps around the edge so the tent can be banked with snow to prevent winds from sweeping underneath and snugly closing doors.

Check Lists

Most campers have their favorite stories, usually told in the third person, of things left behind on long trips. These can range from the silly and embarrassing (such as toilet paper) to the more serious (boots or stove). The best way to avoid adding your own story to the record is to create a personal checklist of all your own gear, ranging from the apparently obvious– skis– to such minutae as the contents of the toilet and medicine kit.

It is important to itemize everything down to the last piece of clothing for two reasons. The main problem we all face when heading out for a trip is simply forgetting something because we do not use it every day. This is more a problem for beginners but even experts have been known to rush out of the house without their ski boots. In addition it is a control on things that are used up or damaged during a trip and not replaced immediately. If you check everything against a list ahead of time you have a chance to repair or replace the item.

Following is the suggested list for an overnight pack but it should be treated only as a guide to each individual. You should create your own list around equipment you have or may need for particular trips.

basic contents of a day kit
change of underclothing
sleeping bag suitable for coldest weather likely
ensolite pad
mukluks or other warm boots for camp
water bottle (plastic or aluminium)
bowl, cup, spoon, fork and knife
sunburn cream
personal toilet kit with any medicines you need personally

In addition, there is gear which is needed by a party and would normally be distributed between members to equalize the weight and bulk. This would include:
tent
stove and fuel
shovel
one large, first aid kit
food, including survival rations
cooking pots and utensils
pot cleaning cloths, pads and paper towels
large, collapsible water jug

Eating Out

Food becomes a key part of any trip lasting anything more than half a day and during the winter it should be something hot (if possible) and nourishing. While the menu for a day trip can be relatively haphazard, and hopefully fun, longer trips require a bit more thought or else good instincts built up over years of experience. On a long trip the body is running on its natural reserves if they are not replenished in amounts at least equal to what has been burned. A balanced diet must include carbohydrates, proteins and fats totalling more than 4,300 calories a day. A good ration is about a kilogram (2.2 pounds) in dry weight of food per day and this will bulk out somewhat when water is added to make soups and stews. In addition, many wilderness travellers add a vitamin pill per day to their menu to cope with any deficiencies caused by the change from a home diet.

Actually, water is first on the list of priorities since one can survive several days without food but much less without water. Eating some snow will not drop you in your tracks as some fables have it, but eating a lot of snow to get a relatively small amount of liquid will chill and tire your body. (Snow, especially if it is light and powdery, is more air than ice.)

The best way to cope with the water siutation is to start off with a full metal or plastic bottle of water per person and when the container gets about half empty pack it tightly with the wettest, densest snow available. As that mixture sloshes around it will melt into water by the time you are ready for another drink. This system is not likely to keep up with your thirst however and at night it will be necessary to melt enough snow to refill all water bottles completely. Leave them between sleeping bags and they won't freeze. If you are in a large group it may be more convenient to fill a plastic half-gallon jug for the night.

Naturally you will look first for unpolluted running water. Even in the winter there are a suprising number of spring-fed streams which remain open, though some have to be located by digging through several feet of snow and chopping a bit of ice. Just be extra careful not to fall in. Instead try dipping from a distance with a cooking pot tied to the end of a ski pole and rope yourself with climbing rope or nylon parachute cord before clambering down steep river banks.

Next in priority is the so-called survival food. This can range from the classic chocolate bar stuffed in a corner of the sack through Dextrose cubes for a burst of energy at the end of the day to plastic tubes of honey, pemmican bars, dry fruit, nuts, dry sausage and tea. Obviously some of these are typical lunch items but just make sure you have enough left over to provide emergency rations if for some reason you have to spend an unexpected night out.

The classic lunch and the one most likely on a long trip is the simple combination of some dried meat like salami, liverwurst, smoked ham, tinned or smoked fish, hard bread (such as foil-wrapped pumpernickel), some dried fruit and nuts and a piece of chocolate or other sweet. Water in your canteen may be made more palatable by the addition of powdered fruit mixes. While you may not want to take the time to cook a lunch on a long trip, the mid-day stop on a day tour is often a highlight of the short trip. You will almost certainly have dead wood at hand (or else may carry a small stove) and the burst of heat will be welcome if there is a chill wind blowing.

The leader picks a sheltered spot which will catch the noonday sun and sends members of the party to snap off dry branches while he opens the pack and spreads out a light tarp as a seat. In some cases the fire may be more ceremonial or a source of heat than a necessity for cooking since the cook may have stowed a hearty stew in a thermos and packed it in ready to eat. At the least the thermos will contain a thick soup or may offer a chili, beef stew or any other concoction which will pour into the bottle. This may be backed up with whole wheat bread sandwiches generously loaded with butter and egg, cold meat, cheese or the kids' favorite — peanut butter and jam.

Cookouts can include wieners, hamburgers and those with hearty appetites may want to grill a steak and munch it on a large slice of toast. If the weather is nice you may even want to play around with shishkabobs of meat marinated the night before.

From New Brunswick come three suggestions for meals which can be prepared ahead of time and reheated or cooked over the campfire.

Shirley's beans: a recipe from the Miramichi lumber camps.

The day before the trip start with a crock half full of beans, then add a medium-size onion, one-quarter pound salt pork, three tablespoons of brown sugar, one-half teaspoon of pepper, one teaspoon of salt, one heaping teaspoon of dry mustard, one-half teaspoon of ginger and one-quarter cup plus two tablespoons of molasses. Then fill the crock with more beans. Add boiling water, cover and cook at 350 degrees for seven hours. Since it will be difficult to bring the food hot in the crock you should start a good fire about two hours before lunch time, then place the crock in the embers and heap them around the sides. Then take an hour or so to practice technique or take some photos in the area. At the last minute break out some wieners and roast them over the open fire, then serve the beans with already buttered bread you have wrapped in aluminum and heated at the edge of the fire.

Ragout d'Acadie: an outdoor stew.

The day before the trip prepare the meal. Take one pound each of fat beef ribs and lean stewing beef, cut in pieces, coat with flour, salt and pepper and brown in butter. Place in a pot and add: five medium potatoes cut in quarters, five carrots cut up, one medium turnip cut up, one small onion cut in chunks, one large can of stewed tomatoes, one teaspoon of salt and one teaspoon of pepper. Add water until the pot is half full and boil for one hour. Then add a small cauliflower cut in small pieces and one-half cup of chopped green onions and boil one more hour. This stew also requires an hour or more of cooking in the crock in embers or else a faster heating over a gas stove.

A quicker meal is Carleton County Potato Pancakes.

Prepare ahead of time. Chop up one pound of fresh or frozen fish fillets. Add three beaten eggs, two tablespoons of flour, two tablespoons of grated onion, one tablespoon of chopped parsley, two teaspoons of salt, dashes of nutmeg, pepper and tarragon, two cups of finely grated raw potatoes. Form into patties and wrap in foil. Pack some applesauce. At the campfire fry patties in hot cooking oil for three or four minutes on each side and serve with applesauce.

Liquid refreshment can vary from the Canadian woodsman's classic kettle of tea to the thermos or pot of coffee to the skier's wineskin loaded with whatever suits the individual's taste. However, a change of pace is provided by this recipe, also from New Brunswick:

Keswick Spiced Cider.

For each cup of apple cider add two teaspoons of honey and one-quarter teaspoon each of nutmeg, ginger and lemon juice. Heat until steaming, pour into warmed mugs, then add a cinnamon stick for swizzling. This can also be packed in a thermos for a quick break.

The dessert course can be as simple as a chocolate bar or can range into cakes and cookies provided they are packed in such things as plastic boxes or tins to prevent crumbling. On a day trip you can throw in fresh fruits provided they are wrapped to prevent freezing, a proviso which should be applied to everything. In addition, the wrapping should be done with an eye to prevention of any spills so you will probably use generous amounts of plastic bags. Fuel and stoves should be well wrapped and kept as far away as possible from any foodstuffs.

To these standard menus one can add such specialty items as fresh maple taffy garnered during visits to sugaring off ceremonies at maple bushes during the spring and the fruits of ice fishing which can be devoured on the spot if you have fire and pan or grill.

Breakfast and dinner for the winter camper present a few logistical problems, especially when the cooking is done on a small stove, placed on a piece of ensolite in a tent. A hot cereal dish may be made by mixing powdered milk or diluted tinned cream with water and pouring in an instant cereal. You can enliven this by adding some sugar or dried fruit. Tea can be drunk strongly laced with honey, an advantage for the energy conscious skier. If you have time and fuel there are extensive possibilities in the freeze-dried food range, including scrambled eggs and omelets, with bacon chips and tinned bacon.

The night meal is the major one for wilderness travellers and will also probably be a one pot special because of the fact one dish would be cold before a second could be cooked to make a more traditional dinner. Stews tend to be heavy favorites with a soup base to give the water some extra nourishment, then a starch such as potatoes, noodles or instant rice and possibly some dried vegetables before the meat is added. The meal will probably start with a straight soup, then the stew dish and be rounded off with a chunk of cheese, a handful of nuts and some sweet. Along with the basics consider packing some herbs and spices to add a personal touch. For example, curry powder or tomato sauce will both liven up a stew. And for drinks there are the standard fruit powders plus instant tea or coffee and chocolate. You might experiment with such things as serving jello warm and liquid as a dessert beverage.

Navigation

For the skier accustomed to following well marked and often well-worn trails around a resort, navigation might seem to be a completely unnecessary skill. But the moment he strikes out for a run in bush country, even on a wilderness trail marked by a club, he begins to navigate, whether instinctively or consciously. It may simply mean following a wagon road through a small bush until you hit the concession road and realize it's time to turn back; it may be that you will follow a river bank; or the navigation might simply mean keeping a landmark such as a farmer's windmill in sight.

Such simple methods are adopted almost naturally, even by city dwellers little used to foot travel in the country. The interesting part begins when you make trips of more than a mile or two, and especially when you plunge into heavy bush country where no landmarks are visible. In many cases you will ski into the wild country for a couple of hours, rest and have a bite to eat, then ski back out on your now hardened tracks, enjoying the speed of a packed run.

But what do you do if a wind has kicked up while you were travelling in or if it has started to snow heavily? Your tracks could vanish in less than an hour. Or what do you do if you want to cut the trip short by taking a shortcut to a road you know is only a mile or two away through reasonably open bush country?

Do you trust your "instinct for navigation?" If so, you could be in for a nasty surprise. Most of us like to think we can walk, or ski, a straight line, especially when stone sober; but some scientific tests have proven that people are incapable of holding a true course unless they have some steady clues. When you are wandering between the trees, evading obstacles, or going over rolling countryside, you often see nothing but a constantly changing panorama. In this case you will almost certainly travel in circles, just as lost people do the world over.

Even the apparent natural instinct of a professional guide is nothing more than familiarity with his home ground. It's no different than your ability to navigate through your own living room in pitch dark or your inability to do the same thing in a strange room. You probably recall reading the stories of explorers who regularly picked up native guides in one area, then dismissed them and hired new ones in the next mountain pass.

Seasoned explorers or city dwellers with a little practice, some common sense and cool heads can navigate anywhere with the right equipment. The basic tool is a map. For most cross-country skiers this may simply be a few wiggly lines on a piece of paper representing the routes someone had laid out in a given area. Or it may be a topographic map showing hills and valleys, forest and open land, rivers, roads and other natural features present when the photo mapping plane flew overhead. The topographic sheets, printed by the federal Department of Energy, Mines and Resources and available through many provincial government offices as well, are the most detailed and most useful for wilderness travel. Also useful, particularly in mountain regions, are aerial photos, especially if taken in winter.

Unless you are travelling in country with highly visible landmarks and there is no risk of fog or snow to obliterate them, you need a compass. This is the simplest device available to help you move in a constant direction. Even on familiar terrain a compass can be useful if you want to make a shortcut from one trail to another or cut through the bush to a nearby road. A compass, whether it costs one dollar or over $100, is basically a magnetized piece of metal balanced on a pivot and

Compass selection. From left: precise bearing compass, wrist model, simple pocket compass, lapel pin-on type, rugged compass used in armed forces survival kits.

enclosed in a non-magnetic case of plastic, brass or aluminum. The differences between the dime store and the more expensive varieties include things like sturdier materials, liquid damping, luminosity and sighting devices.

To some degree all these are useful features for the bush traveller, who needs to get an accurate reading in the shortest possible time. A few years ago your compass would have been a simple device, like a pocket watch, with a needle which swung back and forth for several seconds, then shakily settled into one position, which you would accept as North. Then you would look across the compass face for the direction in which you wanted to travel, pick it off the letters and numbers marked around the dial and line up a distant object as best you could.

Modern compasses have liquid-filled capsules which settle the needle into position quickly and many offer sighting devices which allow you to take precise bearings and pinpoint your location on a map. At one time compasses were marked with the cardinal points— north, south, east and west— and the various intercardinal points. These ranged from the simple northeast to north northeast to north by north northeast and so on as navigators tried to give ever more precise directions. Except for the basic directions, this system has been replaced with 360 degree marking. Although you may not automatically react with the word ''west'' when someone throws the bearing ''270 degrees'' at you, this is a quicker and more precise method of charting direction. For simplicity's sake, at first just remember north is at 360°, east is 90°, south is 180° and west, 270°.

The traditional compass still has a needle pivoting around the face and one end of the needle is marked with letter N or is colored red, black or blue to indicate north. An increasing number of compasses now have no needle but whole dials which rotate – and they are quicker to read.

The easiest way to keep your compass handy but safe is to hang it around your neck with a light, nylon cord and tuck it under your jacket or sweater. Many wilderness travellers stash a second compass deep inside a pack or pocket as travel insurance. Some designs allow the instrument to be pinned on the front of your jacket or strapped on your wrist like a watch and these are useful if you are following a winding path. With this type be particularly careful to keep the device away from steel or iron objects, such as pocket knives, which can deflect the magnetized needle.

The third tool of navigation is a watch. While skiing there is no easy way to measure how many kilometres you have covered unless someone has marked the trail or you can pinpoint your location on a map. Such travel is usually best measured by the time it takes to cover a given distance, which varies with the individual. A strong, expert skier might slip around a trail in one hour, but a novice could take more than twice as long. After your first trail, you will get an idea of how many kilometres per hour you can cover and from there on, it's a matter of finding how long a given trail is and applying you own rate of travel to estimate how much time you need. With experience you will gain speed and awareness of variables like steepness of terrain, snow conditions and the need for rest stops. In a group never forget that the speed and range of your trip are governed by the slowest, weakest member of the party. On a day trip, set a point of no return on your watch and obey it as a pilot would his fuel gauge. If you start at 1 P.M. and darkness falls at 5 P.M., you should be at least half way around a loop by 3 P.M. or turn back at that time.

In a pinch, a watch (though not a digital model) can serve as a crude compass. If you aim the hour hand in the direction of the sun, South will lie directly between the hour hand and 12 on the dial. For example, if it is 8 A.M., South will lie directly over the numberal ten on the watch. At noon, the sun will be sitting directly over the direction South.

If you are going to be bashing around in the bush and possibly falling in the snow, you should have a shockproof and waterproof timepiece on your wrist. Although you may not be tempted to wear a dress watch into the woods or to buy an armored skindiver's model for a few trips only, you might consider a cheap but rugged pocket watch which can be secured to a belt loop or safety pin with a length of nylon cord.

Beyond this basic equipment you should include a map case. It can be as simple as a clear plastic bag or could be one of the plastic envelopes with self-sealing openings, neck cords and pencil pockets sold in many outdoors shops for three to four dollars. Inside this you may toss a six-inch, clear, plastic ruler or blow another four dollars on one of those handy devices which you can roll across the map, especially around curves, to get a quicker measurement. For more precise navigation you might even include a small protractor, which can be placed on the map to provide compass bearings.

Along with the basic equipment you should pick up and commit to memory a few basic skills, increasing the number as your trips become more challenging. Trail marking is probably as old as human settlement and no doubt the cave dwellers scuffed some marks in the dirt with their toes or broke off a few branches as they walked along to mark a return route to shelter or food. Primitive trail markers, such as axe blazes on trees, are still popular in folklore but are losing favor with people like foresters, who see them as open sores, inviting infection of the trees. Other natural systems include stone or snow cairns on open ground, marks scratched on rock faces and pointers made from wood and attached to a pole stuck in the ground.

Now more permanent, more visible and less damaging markers such as paint blazes, fluorescent painted metal or plastic strips or signs and lengths of orange surveyor's tape mark well-used trails. At a resort it is usually enough to follow these markers, remembering to keep following the right color after every intersection in the trails. If you are laying a trail, don't forget to mark both sides of every tree or you will have a one-way route and a devil of a time finding your way back. On more complicated routes you may also need a map to help you pick your way through interconnecting trail networks and again it is often just a case of matching the color of the line on a map to the color of the markers.

Once you start heading for little used trails or try some bushwhacking on your own to explore the back country it is time to learn some details about maps and how to use them. In a pinch you can make your own maps and they may be all you need. At the very least, you will probably have a general road map of any given area of the country and from this can create your own local map with a pencil and piece of paper. It's not a bad idea to carry a pencil and notepad when visiting a resort for the first time, since some owners only post a map at the entrance and if you want a copy you'll have to sketch it there.

A highway map will give you a general outline of the settlements, roads, and large watercourses in an area, but it will not provide the details useful for locating yourself over distances of a few miles. Sometimes you can sketch a simple map, but many times you don't have all the details. For this you need the topographic maps. At first glance, these sheets of lines, names and numbers can be intimidating. In addition to the usual lines for roads and railways, they are covered with a grid of blue lines and a mass of wavy brown lines which seem to wander all over the place.

The blue vertical and horizontal lines, each ending in a number, are used by professionals such as surveyors and pilots to plot exact locations and communicate them in a simple, numerical form. For most travellers, the fact that the lines form a grid makes it easy to calculate rough distances, especially if they are on north-south or east-west routes.

The wavy, brown lines are called contour lines. These are the map-maker's way of translating the hills and dales of the countryside into something readable on a flat surface. Spaces between the lines indicate a change in elevation, such as twenty-five feet on detailed maps. With some practice, you will learn to translate a closely set series of lines into a steep hillside and a series of rough circles into a hilltop. For skiers planning trips across unfamiliar country, such maps are invaluable because they show the steepness of the terrain and suggest routes around cliffs and up gently terraced valleys. With a pencil and compass, you can plot a route across a map on the living room table and be prepared for the twists and turns of the trip even before you snap on your skis.

If you are unfamiliar with the topo sheets as they are sometimes called, it's a good idea to get one of the area where you live or holiday and to try navigating with it as you travel along familiar roads. This will give you the feel for translating directions and spotting such features as hills and buildings from the symbols on a map.

In the Canadian topographic series there are two scales of map which will be of greatest use. The 1:125,000 scale (one inch on the map equals 125,000 inches on the ground or about two miles) is handy for locating general areas such as river and lake systems and simply for getting the lay of the land. The 1:50,000 series (1¼ inches to 1 mile) is the type most commonly used for actual wilderness travel, since it locates just about every creek and cabin in the bush.

Topo maps and free indexes and map lists are available from the Canada Map Office, 615 Booth St., Ottawa, Ontario, K1A 0E9. Maps also can be obtained through provincial government departments responsible for recreation, conservation and natural resources and from map dealers across the country. The Canada Map Office can provide you with a complete list of suppliers.

Once you have the tools for the job, you need to learn some fundamental skills of navigation. Basic but commonly overlooked is a method of finding your way

Wilderness travel demands the ability to navigate, usually by map and compass.

back to a starting point if there is no obvious landmark. It may sound silly, but you can travel all day into the bush, then back to the road where you started and find yourself "lost." This will happen when you work your way back to the road satisfactorily (by reversing the compass bearing you took on the inbound leg of the trip) but have enough deviation in your return course to be out of sight of your car. In such a case you won't know whether to turn left or right to walk down the road to the vehicle. The problem becomes even more difficult when the point you are returning to is a single target such as a cabin.

In each case, you either have to find or create a base line. You may have a natural base line such as a road, railway, lake, river, hydro line or cliff which is close enough to your return point that it will serve as a signpost when you head back. If no such line exists you may have to create one. In the bush you can string a long series of blazes– with colored tape around trees– out for a mile or more in two or even four directions from a base camp. Just make sure they indicate which way leads back to camp. In open country you might have to firmly plant tall, colorfully marked stakes. Whatever system you use just make sure the markers are close enough together that you won't wander through the base line without spotting the indicators.

From that base line you will take a line of travel at right angles to head into the bush or the mountains. For example, the base line might be a river which runs east and west and you will head due north from a cabin on the river bank for a day of exploring the bush. Coming back may be as simple as following your ski tracks in the snow or it may be complicated by newly fallen snow or you may simply want to try another route back. In this case, you should not try to simply reverse the direction and head due south because the twists and turns you will make in rough country could put you off course enough to end up on either side of the cabin. It's safer to make an intentional deviation of several degrees so that when you hit the base line you know which way to turn to head for the cabin and a hot supper.

If you have a sighting method on your compass and some prominent landmarks, you will be able to navigate with more confidence by creating lines of position or by using triangulation to locate yourself. A line of position is like one of the latitude or longitude lines already drawn on a map. You can create your own lines of position using a compass and landmarks. At your starting point or base camp take a precise compass bearing on some prominent object, such as a distinctive hilltop or mountain peak which lies in your general direction of travel for the day. You might, for example, get a reading of 50 degrees. Then you could strike out on a wandering course and whenever you wanted to get a precise route back to the starting point simply keep moving until you reached a place where you could get a bearing of 50 degrees on the mountain. As long as you moved in such a way that you kept that bearing you would be on a line between camp and the mountain.

In another case you might be lost but have a map of an area and be able to see some distinctive natural features. Here it would help to have a compass with a sight and a straight edge for marking lines or else a ruler and protractor. You would take a bearing on one target, such as the lone mountain peak in an area, and would trace a line on the map from that peak at the same angle as your compass reading. To place yourself more precisely you would need a second and if possible, a third bearing, perhaps on a distant waterfall and a lake you would also locate on the map. Where the lines intersected on the map is where you would be. This is triangulation.

Before striking out to navigate with a new compass, you should have a basic understanding of how it really operates. The needle of a magnetic compass rarely points to true north. Actually, the needle aligns itself with the Earth's magnetic field at the point where it is being used and even this field doesn't run in straight lines like the grid on a map. Instead, it fans out in curving lines from a fifty square mile area on Bathurst Island in northern Canada. Only along the agonic line, which runs from magnetic North south through Lake Superior, is the magnetic pole more or less in line with true north.

In Newfoundland and British Columbia, the variation (or declination, as it is technically known) is thirty degrees and in parts of the far north, it is so great that a magnetic compass is difficult or even impossible to use with any accuracy. So unless you live in Ontario or Manitoba, the declination from true north is going to vary enough that you should consider it when navigating from maps. In the case of topographic sheets you will find the declination marked and graphically illustrated in a corner of the map and you can make appropriate corrections to your compass readings. If you are east of the agonic line, you will add the number of degrees of declination for your area to any bearing you get to have a true bearing for use on a map. If you are in the west, you will subtract for a correction.

If you live on the east or west coast, you might consider getting a compass with a small screw to make semi-permanent corrections for declination. This will save you the time of adding or subtracting a certain number of degrees from each bearing. In serious navigation, declination should not be overlooked because a difference of twenty degrees could put you in the wrong pass of a mountain range.

Two skiers pause for a moment to watch a fresh snowfall at the edge of a sheltering woodland.

However, if you are simply heading into the bush for a day, without a detailed map of the area, it is usually sufficient to take a simple bearing from your base line and follow that in.

Navigation by natural signs is a favorite topic of camp counsellors, who can explain in great detail how you can take bearings from Polaris, the North Star, or from the sun or from moss on trees. Of these the North Star is the most faithful compass but is not particularly handy since you have to wait till dark and a clear night at that. If you are still out and lost at dark, you will probably be huddled in some temporary shelter trying to keep warm.

The sun does lie due south at noon, but it does not regularly rise in the east or set in the west. In winter it travels from a point somewhere in the southeast to a point somewhere in the southwest quadrant of the sky, while in summer it will be north of east and west. So navigation by the sun can lack precision, but it will give you a general idea of the directions and that may even be enough to get you back to something like a familiar trail. Even when the sun is obscured by clouds there are ways of finding it. On skis you can sometimes do this by skiing across a clearing. The side of the clearing where your skis sink the deepest will be the north side because this will have received the most heat from the sun. The south side would be crustier because it was shaded by trees.

There are other natural features and signs which you will pick up, particularly when you become familiar with an area or on how to pick up details from topo sheets. For example, you might come to a river you know flows from east to west. If the water is open or you can bash a hole in the ice, you will get a peek at the current.

Most Canadians are familiar with methods of finding their ways around built-up areas. Navigation off the beaten path isn't that much more difficult, it's just different and it takes some practice. You can pick up some good experience just using a map and compass in familiar areas to get the feel of these tools and, if the idea appeals to you, consider joining one of the orienteering clubs which make navigation on foot or on skis a weekend sport.

Two useful reference books which deal with navigation in detail are: *The Wilderness Route Finder,* by Calvin Rutstrum and *Be Expert with Map and Compass,* by Bjorn Kjellstrom.

Winter Survival

A typical Rocky Mountain ski trail leading to a remote mountaintop campsite.

In recent years the word survival has taken on new meanings as legions of city dwellers head for the wilderness and find they lack the skills common to the most primitive aborigines. This discovery has spawned a whole new industry, the survival school, as people used to ready-made food, clothing, shelter and heat struggle to re-learn abilities lost over generations of urban life. The concept of survival as a skill which can be taught over a short period of time seems to have its roots in the military training exercises which began in the Second World War. For example, the Outward Bound schools trace their roots to training sessions given sailors to help them survive at sea if their ships were torpedoed.

Various types of survival courses were and still are given to airmen who might have to ditch in uninhabited areas and to troops trained to penetrate and live far behind enemy lines. In postwar years a few military veterans gave similar courses privately, usually to hunters and fishermen. During the 1960s, as wilderness sports like hiking, canoeing, snowmobiling and cross-country skiing became popular, the number of these courses increased sharply and the whole concept of survival training gained considerable publicity. Now it is common to see articles on survival in newspapers and magazines, programs on television and survival courses offered in such institutions as community colleges.

Often ''survival'' is an overdramatic word for what is being taught. Actually the students are usually learning the basics of wilderness living: the sort of techniques often used by our own ancestors as little as a century ago and still part of the life of many northern dwellers. A businessman used to nothing more rigorous than commuting through the occasional snowstorm and shovelling his driveway would be risking his life to go for a walk in the Arctic, even if he packed all the right equipment. An Eskimo walking just over the next ice ridge however, might use a piece of bone shaped like a crude saw to cut snow blocks for an igloo, light a koodlik lamp fueled with fat, munch some seal meat or fish and sleep comfortably, wrapped in animal skins.

As more and more people born and bred in cities follow the urge to rediscover nature and particularly to explore its frozen beauty on skis, they need to learn some of the ways of wilderness life. At the least these may keep them warm and dry some stormy night when they can't make it back to permanent shelter. These skills might even save them from frostbite or worse.

The most important thing you can take into the wilderness is a cool head and a realistic but positive attitude toward your own abilities. This survival psychology means recognizing your own limitations and not tackling a route beyond your own capabilities, but at the same time, not losing hope if you become lost or injured. Armed forces instructors say people cope better with survival situations if they are prepared for the idea. Reading about techniques, and particularly practicing them, help people to form some mental attitudes and absorb some skills which will be ready if they are ever needed. On the other hand, your worst enemies include irrational fear and hopelessness, which can let you give up fighting even though your body could carry on.

Sometimes you can draw hope by remembering tales of endurance and survival by explorers and marooned travellers who used whatever tools they could make or find to build shelters, find food and even improvise means of travel.

If you are in a group, and you should be if you are touring in the back country, you should either have or adopt a sense of group psychology if the going gets tough. There may be a natural leader, often the most experienced outdoorsman in the group, and he should give direction to the less experienced members. He may direct one person to gather material for shelter building, another to find dry wood for a fire and someone else to organize the equipment so nothing will be lost or soaked in the wet snow.

The possibility of facing some kind of survival situation should not be ignored by anyone. Conceivably you could become at least temporarily lost in a storm and have to bivouac overnight without a tent and sleeping bag or someone in the group might shatter a ski or suffer an injury, delaying the return.

First you should study and, if possible, practice some of the basic wilderness skills such as finding or making shelter and fire. These two things will enable you to last several days even with no food and little water. This doesn't necessarily mean enrolling in a course. There are many good books on the subject and plenty of open country in which to try your hand with these new skills.

Another key to surviving in case of accident can be getting help in a hurry. Help can only come if someone is missing you and knows where to send a rescue party. Many long and costly search and rescue missions could have been eliminated if people heading into the wilds had taken a minute to leave word with a friend, relative or even at an official post such as a ranger station. You should leave specific details of the route you plan to take and when you expect to return, making some sort of allowance for minor delays.

Equipment
Before leaving on any trip you should prepare some equipment as outlined in the

chapter on touring and winter camping. Of course you need a map of the area and a compass and the knowledge of how to use them. A sharp, well-sheathed hatchet should be stashed somewhere in your rucksack. With this primitive but highly efficient tool you can cut small trees to make a lean-to shelter and chop up dead branches for fuel. For many outdoorsmen of a traditional bent, the axe is the last tool they would give up. Of course if you are beyond the tree line, in the mountains or far north, you will replace the hatchet with a snow saw for cutting blocks of snow. With these you can make a snow shelter or even an igloo.

In addition to the hatchet you can pack a knife, which will serve for making tinder from dry wood, repairing damaged wood skis and slicing your dry sausage. A useful type is the Swiss Army knife, loaded with such tools as screwdrivers, awls and even hacksaws. Matches of course are essential and you should carry them in at least two, separate, waterproof packages. The first package will be for lighting campfires or your stove at lunch as you would normally expect to. The second is an emergency reserve. Use ordinary ''strike anywhere'' matches and avoid the ''windproof'' and ''waterproof'' types that need special surfaces for ignition. If the surface is damaged the matches are useless.

If you feel at all unsure about your capabilities at fire and shelter making, you could pack a pocketbook on survival in a plastic bag. If all else fails the paper will make good tinder. A better idea for tinder is to stash a few of the dry, solid barbecue fire starter cubes in a couple of layers of plastic or to use a candle stub.

A first aid kit can mean the difference between returning from the trip with a minor discomfort or being immobilized. For starters you should read a good book on wilderness first aid or at least the St. John Ambulance manual. Then adopt a packing list in such a book or adapt it to your own needs. As a minimum you will need bandages, scissors, tweezers, disinfectant, ointment and painkillers.

A repair kit will contain such items as brass wire and strong tape for making emergency repairs to equipment, several binding screws, screwdriver and pocket tool for making holes in the skis to allow repairs. Of course you should carry a spare ski tip and might look for the metal type which incorporates a folding snow saw. In addition to your normal lunch you will add at least a small emergency ration for everyone. This might include an extra length of sausage, chocolate bars and some Dextrose tablets.

If you are well equipped, a night on the trail will be more of an adventure than a true survival experience.

Time
Time is the biggest factor in creating many of these unexpected nights out. Some skiers simply overestimate the ability of themselves or others in the group to complete a long circuit in wild country. They fail to make allowances for heavy snow and muscles not used to the strain of such a trip. Some time in the late afternoon the leader should take a hard look at the time, should know when darkness will fall and must estimate whether it is safe or even possible to make a dash for home. If not, the party is better to take the last few minutes of light in searching out a good location for a camp and making preparations for a night out.

Shelter
Shelter is the first priority. If you know what to look for and what to do, there should be little problem. For example, just remember the last time you were walking in the woods when a shower struck and you found dry shelter beneath a thick pine or spruce. The heavy boughs of a coniferous tree will give you shelter from wind and snow during a winter's night.

At the very least you might dig under the snow-laden limbs of the largest, thick-

The classic woodland survival shelter, a lean-to made of branches with a mattress of spruce boughs and a reflector fire in front.

est tree you can spot and find a place with only a thin layer of snow. Or you might discover a huge tree recently blown down and still holding its needles. You can trim off a few branches to make an opening (away from the prevailing wind of course) and snuggle under. Assuming you haven't forgotten a good supply of matches, the best shelter will be a classic lean-to facing a fire.

If it is to shelter only yourself, look for a couple of trees about seven feet apart and with level ground between them so you can stretch out under the roof you are about to build. Cut a ridgepole, and wedge that between the branches of the two trees about four feet from the ground. If no supporting trees are available, you can brace one or both ends of the shelter with a bipod or tripod arrangement of sticks lashed together at their tops.

When the ridgepole is secure, lean the roof support poles about one foot apart and at a forty-five degree angle to the ridgepole. Then thatch the roof with a six to twelve-inch layer of coniferous branches which you can easily strip off with your hands. Start at the bottom of the shelter and with the tips of the branches facing the ground, work your way up to the top with each layer of branches overlapping the layer below. Then thatch in both sides of the shelter.

Next you will build a floor or ''browse bed'' of soft evergreen branches, both to give you a decent mattress for the night and to insulate you from the cold below. Lay at least a six-inch layer with the bottom sides of the branches up so the sharp butt ends will be face down. If you have the time, lay a log in front of the bed both to keep the branches in place and to give you a place to sit.

While you collect wood for the shelter, you should also lay in a supply of dead wood for a fire. If you have enough fuel, you should build a fire the length of the shelter to warm your entire body.

This is the style for a one-man shelter. If more than one person is going to spend the night there, it will have to be deep enough so each person can sleep with either their head or feet toward the fire.

Of course if you have packed a light, nylon tarpaulin it will be much easier to rig an emergency shelter and it will be more windproof. If you thought to add a reflective-coated blanket, this will make the floor more secure and draft-proof and will help bounce back your body's heat. A few people, usually those with mountaineering experience, carry a bivouac bag, which is a large sack into which you can stuff yourself and sleeping bag, if you have it, to pass a night out of the wind.

Another type of natural shelter sometimes available is the cave. This is solid protection but not always easy to find and often damp or lined with sharp rocks or boulders. At times it is already inhabited. However, it you are travelling in hilly country where the snow is deep, you can make your own cave in the snow and pass a night undisturbed by the wildest blizzard. The only problem is that it takes several hours and some effort to build a good shelter. But if you are stuck for the night and have your flashlight handy, you can dig at least a respectable one.

A snow cave is shaped like a classic igloo but is carved, instead of built out of snow. Ideally, you should tunnel into a thick bank of snow, then start scooping out a dome-shaped room. This is a wet job and you should wear a parka and overpants. It is also slow going with hands alone and easier done with a small shovel. Once inside, poke one or two small ventilation holes through the roof and protect the entrance from drifting in with some snow blocks to act as a snow fence.

The cave will be warmest if you keep the tunnel entrance low and carve out a sleeping platform a foot or two higher up. Snow is a good insulator of course, as the relative warmth of the cave will show. But it is cold to sit on directly. If you have no branches or insulating pads to put beneath your body, use a packsack or even plastic bags to ease the chill. Don't worry about freezing to death in your sleep; the cold will wake you up first and you'll toss, turn and if lightly clad, shiver a bit to turn a few more calories of fat into body heat.

On flat snow, such as on a glacier or in the Arctic, you may have to make a trench or igloo. The trench is simply a ditch dug a couple of feet or more deep and covered with whatever is handy. If there is at least some brush handy, you might use some of it to line the bottom of the shelter and the rest to make a roof with the aid of skis and poles. On top of that you would add a layer of snow to make it windproof. Or if there is no shrubbery at all you could carve snow blocks from the packed surface and lean them against one another to form a peaked roof. If the snow is too shallow even for that, you may have to cut snow block walls and roof them with other snow slabs.

Igloo building takes even more time than cave-digging and it's the sort of thing you might want to practice. The secret is to create an ever ascending spiral of snow blocks rather than simply laying rows as you would brick up a house. Obviously you have to bevel the blocks and gently tap them into place so they will hold. A snow saw and knife are a necessity and a detailed description of the technique is helpful. There are good instructions in the Canadian Forces booklet *Down but Not Out*, a paperback on survival for stranded airmen.

Keeping Warm
Keeping warm while you are holed up for the night is important. Certainly you want to prevent any of your extremities from suffering frostbite and, if possible, you also want to get some sleep (for which you'll need to prevent an excessive loss of body heat).

In cross-country skiing you generate a steady flow of heat so that you need little clothing while on the move. A few moments after you stop moving, the last of that excess heat will have evaporated and been blown away by the wind. You will probably react by pulling your toque down over your ears and the back of your neck and putting up the hood of your jacket if there is one. Then you will switch to warm mitts and pull on overpants to insulate your legs. The down or polyester filled ski jacket will go on over your light jacket.

As the cold moves in, your feet will probably feel it first. Unless you had room for a pair of mukluks in the day pack, you won't have much extra insulation. Look around and use your imagination. Once you have settled in place for a while, you could partially fill the packsack with the tips of pine branches, slip your feet inside and draw the top snug around your calves. Then pull the nylon tarp or space blanket around your body to act as a further windbreak and toss another couple of sticks on the fire.

Remember, it's the thickness that insulates you against the loss of body heat and in a pinch, you can even stuff pine needles, bark, moss, feathers, animal skins or just about anything else you can lay your hands on under your jacket or around your shelter. The great enemies of any insulator are wind and water. Wind, as you can tell by its effects on your face, wipes away the heat as fast as it can radiate. One answer is to wear a windproof outer shell, such as nylon or one of the cotton-nylon weaves, and the second is to get out of the wind as fast as you can.

Water can hit you from both sides. On the average the body evaporates 1 ½ pints of water– almost one litre– per day. That moisture can clog the tiny air cells in any clothing, especially down-filled, and act as a heat conductor. To avoid that, you need clothing which is water resistant (but not waterproof, most of the time) to allow evaporation right through to the outside and you need to be able to zip open your clothing when heat builds up. On the other hand, you may need highly water resistant or even waterproof clothing such as a poncho or cagoule if you could hit rain.

You just may not be able to keep your feet completely dry during the day and the best answer is to have at least one pair of dry socks stuffed away in the pack.

Fire

The answer to your heat problems of course is fire. On a long trip you will have a gas stove and several aluminum Sigg bottles topped up with fuel, but on a day trip you might carry nothing more than a couple of waterproof containers of matches. Such brass and nickel containers are available in many sporting goods stores or you might use one of these as an absolutely safe package and use a more capacious thirty-five mm film container for the main holder.

Primitive methods of fire building look good in books and may be fun to practice during the summer when you have an afternoon to while away, but they should not be counted on under adverse conditions when you need heat in a hurry and everything around you is wet. Here it helps even to carry some fire starter such as barbecue cubes or a candle or even a couple of pieces of Kleenex. Then you need a large pile of dry wood such as the dead, lower branches which can be snapped off most trees and the frequent dead tree you will find in real forest.

As you gather your wood you try to get at least three thicknesses. The tiniest, driest twigs you can find in sheltered places around tree trunks will be your most likely fire starter. If necessary, you can make fuzz sticks by starting but not cutting free a series of shavings on a stick from which you have removed the damp bark. Of course, the woodsman's emergency fuel source in many places is the birch tree, one of the few woods which will burn even when it is wet. You wouldn't strip a tree unless it was an emergency any more than you would slash pines to make a lean-to, unless your safety depended on it– but these are the things you should know about just in case you need them. The fine birch bark will make an excellent tinder and the branches will burn fiercely.

The next size of fuel will be pencil-thick branches or heavier branches split open with a knife or hatchet to expose their dry interiors. Then come the heavy

Mike Exall, ski and survival instructor at Toronto's Seneca College, coaxes life from a fire with a few full breaths of air.

pieces, including small logs and even stumps to hold the heat through the night. You will have stamped down the snow in the area of your camp, but the heat of a fire will melt the snow and your sticks will disappear if they don't have some sort of base.

The most secure base would be a platform of rocks, but you'll probably have to settle for a double or triple layer of green branches which will be slow to burn through. If you can build your shelter about four or five feet from a cliff or even a snowbank, you will have a natural reflector. Otherwise you can improvise a reflector by stacking birch branches or peeled sticks between upright stakes on the far side of your blaze. With a full-length fire in front of a well-made lean-to, you can spend a reasonably comfortable night. As the fire dies down from time to time, the chill will awaken you long enough to throw a few more logs on the embers and you'll roll over to warm your other side. You should automatically store some dry tinder in a secure corner of your sleeping quarters in case you have to re-light the fire in the morning and you should cover your dry firewood with a few evergreen branches to keep it clear of snow which could fall during the night.

When you awaken in the morning you will appreciate a hot drink and to make one you'll need a metal container. Some outdoorsmen pack some of their supplies in a coffee or nut can which has a plastic top and with a piece of wire they can rig a handle, then suspend it over the fire with a stick. At the least you will need a metal cup to melt some snow and boil up some tea from the bag you slipped into your emergency food packet.

Accidents and first aid

Cross-country skiing is not considered a high-risk sport, but if you take to bushwhacking there is a chance that some day you will run into something solid, get caught in a severe cold snap or will damage your equipment. Equipment breakage can range from the annoying to the serious. For example, shattering a bamboo ski pole will be unsettling at the least and could cause an injury if you fall on the splintered shaft. But you may be able to repair the damaged pole in a few minutes with the strong tape you carry. Otherwise you might settle for a slightly slower pace and just keep going with one pole. If you still have a long distance to cover, you can simply cut yourself another pole from a handy sapling, taking time to slide the basket from the old pole onto the new one.

A damaged ski is more serious. Tip breakage is the most common problem if a wood ski rams a rock or tree trunk and this is often quickly repaired by sliding on an emergency ski tip. If for some reason you forgot to pack one, you may have to resort to the trick of sliding a mitt over the end of the ski or to some fancy taping and bracing with jury-rigged splints.

Should a ski be shattered by a severe fall, you may have to start using some imagination and whatever gear you packed in your repair kit. For example, you may be able to lash the tail back in place with tape or spare screws and a rough board cut from a small tree. Theoretically, you could even hack a new ski from some dead hardwood, steaming the tip over a boiling billy of water to bend it up; but this would be time consuming and possibly dangerous unless you had adequate food and shelter. Some bush dwellers have rigged their own snowshoes in an emergency, using bent saplings and whatever lacing material they could find or create. Again this is not a task to be started lightly, for you will have to make the webbing strong enough to take your weight.

Personal injury is something you don't want to dwell on but should be prepared for. Many problems can be avoided by a few simple precautions. For example, if you are skiing in heavy brush and especially if you are tackling some downhill sections, slide your hands out of your pole straps. This could save you from a nasty dislocation if a pole basket should snag something. Frostbite, particularly on an exposed face, is a possibility when you are skiing on cold days, particularly if there is a sharp wind whistling out of the north. In such weather, a hood tied under the chin, a scarf across the face or possibly a balaclava wool face mask will save you problems. For extreme climates there are even down-filled masks.

The simplest ways to avoid frostbite are to stop and warm your face if you feel it getting very cold and for members of a group to watch each other's faces for the telltale white blotches indicating frostbite. Unless you are in a state of collapse or woefully underdressed for the climate, there is little excuse for getting a serious case of frostbite on your extremities. If you are starting to lose sensation in your hands, simply put on the warm mitts you carry in your day pack. Or at the least jam them under your armpits where they will find plenty of warmth. In the case of feet, try skiing faster or simply bouncing up and down on your skiis or even taking off your skis and doing a quick dance on the hard snow. The problem might also be wet socks and it might be time to change to the dry pair in your pack. If someone in your party has feet that are turning white with frostbite, get the warmest member of the group to take those feet under his armpits or against his stomach until they thaw out.

By now everyone should know that rubbing snow on frostbite will do more harm than good. If you have a case of serious frostbite on your hands and the flesh is frozen solid, avoid rubbing anything on the skin since this will only damage the hardened tissue. The skier should be evacuated – walking or skiing if necessary, on a frozen foot – to a place where the frozen part can be kept in water of about forty-two degrees Celsius or 108 Farenheit until thawed and where there is no danger of re-freezing. Treat a frostbitten part as you would a burn by wrapping it in a sterile dressing. The patient should be given extra clothing, warm drinks and food.

Hypothermia is the new catchword among outdoorsmen and is a more accurate term to describe what we once called exposure. It is Greek for "too little heat" and expresses what happens to the body when it is losing heat faster than it can be regenerated by burning food and fat reserves. It is more serious than frostbite since it involves a chilling of the body's core and can be a killer even in above freezing temperatures. Most people have had a brush with it when they got caught in a cold, driving rainstorm with only light clothing and suddenly found themselves shivering uncontrollably. If the heat loss continues past a certain point, the heart begins to beat aimlessly and death follows.

Violent and uncontrollable shivering is a good sign of hypothermia. So are poor co-ordination, which often shows up in a slow and stumbling pace, thick, slurred speech and a deep feeling of cold and numbness – all of which can impair the ability to react wisely to the impending problem.

All outdoors travellers should react to these signs and if one member of a party is starting to show them, get that person warmed up fast. Usually the two major problems are dampness wicking away heat from the body and wind evaporating it from there on. If there are fresh dry clothes, put them on and get out of the wind. Hot food and drink are the best cures, but shared body heat, nude body to nude body in a sleeping bag also makes a quick heat transfer and will help bring someone around. Like frostbite, hypothermia is the sort of thing that should not happen to a properly equipped and led party, but might easily be an additional problem for someone stranded or already suffering shock from an injury.

Anyone who travels on ice during the winter is taking a risk of dunking. At the worst this may only mean a wet foot as you scamper and slide to safety, but even this can pose serious problems. One immediate solution is to immediately roll the wet part of your body in dry, powder snow if available, as this will blot up some of the water. With luck and reasonably water-repellent clothing, you may end up with nothing worse than an armour plating of ice which can be brushed and scraped away. However, you will more likely have to find some immediate shelter, get into any dry clothing available and possibly build a fire.

Snow blindness should not be a problem for any skier equipped with a good pair of sunglasses, preferably of dark glass if you travel in the high country. If you do find your eyes swollen and sore after a day on the snow, you should have some antiseptic eye ointment in your medicine kit to ease the problem. Somehow your sunglasses may be lost or broken and you don't have another pair in your pack. In this case you may have to make your own eye protectors by tying a strip of some material such as nylon or even tree bark in front of your eyes and cutting small slits for vision. Of course you will have to travel carefully because of your limited vision.

Sunburn can be a serious problem in spring skiing or at high altitudes, where there is less filtration of the sun's rays. Every skier should carry one of the tiny tubes of suntan lotion available in drugstores and ski shops and should get a sun-screen lotion if touring at high altitudes in the spring.

Another problem for high altitude parties is mountain sickness or the more serious high-altitude, pulmonary edema. Altitude sickness can strike most people not used to the change in elevation, but again most people become acclimatized to it. Edema is usually only a problem in high ranges (above 10,000 feet) and involves fluid building up in the lungs. Immediate evacuation to a lower altitude is the cure.

Other injuries which might strike a skier are dislocations and fractures. Often it is better to try to replace a dislocated bone in a socket and endure a few seconds of extra pain rather than try to hobble back on the trail. In the case of fractures, someone will have to splint the injury as best possible with bandages or possibly with a splint made from a split open tree branch. A broken arm may be lashed to the torso and one broken leg to the other good one in a pinch. If you carry in your pack a piece of wire mesh splint made for such emergency use, then things may be a lot easier.

Under such circumstances you may have to organize an evacuation of the injured person. Unless you are so well equipped that you have a roll-up sled, you will have to help the victim walk or ski out or you must rig some kind of sleigh. It won't be easy, but with tape and nylon cord, the skis and ski poles of the injured party and some branches, you can fashion a crude sled. This should be padded with extra clothing, sleeping bags and even branches to make it more comfortable. The rider should be well dressed and wrapped in a waterproof tarpaulin if possible.

There are many publications on survival and if you are interested in the outdoors, you will probably want to obtain at least a couple for reference. Among useful works are: *Down but Not Out,* the Canadian Armed Forces manual already mentioned; several of the Bradford Angier series of books, including *How to Stay Alive in the Woods, Skills for Taming the Wilds* and *Being Your Own Wilderness Doctor; Wilderness Skiing* by Lito Tejada-Flores and Allen Steck, published by the Sierra Club; *First Aid,* the manual of the St. John Ambulance Association.

The following is a suggested list for a toilet and first aid kit. You may want to add some personal medications such as those for allergies. Never count on being able to buy what you need on the road. The kits should be packed in metal or tightly closing plastic boxes.

Toilet Kit
suntan lotion
Uval (total sunscreen)
Solarcaine (sunburn lotion)
sewing kit of needles, threads
   and thimble
cuticle scissors
nail clippers
nail file
tweezers
comb
metal mirror with cord for hanging and
   hole in middle for emergency
   signalling plus
instructions for signalling.
toothbrush
toothpaste tube, in plastic bag
safety pins
toilet paper
Kleenex
plastic tube of liquid soap

First Aid Kit
disinfectant (such as Merthiolate)
cream for cuts and scrapes (such as
   Ozonol)
222s or 292s if you can get a
   prescription
ASA tablets for a mild headache
tetracycline (or other antibiotic)
opthalmic ointment
sleeping tablets
Locomotil
triangular bandages
tensor bandage
2 inch bandages
bandaids
gauze compresses
2 inch roll of tape
eye pads
sterile plastic bags
St. John Ambulance First Aid manual

The Elements of Winter

"Mon pays c'est l'hiver," (my country it is the winter) sings Quebec songwriter Gilles Vigneault.

Canada has been given – some would say blessed and some would say cursed – with one of the snowiest climates of any country in the world. On Rocky Mountain glaciers and in the high Arctic you can find snow, some of it skiable, all year round. Excepting such balmy spots as the southwestern corners of Ontario and British Columbia, the land is white for upwards of three months each year.

Anywhere from September to October snow makes its first, somewhat hesitant appearance. One cool autumn day a few snowflakes drift down from a slate-colored sky – vanguards of the billions to come in the months ahead. From then until the hot sun of May hunts down and melts the final patches huddled on north slopes and deep in the bush we will walk in it, shovel it, try not to get stuck in it and hopefully find some idyllic minutes playing in it.

For the skier even winter has its seasons. At first there is a tempting little layer of snow on the ground when you awake one morning in late fall. It is time to step up the tempo of that exercise program you have been toying with since late September when the canoe and packsacks were stored. You gauge the snow still a bit too thin even for a run across a nearby golf course and settle for a check of equipment. Are the skis tarred, the boots waxed and the long johns where you can find them? How is the wax kit? Maybe it's time to replace that stub of violet you nursed through last spring. You settle down one evening with a pile of maps and start planning some tours for this winter, then you reach for the phone book wondering who might be interested in joining a trip.

That first layer will melt away but soon be replaced by more determined snowfalls. In the short days of early winter you head out, watching for rocks and stubs of pruned underbrush just beneath this thin snow cover. The fields are full of weeds, their heads still laden with seeds not yet buried by the snow. You skirt the thin ice of streams and rivers but look for broken areas which indicate a beaver or muskrat has been passing by.

January and the cold reaches its deepest point. Some days it is so cold you don't venture farther than a nearby park where you join dozens of newcomers to the sport testing their Christmas present ski outfits and making tentative attempts at kick and glide. Other days you try tours in forests, counting on the trees to break the force of the bitter north wind. Even so, you carry a down-filled parka and warm-up pants for the lunch break in a thick pine grove. With little encouragement a gray Canada Jay flutters in to take a handful of bread crumbs. Then you finish the thermos of tea and head back for the road, listening as you go to the trees creak in the wind and the cold, dry snow echoing the sound from beneath your feet.

By February and March your leg muscles will be firmed up and your wind capable of sustained runs through the heavy snows which now blanket everything in sight. The days are a bit longer and warmer and you poke through the bush, following the characteristic two wide, two narrow tracks of a rabbit you flushed from its hiding place under a spruce. You deliberately detour through a grove of apple trees, hoping to flush a grouse and as usual, the bird spots you first and the sudden burst of sound from its frantic wing-beats jumps your heartbeat. With temperatures a bit milder, you join the ever increasing numbers taking a week or two of winter vacation and looking for a friendly lodge with trails for good excur-

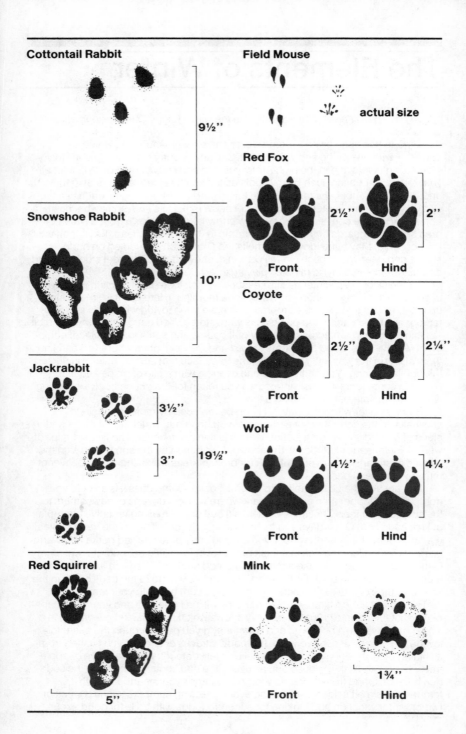

Cottontail Rabbit — 9½"

Field Mouse — actual size

Snowshoe Rabbit — 10"

Red Fox
Front — 2½"
Hind — 2"

Coyote
Front — 2½"
Hind — 2¼"

Jackrabbit — 3½", 3", 19½"

Wolf
Front — 4½"
Hind — 4¼"

Red Squirrel — 5"

Mink
Front
Hind — 1¾"

Otter

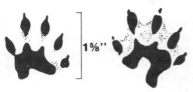

Front   1⅝"   Hind

Ruffed Grouse

2"

White Tailed Deer

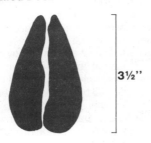

3½"

Moose

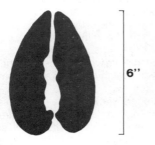

6"

Caribou

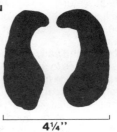

4¼"

Elk

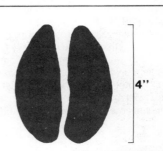

4"

Lynx

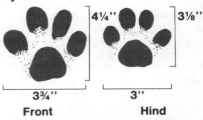

4¼"   3⅛"

3¾"   3"

Front   Hind

House Cat

both are 1⅛" x 1⅛"

Front   Hind

Bob Cat

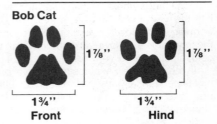

1⅞"   1⅞"

1¾"   1¾"

Front   Hind

sions. If you can round up a couple more experienced skiers, you might even try your hand at winter camping, with a one-night outing for starters and a longer trek after that. It's also the season of races: everything from the Canadian Marathon to a local fun race present a variety of choices that would more than fill up the time you have free.

Late March and early April are the seasons of the tubes. There are tubes of sticky klister waxes to grip the wet snows and tubes of suntan lotion to protect your winter-whitened face from the powerful combination of direct and reflected sun. If you are touring in the mountains you will come back with a face tan as dark as that of a Caribbean tourist. This is the season when the world begins to come alive. Animals are active in the woods and overhead crows are starting to migrate north, the harbingers of spring with their raucous calls. You hide under a pine tree and try to draw them in by mimicking their calls and are rewarded by a flurry of wing-beats overhead. As the days lengthen, the snow becomes pure corn in the morning and you are whizzing across nature's ball bearings. But by afternoon it has turned to slush. At streams you hesitantly poke the remaining snow bridges with your poles, trying to gauge if they will get you across. You make it, but find the bridge virtually vanished when you return that way two hours later. Across the fields you dash, a light jacket tied around your waist and sunglasses steamed up from the heat as you twist and turn among the bare patches. Finally, you unsnap the bindings for the last time, at the edge of a muddy road, and carefully pick your way back to the car.

Snow

Snow. A single flake of it can be so tenuous that it melts in your hand before your eyes can analyze its complex, crystalline structure. But let that flake get together with a few hundred trillion of its friends and you may never see the end of it. Snow that fell millions of years ago remains in a compacted form in the polar regions. Even the snow on mountain tops is dubbed eternal for more than poetic reasons.

Old snow is called firn, a German word meaning "of last year." This is dense snow in which the air spaces between the ice particles have been greatly compressed but there is still enough air that the stuff has not yet turned into the solid form: ice. There are many other evocative words associated with snow. For example, sastrugi are long, sharp ridges in the snow formed by wind erosion and snow, barchan are U-shaped snow drifts or snow dunes formed by fresh, blowing snow. Hoarfrost and rime are ice particles separated by trapped air when water droplets cool suddenly. For example, rime is the traditional decoration on an arctic explorer's parka after his breath has been frozen around the edge of the hood seconds after it is expelled into the frigid air.

We know that snow is formed at high altitudes when water droplets form around such things as passing dust motes in the sky. All snowflakes, and ice particles as well, are hexagonal– six sided– but no two are the same. At high altitudes most of the condensed water is snow, but much of it melts by the time it reaches lower altitudes where the air is warmed by the sun. When the snowflakes do make it all the way down, they may arrive in any of a dozen or so classified forms ranging from big, soft snowflakes so beloved by movie makers who try to imitate them to the tiny particles known as diamond dust, which float through the air on some cold, clear days.

In those first few minutes after arrival on ground, snow may be as much as ninety per cent air trapped between a multitude of ice crystals. This is the fresh powder snow favored especially by downhill skiers who float on its elusive substance. Within a short time, snow begins a process of metamorphism in which the fluffy flakes begin to change into rounded granules. The process is often called

In the western national parks dogs are trained to search for people buried by avalanches.

settling because the snow pack begins to lose air content and literally settles closer to the ground. Such exterior forces as wind or the passing of skis can greatly speed up the process. If the snow is at a high enough altitude or latitude, it will become firn and eventually may become ice as the air is displaced.

Insignificant in small numbers, snowflakes can take on awesome proportions as they add up. For example, twenty-five centimetres (ten inches) of snow will put as much as ten tons pressure on the roof of an average house and you may have to shovel a ton to clear your sidewalks and driveway after such a storm.

Avalanches – One of the most impressive forms in which a skier can ever encounter snow is as an avalanche. It is one of nature's greatest destructive forces, ranking right up there with the hurricane, earthquake and tidal wave. Avalanches have been recorded at speeds of 360 kilometres per hour (225 m.p.h.) or about twice the world speed record on skis. When a big slide comes down, everything moves: century-old trees, boulders as big as houses, houses themselves, churches, schools, trains and any other structures not specially designed to let the snow roll over them smoothly. The forces are known to exceed 100 tons per square metre. Snow slides have their worst record in well inhabited alpine regions, particularly Europe and now the West, as more and more people settle and ski there. But even Easterners might look at snowslopes with more respect if they remembered two Scarborough (metropolitan Toronto) girls killed in a slide on a twenty-metre (seventy-five foot) long toboggan slope and a skier at Blue Mountain who had to wait for hours until he was rescued by friends from a relatively small slide on a little used trail.

Much is known about avalanches and the fact that they result from any of a series of factors influencing fallen snow, including degree of slope, sun, wind, sound and movement of such things as skis. Most important of all is the snow structure itself. Fresh, fluffy snow can slide quite readily because of its own instability on a slope and often does during a storm, but once it settles for a few hours the arts and science of predicting avalanches get much trickier.

Snow can be affected by a process called sublimation, in which the ice crystals at the extremities of a snowflake vaporize and then re-freeze nearer the centre of the crystal. This is destructive metamorphism. Then these granules can undergo constructive metamorphism in which they literally grow cup crystals a centimetre long. The crystals form a highly unstable layer beneath the even, white surface which the skier sees before him. In effect, they create a sub-surface of ball bearings beneath an expanse of snow and it may take no more than the bark of a dog, a puff of wind, a few more seconds of sunshine or the movement of a skier to break the tenuous bond and send tons of snow sliding downhill.

Experts have spent years trying to find ways to forecast and prevent avalanches, but Fred Schleiss, the avalanche analyst who decides when traffic can safely move through the Rogers Pass in British Columbia, says much is still unknown. He says even the experts work on sixty per cent technology and forty per cent art.

Peter Scharer of Vancouver, an avalanche expert with the National Research Council, says part of the expertise in predicting avalanches is simply gut feeling and that is what makes a good mountain guide. The researchers have their ''snow plots'' where they can slice away at the snow pack every day and look at the crystal formation. The guide goes by his training and experience with certain slopes and weather conditions. He will try to confirm his suspicions by jabbing an inverted ski pole into the snow, looking for an unstable layer below. He may even take a calculated risk and try to guess where the shear line or upper limit of an avalanche would be, then stamp his skis there to see if he can trigger a small slide. It is a demanding task and even guides get hurt once in a while.

For the cross-country skier going into potential avalanche terrain, and basically that does mean the West, ignorance imposes a high risk. The safest measure is to hire a qualified guide who knows the area. The next best – and a distant second for people unfamiliar with mountains – is to check with experts such as National Parks Service snow specialists in the area. They know the usual avalanche patterns for an area and often can warn you of particular hazards in a given area. As well, they may be able to map out a safe route for your party.

You should regard any slope steeper than fifteen degrees as having some avalanche potential and treat it with at least some respect. This respect should increase after heavy snowfalls or rains which can make conditions suddenly unstable. Most cross-country skiers will be travelling the flatter mountain valleys and won't run the same risk as alpine oriented touring parties, but even so they should watch out for hazards. When an avalanche sweeps down a slope it often keeps going right into the valley and can hurl shattered trees and debris more than a kilometre across the valley bottom.

If you are travelling in avalanche country, there are some precautions to take and things to keep in mind when you are near slopes. One of the simplest protections you can carry is fifteen metres (fifty feet) of brightly colored nylon cord known as avalanche cord. When you are skiing on a slope you think could avalanche, let the cord run freely behind on the principle that if you are buried there is a good chance a piece of nylon will remain on the surface and direct rescuers to you. As in many wilderness skiing situations, you should remove your pole straps; in this case, it is so you can cover your face in a hurry if the choking powder snow flies up or so you can make swimming motions as you try to stay near the surface. A well equipped party will carry avalanche probes and shovels for locating and digging out anyone trapped by sliding snow. The most expensive ($100 plus) and one of the most effective protections are the small radio transmitter-receivers sold under such names as Skadi and Pieps and used by helicopter ski parties which are constantly in avalanche country. All members of a group carry one tucked underneath their clothing and set to transmit a beeping radio signal. If one person is buried, the other members switch to "receive" and use their sets as radio locators.

Of course the best route in avalanche country is around any area that looks as if it could slide, but this will inevitably become a question of judgement and you will feel pressed by falling night, an empty stomach and other factors. If you are crossing a slope with a possible hazard, each member of the group should go separately and the others should watch carefully. In case one skier is buried, the others should keep watching, then start digging and probing in the area below where the person was last seen. Form a straight line and probe with the tails of skis if necessary. At the same time don't forget there could be a second avalanche, so you should keep an eye peeled above.

If it is you who are caught in a slide take hope and remember the words of Fred Schleiss: "There's no slide I've triggered that's outpaced me in the first five seconds." In other words, if you are near the edge of the avalanche there is a chance you can ski down and to one side enough to escape all or most of its effects. In any case, try to stay on your feet and if the snow is already moving around you, dig your poles in uphill and try to hang on. If you go under, keep your hands near your face and try to remember to cover your face with one hand and reach straight up with the other. The most important thing is to cover your face, then quickly scratch out as much of a breathing space as possible. People have survived as long as ten days buried in avalanches, but have also suffocated in a few minutes if the snow seeped into their mouths or formed a solid mass around their heads.

All that is not to terrorize people from ever going within a mile of a mountain but rather to instill a certain respect and awareness of avalanches. Once aware, you stand a far better chance of being alert and learning more about the subject.

Ice

All snow is ice and air and if given enough time will become solid ice as air pockets between ice particles disappear. Given certain conditions, such as very high wind, this may happen almost instantly. Mountaineers at high altitudes have found that gale-force winds will pack the snow so hard that it virtually becomes ice in seconds and has to be chopped away from equipment with an ice axe.

The cross-country skier is more likely to find ice beneath his skis as the result of other skiers packing a trail. As each ski passes over the snow, it briefly melts the surface with friction and leaves a microscopic trail of water which immediately refreezes. In addition, it packs the snow and speeds up the process of sublimation which also leads to ice formation.

Most back-country skiers will also run across ice in the form of frozen lakes, rivers and streams and will probably use the flat, snow-covered surface as a place to pick up a bit of time on a long trip. It is worth remembering that a smooth surface, like the even surface of a slope before it avalanches, can be deceptive.

The times of greatest hazard, of course, are in the fall freeze-up and during the spring melt, but few ice surfaces can automatically be considered completely safe at any time. In the middle of winter a fast current will be nibbling at the underside of the ice on a river and may leave only a shell of snow on the top. Lakes are sometimes fed by streams which pump a steady flow of water to one area and create a thin spot in the ice. Narrows between two lakes or in the course of a river are notorious for having weak spots where the current is a bit faster and have claimed many a snowmobile, passengers and all. Experienced travellers will check the ice conditions with residents of the area if possible, and will find out something of the weather patterns just before the trip. As they travel, they will make frequent stabbing checks of the surface ahead with the tips of their ski poles. Sometimes a pole will penetrate the snow and turn up slush beneath. This bears further checking. Is it just a layer of water atop the solid ice or is the ice below unsound? If for some reason you absolutely have to cross ice that appears rotten, you may be better off to carry a stout sapling, as long as you are tall and hold it crosswise. If you go through, the pole will probably hold on either side and prevent you going right under. Another good precaution is to rope up all members of a party.

A complete dunking far from shelter can be disastrous, but even a wet foot can pose a severe threat of freezing. One reaction taken by some northern dwellers when they put a foot through the ice is to immediately plunge it into soft, dry snow. The snow, if full of air spaces, will act somewhat as a blotter and can absorb part of the moisture. This is another reason to carry a change of socks in your pack: they could save you from a frostbitten foot. Once badly wet it becomes a matter of judgment. If the weather is not too frigid and you are not too far from shelter, it may be worthwhile to make a dash for camp or car. All members of the party should contribute some warm clothing, especially that in the packs and strip off all the wet clothing possible from the victim. Then set out at top speed and keep an eye on the wet person for signs of frostbite. The alternative is to immediately make an emergency camp and start a roaring fire. There will be a time consuming wait while you carefully dry out his clothing without burning it up.

Weather

Wind, cloud, sun and temperature all govern the lives we lead, especially if we are spending them out of doors. They are part of the weather patterns which dictate whether or not we will be able to ski, and if so, what the conditions will be like.

Fallible as they are, the weather reports from government meteorologists are still the best indicators most of us can find to get at least a general idea of the weather for our area. These reports tend to paint the picture in broad brush strokes and will tell you if a warming trend is in the air or if cold weather will continue. They can also forecast major storm fronts and alert you to possible hazards. Sometimes it takes a bit of research to get the report for the area you plan to ski. Some radio stations, particularly CBC, will occasionally carry forecasts for a wide area beyond the city where the station is based. Sometimes there is a government weather station you can phone for up-to-the-minute information on specific localities.

Sometimes weather reports are not available and in areas such as mountain country, they may be of little specific use. Within a given weather system there are frequent local variations: in the mountains you may have sun in one valley and a storm in the next, and lakeshores often have more cloud than areas a few kilometres inland. Winter weather can have a drastic effect on your skiing, especially if you are going off the beaten track. If a severe storm is brewing, you probably wouldn't want to stray more than a couple of kilometres from the base and certainly wouldn't risk heading out for a day or two of winter camping. If the weather has been steadily warming, you would seriously reconsider any trip into the mountains where wet snow could double the time of travel and increase the avalanche hazard.

Every skier should develop a bit of weather sense to augment forecasts that may be already outdated by sudden changes or may not be valid for a specific area. Just as you learn to gauge the type of snow before applying wax in the morn-

The first part of making camp in deep snow is creating a solid platform for the tent. This means stamping down the snow with your boots until it becomes as hard as earth.

ing, you should learn to scan the sky for cloud signs. There are plenty of standby signs for bad weather: rising wind, sharp changes in temperature and build-up of clouds. However, strong winds in one area or under certain conditions may mean different things. In one part of the country they could be the sign of an impending storm and in another area they may be a sign that the weather is clearing. Or they may occur before, during and after a storm.

Forecasting local weather is best learned by observation and experience, but many useful tips can be gleaned from true experts such as guides and rangers who live and work outdoors and are used to keeping a weather eye for their own safety and comfort. Many mountain guides carry a pocket altimeter, which is just a barometer with the dial working in reverse. In other words, a rising altimeter (if you are stationary) means a falling barometer and the probability of bad weather.

Temperature – Most of us are constantly curious about the temperature around us and for skiers the concern is even more justified. Certainly this, along with the condition of the snow surface, dictates what kind of wax we should begin with on any day and the kind of clothing we will wear and pack. The temperature may also affect the choice of route. A sheltered route among the trees would be more appropriate on a cold, windy day. If the temperature is rising and there is a possibility of precipitation, we might also pack rain gear as a precaution against a shower. When the wind is picking up, the temperature is dropping as a result of the wind chill factor. For example, the air temperature according to your pocket thermometer could be five degrees C (forty degrees F) but with a sixty kilometre (forty m.p.h.) wind your exposed flesh would feel a temperature of minus eleven degrees C or ten degrees F.

On a minus twenty degrees C day with a fresh breeze, there will be danger of exposed skin freezing in as little as one minute and you should take great care to cover even your face with a scarf or mask. In truly extreme cold, such as is rarely found in the lower latitudes of Canada, not only the outer skin but the lining of the lungs could suffer damage. When the temperature starts getting into the minus forty degree C range, you should use caution about moving quickly and drawing in great breaths of air.

The other side of the coin or the clouds as the case may be is the warmth from the sun. This is the life-giving force which powers our world and creates our weather as it evaporates the water which makes the clouds which make the rain and the snow we ski on. From December through January it seems to vanish from the sky and in the high North it is almost completely absent, creating a period when people can work and move about for only brief periods without artificial light, heat and insulation. The legendary resistance of the Eskimo to deep cold is largely a result of his knack for staying out of the cold and beneath a warm layer of fur and insulating snow as much as possible during the deep winter.

For many centuries man, particularly in northern latitudes, has respected and even worshiped the cycles of the sun as it drew further away from his land, then slowly started its trek back across the sky, melting the snow and warming upturned faces. Despite the artificial environments we create in an attempt to ignore winter, Canadians are still affected by the changes and, like other peoples, celebrate the return of Old Sol. Since the distant past, Europeans have marked the lengthening of the days in January and February with celebrations such as the famous Fasching of Germany. These celebrations have been transplanted to the New World and take such forms as the carnival in Rio, the Mardi Gras of New Orleans and the *Carnaval d'Hiver* (Winter Carnival) of Quebec City. In recent years the winter carnival has become a new part of life in many towns and cities across Canada, as people relax and let their hair down after a couple of months of cold and snow. For many skiers it is a time not only of celebration but competition – both serious and friendly – as people race for trophies and personal satisfaction. Many carnivals have cross-country races as part of their programs and draw both the trained competitors and erstwhile spectators who decide to try their newly developed skills in a run of a few kilometres with their neighbors.

Winter Photography

Photographs provide some of the best souvenirs of any trip, especially a tour through winter wonderlands of snow-clad trees, soft drifts and sun-sparkled snow. Winter photography is not quite as easy as snapping a family photo in the back yard. The extra equipment to carry all day can prove a bit cumbersome until you find a good place to stow it and picture taking can get tricky when you are trying to get a good shot of friends as they move quickly along a winding forest trail while you are fumbling with gloves and the focusing ring of your lens. However, even a passably good snapshot is worth the effort since it will provide a clear memory of that favorite trip for years to come.

Almost annual technological improvements in photo equipment make the preservation of those memories ever easier. One has to admire the photographs taken during the period up to the 1950s. Professionals and many ambitious amateurs lugged anywhere from ten to thirty pounds and more of view cameras, lenses, tripods and film in metal cases in addition to their skis and winter camping gear. They took few action shots with those cumbersome cameras but endurance and patience has rewarded them and us with some stunning winter scenes.

Now it is no longer necessary to pack a case of heavy equipment and freeze fingers in the recording of your exploits on skis. Even professionals rely on fine-grain film in highly portable thirty-five mm cameras. Most amateurs use this size film and many persons are satisfied with the results of the 110 ''pocket camera'' snapshots.

The technological squeeze play has produced some marvellous results for the wilderness traveller. Designers are steadily reducing the size of viewfinder style thirty-five mm cameras and many of them now fit comfortably under a ski jacket let alone in a belt pack or rucksack. One of the better models is the Konica Auto S-3 which allows the photographer to control the speed of the shutter manually and to override the automatic aperature very simply in order to obtain special effects or compensate for uneven lighting.

Most of the viewfinder cameras sold these days have lenses in the thirty-five to fifty mm range, which provide anything from a moderate wide-angle to a ''normal'' view of the subject. For more specialized shots, such as wide or extreme wide angles or for telephoto shots you are almost obliged to have a single lens reflex camera. This is a bulkier camera, more suitable to packing in a rucksack or carrying under the ski jacket for limited periods, but it provides the greatest flexibility in composition of photos and an unlimited (except financially) choice of lenses. You can slip on a fisheye lens to produce a splendid panorama of mountain tops or a 500 mm telephoto for nature photography.

One of the advantages of winter photography is the great reflecting surface of the snow. On sunny days in particular the light can be so strong, that a fast film – one with an ASA rating in the hundreds – will be overexposed at all but the highest shutter speed and tiniest aperture. This means that you can switch to slower, finer-grained films which in turn can be enlarged to great degrees without extreme loss of sharpness.

On the other hand you have to be careful with exposure to avoid the extremes of contrast that come with very bright light on a combination of white and dark surfaces. You almost need one exposure to get the nuances of light and shadow on the surface of the snow and another to bring out the details of clothing and

With a little luck or some skill in tracking a skier may find deer taking shelter or browsing in the woods. This western Mule deer is poised for a quick escape from such an intrusion.

equipment. If the skiers are in the distance and won't be seen in detail on the final print you will usually settle on an exposure weighted in favor of the snow, but if the skiers are close you may want to take a separate light meter reading on their faces. This is where a camera that can be manually controlled is useful.

High contrast can be used for dramatic effects. For example, shooting skiers backlit by the sun will produce sharp silhouettes. Another trick is to set the camera for a high shutter speed and the smallest aperture, then shoot to include the sun in the picture. The result will be a star image as the lens creates a controlled flare of light. At times you may want to add yellow, orange or even red filters when shooting with black and white film to increase contrast and bring out the texture of tree bark, mountain rock or wind-blown snow. The best way to get the desired effect is to have a bit of experience so it is worth shooting and processing a roll of film with different exposures before setting out on a trip you want well recorded.

While it is sometimes tempting to think of a Canadian winter only in terms of light and dark, there is plenty of color to provide memorable slide shows. Modern ski fashions produce groups of skiers garbed in all hues of the rainbow. Color film is also a good way to record that springtime tan. In addition to the colors of skiers, nature provides a range of greens in its spruce, balsam, fir and pine, the blue of snow in the shade of early morning or late afternoon and the blaze of orange and yellow from the rising and setting sun. Look for such color combinations as old wood set against a white snowfield, the gold of weeds against fresh snow in the early winter, reflections in open water and of course the blue of a clear winter sky as a backdrop for any panorama.

A word of caution about handling film and equipment in winter. Even with modern chemicals and lubricants delicate mechanisms can be slowed or even solidified by extremes of cold and film can become brittle enough to break if handled roughly. It is a good policy to sling a camera under the ski jacket, either beneath an arm or in front, to warm things up before shooting. This will help ensure the shutter is giving the exposure indicated and that the film will not be damaged during a rapid winding.

Car and Skier

Aside from a well-waxed pair of skis, your major method of transportation in the winter will likely be a car. If you are dedicated to searching out wilderness areas you may invest in something with four-wheel-drive, four big snow tires and lots of cargo space. Another variation on the travel theme is the camper van which has plenty of road clearance and provides overnight shelter if you have lots of insulation. However, most of us choose our vehicles for urban and highway driving and that means something that will cruise a freeway with respectable speed and at least moderate comfort. If we make regular ski trips in winter (and probably canoeing or camping trips in summer) we look for a car or station wagon with reasonable road clearance and cargo space and at least decent handling so it won't misbehave on icy or gravelled roads.

From there on it is a question of equipping the basic vehicle so you can cope with most winter driving situations. The number one priority is good snow tires. You may already have radial tires with an all-weather tread, which is suitable for light snow but not the heavy stuff. If you are doing a lot of driving in the country you should consider not only putting snow tires on the rear but on the front as well to improve the steering on snowy surfaces. In any case, you should carry a set of chains, one of the most useful emergency devices ever known to someone stuck in a snowbank. While full chains are ideal and may be necessary for some parts of the country, the type with two sets of links and a leather strap are effective enough for most situations where you are caught on a patch of ice or a small snowbank.

Of course a snow shovel is another very high priority. If space is at a premium in your car, a folding trench shovel will do most jobs in a little more time. Another effective tool for getting unstuck is a tow cable and this can be a lightweight nylon rope which takes little storage space. For those of us who get caught with a flat battery, and it happens to just about everyone sooner or later, a pair of jumper cables and instructions on how to use them are an investment which will be recouped on the first usage.

At any time of the year you may need a flashlight with fresh batteries and a set of road flares in case of a breakdown in a hazardous spot. If you are going to be messing around looking for things under the car you should have a pair of cotton work gloves and a plastic bag or two as at least minimal protection against dirt and grease. Cloths are also useful, particularly in winter when everything seems to be getting covered with fog or grime. It is handy to have one for wiping the salt spray off windows and lights and a clean cloth for wiping off the inside of fogged windows.

On the liquid side you should keep the windshield washer tank topped up with full-strength fluid from the pre-mixed jugs and should have a reasonably full jug in the car at all times for refilling the tank. On a wet and salty highway this can be almost as important as gasoline. Still on the fluids, you should have a tube of lock de-icer. If your car does not have a rear window de-fogger consider one of the kits now on the market or the cheap and effective frost shields which have been used for decades. Somewhere in the trunk of the car there should be at least a minimal tool kit, containing such things as a screwdriver, pliers, open end wrench, some electrical tape and some wire. If your car is very hard to start you might throw in a can of gas line de-icer and even one of starting fluid which is sprayed into the carburetor.

Long winter drives under poor visibility conditions tax the eyes. You might consider a set of quartz headlights a good investment for the extra visibility they offer, especially under adverse conditions.

In the ski carrying department, anyone with a valuable pair of skis and plans to park on a street for longer than a couple of minutes should look at a rack with locks. Most people discover sooner or later, but in case you hadn't noticed the correct way to carry skis is with the tips to the rear of the car. With road salt and sand an almost constant fact of winter life, no skier should carry equipment unprotected on the roof. In the first place the salt spray messes up any wax job you have started and moreover it will corrode the bindings. For those who have the flat style of roof racks there are now nylon ski envelopes which are light and waterproof.

If you are setting out on a long trip, especially on a nice day, you may not have heavy clothing but if you are planning a long trip, particularly one which will last into the night, you should have a pair of heavy boots and a warm jacket, hat and gloves in the car. Travellers in the north are usually advised to also carry a warm sleeping bag so they can hole up in the car until help arrives. One last warning, oft repeated but oft ignored. If the motor is running on a parked car keep a window open so carbon monoxide can't build up and suddenly knock you out.

British Columbia

Throughout British Columbia skiers will find mountain and forest panoramas.

This province, lying astride the Cordilleran region of North America, is a land of mountains, plateaus and valleys. Cross-country skiing ranges from peaceful rambles along quiet valley bottoms to exciting climbs up the ever present mountain slopes. For the trips over gentle, rolling countryside regular cross-country equipment with rat-trap toe pieces is just fine. However, trips into the mountain regions may require heavier equipment, including hiking style boots, cable bindings and wide, heavy skis to cope with deep snow and steep descents. Ski parties heading into the mountains should be led by people familiar with the area and experienced in guiding skiers through such potential hazards as avalanche zones. This is a skill which is not easily learned and sometimes it is better to hire a qualified mountain guide than to trust your untrained senses.

Though B.C. is better known for such downhill areas as Whistler Mountain, with the greatest vertical drop of any ski resort in North America, and the helicopter skiing regions along the Alberta border, the province has beautiful cross-country skiing. Some resorts are taking advantage of the great wilderness areas in the interior to lay out trail networks running for more than 100 km. Both national and provincial parks offer good cross-country ski opportunities and trails are under development. The provincial Department of Recreation and Conservation notes that pilot cross-country ski touring programs are being carried out and, if successful, may be extended to even more parks. Many experienced ski parties take advantage of summer alpine shelters for camping during the winter and some are reached by chartered helicopter. B.C. residents are proud of the similarity of their province to the ski countries of Europe and the town of Kimberley even went to the length of redecorating its shop fronts in the business section to Bavarian style architecture.

While persons who don't live in the province tend to think of Vancouver Island as a Canadian banana belt where only rain falls, they should look at the central and northern sections. Here a combination of higher latitude and some good elevations create a ski season as long as that on some parts of the mainland.

However it's not quite like the Garibaldi Park area just across the Strait of Georgia where high mountains stop the moist Pacific air and receive as much as 900 cm (thirty ft.) of snow between mid-October and mid-January. During that period park officials simply clear out of the area, let the white stuff accumulate and advise skiers to take the same precaution. Snowfalls of five to six cm (more than two in.) per hour have been recorded for twelve hours straight. Anyone caught in that would end up in chest-deep powder snow and would find travel difficult to say the least. Once the snowfalls taper off and the weather warms up the skiing is delightful and lasts well into spring.

The mountains have a lot to do with B.C. weather and there are enough mountain ranges to create many different weather patterns. Starting at the east is the Continental Divide, which forms the border with Alberta. From this point rivers flow either east toward Hudson Bay or west toward the Pacific Ocean. Here is the famous Rocky Mountain range, but in fact it is only the biggest of a number of mountain ranges which cover the province. To the west is a plateau dotted with older, more timeworn ranges. For skiers some of them will ring a bell: Cariboo, Monashee, Bugaboo, Selkirk and Purcell. Along the ocean lies the Cascade Range, reaching from the Yukon to Washington.

In the east, the highest peak is Mount Robson (12,872 ft). In the west, Mount Fairweather in the St. Elias Mountains near the Yukon border reaches to 15,300 ft. Though British Columbians have the third largest province (366,255 sq. mi.) the population of almost 2.5-million tends to crowd into the flatlands along the coastline or in such areas as the Fraser R. and Prince George. Almost three-quarters of the province is forested but in the cleared areas are some of the richest

		Mean Temperature In Celsius (Fahrenheit)		Snowfall In Mean Centimetres (Inches)
		Min	Max	
Vancouver	Dec	1.1 (33.9)	6.6 (43.8)	14.5 (5.7)
	Jan	- 0.4 (31.2)	5.2 (41.4)	22.4 (8.8)
	Feb	1.1 (34)	7.7 (45.9)	7.9 (3.1)
	Mar	2.1 (35.8)	9.6 (49.2)	5.2 (2.1)
Victoria	Dec	1.3 (34.3)	7.2 (44.9)	11.7 (4.6)
	Jan	- 0.1 (31.8)	5.9 (42.7)	19.1 (7.5)
	Feb	1.1 (34.0)	8.3 (46.9)	7.1 (2.8)
	Mar	1.7 (35.0)	9.8 (49.7)	5.3 (2.1)
Prince George	Dec	-11.6 (11.1)	- 3.7 (25.4)	49 (19.3)
	Jan	-16.4 (2.4)	- 7.2 (19.0)	59.4 (23.4)
	Feb	-11.6 (11.2)	- 0.8 (30.5)	37.3 (4.7)
	Mar	- 7.7 (18.2)	3.5 (38.3)	24.9 (9.8)
Prince Rupert	Dec	0.7 (33.2)	5.2 (41.4)	31.8 (12.5)
	Jan	- 0.8 (30.6)	4.4 (39.9)	34.3 (13.5)
	Feb	- 0.1 (31.9)	5.4 (41.8)	19.3 (7.6)
	Mar	0.5 (32.9)	6.9 (44.4)	19.1 (7.5)
Kamloops	Dec	- 5.6 (22.0)	0.6 (33.1)	29.0 (11.4)
	Jan	- 9.5 (14.9)	- 2.2 (28.0)	30.7 (12.1)
	Feb	- 5.1 (22.8)	3.7 (38.7)	7.1 (2.8)
	Mar	- 1.4 (29.5)	9.7 (49.4)	3.6 (1.4)
Penticton	Dec	- 2.9 (26.7)	2.2 (35.9)	21.6 (27.2)
	Jan	- 5.6 (21.9)	- 0.3 (31.5)	24.9 (9.8)
	Feb	- 3.3 (26.1)	4.0 (39.2)	10.9 (4.3)
	Mar	- 1.7 (28.9)	9.0 (48.2)	4.6 (1.8)
Revelstoke	Dec	- 6.1 (21.1)	- 1.1 (30.0)	119.1 (46.9)
	Jan	- 9.1 (15.7)	- 2.8 (27.0)	131.6 (51.8)
	Feb	- 5.8 (21.6)	2.1 (35.7)	79.2 (31.2)
	Mar	- 3.2 (26.2)	6.9 (44.5)	24.6 (9.7)
Kimberley	Dec	-10.7 (12.7)	- 2.8 (27.0)	40.9 (16.1)
	Jan	-13.7 (7.4)	- 4.6 (23.8)	41.1 (16.2)
	Feb	-10.3 (13.4)	0.7 (33.2)	22.4 (8.8)
	Mar	- 7.2 (19.0)	5.0 (41.0)	15.7 (6.2)

grazing and fruit lands in the country.

Among the big events for cross-country skiers is 108 Kilometre Cross-country Ski Marathon held at the 108 Recreation Ranch in central B.C. The race is organized by Frank Ludtke of Ski Cross-country Ski School, 1451 Adanac St., Vancouver, B.C. and is held at the ranch, Box 2, 100 Mile House, V0K 2E0.

Another active group is the Mount Revelstoke Ski Club, Box 809, Revelstoke. This club is based near one of the beautiful national parks in the province's interior and it holds a number of major ski events plus regular tours through the season. For general information on ski activities contact the Outdoor Recreation Council of British Columbia, 1606 W. Broadway, Vancouver.

Information on skiing, particularly about downhill resorts, and a booklet on accommodation across the province are available from the Department of Travel Industry, Government of British Columbia, 1019 Wharf St., Victoria. A calendar of events, including ski races, winter carnivals and other activities around the province, is available from British Columbia Festivals, Box 34135, Vancouver, V6J 4M1.

A school class in Atlin gets a welcome break from the classroom. The youngsters are learning the basic movements of cross-country skiing.

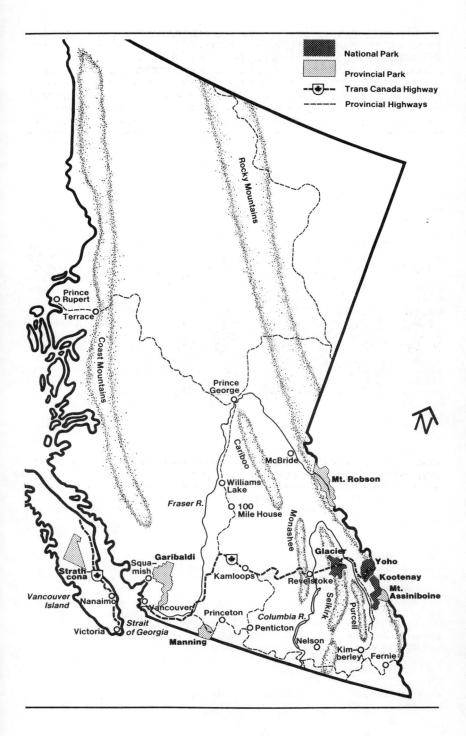

■ National Park	
▨ Provincial Park	
–·–✦–·– Trans Canada Highway	
– – – – – Provincial Highways	

Rocky Mountains

Coast Mountains

Prince
Rupert
Terrace

Prince
George

Cariboo

McBride

Mt. Robson

Williams
Lake

Fraser R.

100
Mile House

Monashee

Glacier

Yoho

Garibaldi

Squa-
mish

Kamloops

Revelstoke

Kootenay

Mt.
Assiniboine

Strath-
cona

Selkirk

Purcell

Vancouver
Island

Nanaimo

Vancouver

Princeton

Columbia R.

Victoria

Strait
of Georgia

Penticton

Manning

Nelson

Kim-
berley

Fernie

British Columbia Trails

Coastal Region

Forbidden Plateau

Location: On Vancouver I. From Courtenay west 19 km (12 mi.) on access road.

Though the southern tip of Vancouver I. has a well-deserved reputation as one of Canada's balmier climates, the Courtenay area half way up the island on the east shore has snow from December to April. Forbidden Plateau is a downhill area that is developing cross-country skiing on some trails and logging roads along the eastern edge of Strathcona Provincial Park. There are trails for all levels of skier in the hilly area. Restaurant, lodging by reservation, food, ski shop, rentals. For information write Forbidden Plateau Resort, 489 Island Highway, Courtenay, B.C. The Ski Cross-country Ski School, 1451 Adanac St., Vancouver, holds lessons, including a kindergarten ski school at Forbidden Plateau.

Mount Arrowsmith Park

Location: From Port Alberni on Vancouver Island follow Cameron Division Mainline to day lodge.

Length: Trails ranging from 3 to 8 km.

Skiing ranges from beginner trails in heavily wooded area arouhd base lodge to mountain skiing and winter camping for the experts. Skiing from December through April at the 3,200 to 6,000 foot levels. Day lodge with food, rentals. Downhill skiing at area. Special event days held through winter. Map at area or contact Arrowsmith Mountain Recreation, Box 265, Port Alberni. Lodging in area.

Cypress Provincial Park

Location: From Lions Gate Bridge at Vancouver, north 12 km (7.5 mi.) on the Upper Levels section of Hwy. 99 to the start of the access road, then 14 km (9 mi.) to the parking lots.

Length: About 21 km in total.

Beginners have 5.5 km of trails ranging from 800 m to 2.2 km. Intermediate skiers can choose from 6 trails ranging from 1.2 to 2 km with a total of 9.5 km and experts have 2 trails of 1.6 and 4.7 km respectively. These trails are located on the south-facing slope of Hollyburn Ridge. They pass through an evergreen forest on moderate slopes at an altitude of about 3,000 feet, most of them along old trails established by early pioneers. Wildlife can be observed in the area. Fog and snowstorms may be encountered so skiers should familiarize themselves with the area by studying maps in advance. Skiers are advised not to travel alone. Maps posted on the trails or on brochures available at area or from Provincial Parks Branch, Department of Recreation and Conservation, Parliament Buildings, Victoria, B.C. V8W 2Y9. Trails offer panoramic views of Howe Sound and West Vancouver.

Two privately owned ski lodges are accessible to skiers on the trails and a government warming hut is open to everyone free of charge. The trails are groomed and patrolled by the Provincial Government Parks Branch which also maintains downhill facilities and snow play area nearby. Areas of avalanche hazards will be posted. Avoid traversing avalanche fracture zones. Keep to the marked trails. Ski and road reports may be obtained during the season by telephoning (604) 929-2358 in Vancouver. Mountainous access road. Chains may be compulsory. Trail system under expansion by provincial government.

Mount Seymour Provincial Park

This 13.5-square-mile park just north of Vancouver along Indian Arm was explored for skiing in 1929 by the Alpine Club, which pressed the government to reserve the area for a park. It is a forested area with old Douglas fir and western red cedar interspersed with more recent coniferous and deciduous trees and shrubs. At higher levels there are alpine fir and pine, then meadows. Skiing lasts from early December through March and sometimes into April. Downhill skiing has been developed along the west side of the park but there are possibilities for cross-country trips to the rugged interior. Skiers should get information from District Superintendent, Mount Seymour Provincial Park, 1600 Indian River Dr., North Vancouver, B.C. V7G 1L3.

Whistler-Garibaldi Region

Whistler ski resort and adjoining Garibaldi

Provincial Park have become synonymous with the highest downhill skiing in North America. The ski resort has a vertical rise of 4,280 ft. to the top of its lifts. In the valleys and passes around the western edge of the 750-square-mile park just north of Vancouver, cross-country skiers have a chance to explore the terrain and find exciting views of the Coast Mountains.

It is a region of impressive peaks including 8,787 ft. Mount Garibaldi which towers over the western side of the park and was named by a naval survey crew which spotted it from Howe Sound in 1860. Ancient volcanoes give the area a unique geological character in western Canada as volcanic cones provide an unusual contrast to the usual rugged granites.

Much of the park is heavily forested. A dense growth of Douglas fir, western red cedar and western hemlock covers the mountain slopes below the 5,000 ft. level. Intermixed are lodgepole pine and stands of birch, alder and cottonwood. At the higher elevations, mountain hemlock, yellow cedar, alpine fir and white bark pine grow in scattered clumps before giving way to alpine meadows.

Two large lakes lie in the western side of the park, providing goals for skiers and to the east heavy glaciation has created a remote wilderness area rarely penetrated in winter. The barrier of the Coast Mountains catches a lion's share of snowfall as the wet air from the nearby Pacific Ocean dumps precipitation by the ton on the western slopes. Park officials generally clear out of the interior during the mid-October to mid-January period when as much as 30 feet of snow will accumulate. Skiers in the region report falls of 5 to 6 cm (more than 2 in.) per hour for 12 hours, which means a 60 to 70 cm or two foot accumulation at one time. A skier heading into the interior at this time could end up in chest-deep powder snow and find travel almost impossible.

Though there are virtually no prepared ski trails in the park, several areas are popular. The Whistler Mountain Ski Club had a booklet of 29 ski trails by Monique McDonald but this is now out of print. If you can obtain a copy it will give good information on the area. The parks service can provide general information on skiing areas and a detailed topographical map of the western park region. Write: District Supervisor, Provincial Parks Branch, Box 220, Brackendale, B.C. V0N 1H0. Avalanche information is available by phone at (604) 898-3024. Lodging information from Chamber of Commerce, Squamish, B.C. V0N 3G0.

Diamond Head Area

Location: From Garibaldi Highlands, just south of Brackendale, take park access road east along Ring Cr. to base camp at park gate.

Length: Main trail of 11 km and numerous side trips from chalet at trail end.

This is a beautiful area and well-suited to cross-country skiers who want to do some exploring. The primary trip follows a rough summer road to Diamond Head Chalet at Elfin Lakes. This A-frame alpine shelter provided by the park has foam rubber mattresses, wood and a stove. It is "first come, first served," so skiers planning trips on busy weekends should arrive early or bring equipment for sleeping on the floor or outside.

From the base camp there is a sweeping panorama of the surrounding mountains, Squamish area and Howe Sound in the distance. It also opens up the possibility of travel to interesting points to the north. Skiers head to the Paul Ridge and Red Heather areas about 5 km away or may tackle the somewhat difficult 5 km trek to Diamond Head. This trip passes the grotesque Gargoyles, figures left by eroding lava and sometimes not completely buried by the snow. The Opal Cone, a disintegrating volcanic mound, is about 6 km away from the base via Ring Cr. From the area you can see the Garibaldi Névé and Manquam L. The lake is an 11 km trek of considerable difficulty.

Black Tusk

Location: Western section of park. Access from Hwy. 99 along Rubble Cr. summer road from a point just north of village of Garibaldi.

Length: About 11 km one way with side trips possible.

Named for a 7,598 ft. peak jutting from a glacier area north of Garibaldi L., this highly scenic area has been made a nature preserve and protected from most man-made changes. There is a steep climb up the trail from a summer road and the trail is rated for experts. Park officials warn there is a moderate to extreme avalanche hazard from the steep slopes on the back of The Barrier cliffs. Skiers should check avalanche conditions with the park service in Brackendale before starting. There are shelters along the way.

The main trail leads to Black Tusk Meadows on the north shore of Garibaldi L. and from there skiers can range through the area. Panorama Ridge overlooks the lake and offers a viewpoint over mountains to the south. To the north are the peak of Black Tusk and the nearby Cinder Cone, an extinct volcano. Just south of the main trail there is an excellent view of the lava cliffs of The Barrier, an immense wall almost 2,000 ft. high.

Cheakamus Lake
Location: Trail follows Cheakamus Cr. south from Hwy. 99, starting about 5 km (3 mi.) west of Whister downhill ski resort.
Length: About 10 km one way.

This is a day trip which starts up a logging road then enters a narrow trail through heavy forest for the last 3 km to the lake. Cheakamus L. is bounded on two sides by mountains which tower as much as a mile above its thickly forested shores. Skiers can continue the 5 km length of the lake and continue up the creek valley south of the Fitzsimmons Range. To the north lie ice mantled mountains capped with the Overlord and Diavolo Glaciers, while the McBride Range forms the southern boundary of the valley.

Fitzsimmons Creek to Russet Lake
Location: Start South from Hwy. 99, about 2.5 km (1.5 mi.) south of village of Alta Lake.
Length: About 15 km one way.

This is a rugged, wilderness trail leading to a small lake in the shadow of massive Overlord Glacier in the Fitzsimmons Range. The starting point is just north of the big Whistler downhill ski resort and the trail winds along a summer road beside the ski hills. It works its way up the narrow valley, then branches south along Melody Cr. before passing through the Singing Pass and across a plateau to Russet L. Skiers should check with park officials about the avalanche hazard, particularly in the Fitzsimmons Cr. area.

Manning Provincial Park
Location: Midway between Hope and Princeton on the Southern Trans-Canada Highway (Hwy. 3).
Length: About 130 km.

The Provincial Parks Branch has designated several trails for all levels of skiers in Manning Provincial Park. There are 3 beginner trails: 4, 5, 6 km; 3 intermediate trails: 8, 16, 19 km; 2 advanced trails: 13 and 58

km. More than one class of trail may be linked together to provide longer and more challenging trips. Most are day trails requiring only a few hours for the round trip. Some are much longer and are suitable for overnight trips for experienced cross-country skiers. Areas of avalanche hazard are posted. Avoid traversing avalanche fracture zones and keep to marked trails.

Ski and road reports may be obtained during the season by telephoning (604) 929-2358 in Vancouver. Cars should be equipped with snow tires and chains should be carried. Manning Provincial Park is the site of the downhill Gibson Pass Ski Area. Day lodge with cafeteria. Ski shop. Tobogganing, snowshoeing, ice skating. An area has been set aside for winter camping.

Any person contemplating camping out must be equipped properly, for overnight temperatures drop well below daytime levels. Manning Provincial Park is located in the Cascade Mountains of southwestern British Columbia, 224 km (140 mi.) east of Vancouver. The park is over 176,000 acres of rugged, forest-clad mountains, deep valleys, alpine meadows, lakes and rivers. Two major rivers rise within the park: the Skagit, flowing west and south to the Pacific Ocean and the Similkameen. Vegetation is varied. Marshland gives way to dry-land stands of pine and near the timberline are several stands of rare alpine larch. Conifers like Douglas fir, western red cedar, hemlock, white spruce and lodgepole pine may be seen in the park as well as some aspen and cottonwood. Considerable wildlife. Historic Dewdney Trail, built over a hundred years ago, is located in the park as are even older routes used by Indians, fur traders and goldseekers of a bygone age. For information, write District Superintendent, Manning Provincial Park, Manning Park, B.C. V0X 1R0.

Kitsumkalum Mountain
Location: From Terrace west on Hwy. 16, then north on access road on west side of Kitsumkalum R. for total of 11 km (7 mi.).
Length: 11 km.

A series of trails has been cleared in an area at the base of Kitsumkalum downhill ski resort in Coast Mountains east of Prince Rupert. (Downhill runs are from 1,200-foot vertical.) Most of the cross-country trails are rated for beginners and intermediates with one very steep pitch for experts. Wooded area with excellent view of mountains. Average winter temperature of 0 to -8 degrees Celsius. Trails cleared and marked by Terrace Rotary Club, which sponsors a cross-country race each February. Base lodge with bar and cafeteria, trail grooming and some night skiing. Lodging in town.

Kitimat Trails

Location: From Kitimat on west coast of B.C., south of Prince Rupert.
Length: Four trails totalling about 87 km with more under construction.

Skiing here is in or around the Coast Range and trails provide access to excellent mountain skiing and overnight trips. There is a 2.5 km trail on the golf course for beginners, training and night skiing. The other routes range from 21 to 35 km with travel time of between 3 to 6 and 6 to 12 hours, depending on snow conditions and the ability of the skier. These are for intermediate or better skiers and include forest roads and powerline trail to the massive Alcan smelter. Skiing is both in forested lower reaches of the mountains and in the high country where touring lasts into June. Overnight camping is usually done in mountain cabins. There are an estimated 800 active skiers in Kitimat and there has been a cross-country instruction program since the early 1970s. Time trials for the Canadian Ski Association physical fitness awards are held three times each winter. For instruction, rentals and information on trail locations contact Eric Lasanen, 82 Clifford St., Kitimat. Phone 632-5558.

Central Region

Red Mountain Ski Club

Location: From Rossland, west 3 km (2 mi.) on Hwy. 3B.
Length: From 1 to 10 km trails.

Straight and loop trails on mostly wooded, mountainous terrain. Suitable for intermediate and advanced skiers. Trails cross open areas at some points. Trails groomed. Potential for high alpine mountain touring and cross-country skiing to remote areas for the experienced skier. Red Mountain-Rossland is one of British Columbia's major downhill ski resorts with a 2,800 foot vertical. Area is open seven days a week, December 1 to April 15. Cross-country instruction and rentals available. Skating, curling, snowshoeing. Guide services may be arranged on request. Babysitting at area. Food at Ski Lodge. Accommodation at ski resort or in town. Maps at ski area. Monte Cristo Challenge Fun Cross-Country Race, 4 km, first week of February. For informa-

tion, write Red Mountain Ski Club, Box 939, Rossland, B.C.

Snowpatch

Location: Penticton area. From Princeton west on Coalmont Rd., 1.6 km (1 mi.), then north on Snowpatch Rd. 6.5 km (4 mi.).
Length: 8 km.

Snowpatch is located at the 4,200-foot level at the beginning of the Interior Plateau, on east edge of Cascade Mountains. The trails are wooded but offer excellent views of Similkameen Valley to the east. Area is protected from high winds and is known for powder snow. Groomed and marked trails for intermediate skiers start from downhill ski resort. Most trails follow old logging roads. Maps at Chalet which has snack bar, rentals, accessories and minor repairs. Hotels in area, at least two offer skier discounts.

Kane Valley

Location: From Merritt south 19 to 24 km (12 to 15 mi.). Various trailheads begin off the Kane Valley road.
Length: 3 to 8 km.

Trails in forest and lake area. Suitable for beginner and intermediate skiers. It is not unusual to see such wildlife as bobcats and moose while skiing in the area. Ski instruction can be arranged by contacting Bill Richards at 378-4030 or Pat Ewing at 378-2013 in Merritt. Rentals available at Corbett Lake Country Inn. Limited downhill ski hill located another 13 km south on Hwy. 5. Accommodation at Corbett Lake Country Inn, phone 378-4334, and at Merritt. Trails are maintained by the Outdoor Club of Rocky Mountain. Club plans further expansion. The club holds junior and senior races, time trials, and a citizen's marathon. For more detailed information contact The Outdoor Club, Box 1958, Merritt, B.C.

Le Jeune Resort

Location: From Kamloops, west 8 km (5 mi.) on Trans-Canada Highway (Hwy. 1), then south 27 km (17 mi.) on all paved highway to Lac Le Jeune.
Length: 160 km.

Enormous system of marked and groomed trails ranging from 2.4 to 64 km. Suitable for beginner to expert skiers. Laid out in rolling wooded ranch country. Instruction available. Downhill skiing on Ridge Mountain, ice skating, snowshoeing. Rentals, guide services. Ski season late November to Easter. Ski packages and season passes available. Spring and summer activities include fishing, trail riding, hiking, swimming and tennis. Accommodation at Le Jeune Lodge or in housekeeping cottages. Dining and dancing. Sauna, swirl pool. Map available at ski shop. For information write Le Jeune Resort, Box 780, Kamloops, B.C.

"108" Recreational Ranch
Location: Central B.C. Just off Hwy. 97, 13 km (8 mi.) north of 100 Mile House.
Length: About 160 km of trails with 65 km groomed and marked.

Trails of about 3, 5 and 10 km. In its 26,-000 acres, the "108" has an ideal combination of rolling hills, flat meadowland, frozen lakes and evergreen forests to challenge every level of cross-country skier. Canada's National Team has trained here and made it their headquarters in 1976. No avalanche hazard. Very stable weather conditions. Ski shop with cross-country equipment sales, service and rentals. Ski school. Night skiing around lake. Warm-up cabins located at two points. Historic buildings scattered throughout. Skating, tobogganning, curling, snowmobiling, snowshoeing, ice fishing on nearby Lac La Hache. Limited downhill facilities in 100 Mile House. The resort has also extensive all season activities, golf course, riding, fishing, boating, etc. Accommodation at 108 Motor Lodge. Heated swimming pool, saunas. Dining and dancing at 108 Clubhouse.

The "108" Recreational Ranch is a combination working ranch and year round resort with the facilities of a small community: chapel, community center, etc. Map of trails available at resort. The 108 marathon, a 108 km race, is held at the end of January. For information write 108 Motor Lodge, R.R. 1, 100 Mile House, B.C.

TH Guest Ranch
Location: From Williams Lake, west 96 km (60 mi.) on Hwy. 20 to Hanceville.
Length: Loop trails. Travel time from 30 min. to one day.

Skiing at the Ranch and around Hanceville. Several packed trails for novice and intermediate skiers and miles of snow on the benches and logging roads. Wooded to open bench land. Elevation changes up to 2,000 feet. Guide services.

The TH Guest Ranch has been an operating cattle ranch since 1879. It has been a summer guest ranch with such activities as trail riding, fishing and in recent years has begun catering to cross-country skiers. Located along the beautiful Chilcotin River in one of the largest cattle raising districts of British Columbia's historic Cariboo. Moonlight skiing, sleighrides. Accommodation in rustic log cabins, some 100 years old. Relaxed, friendly atmosphere, spacious lodge for informal meals with fresh baked bread and old fashioned home cooking. Singsongs and square dancing in the evenings. For information write TH Guest Ranch, Chilcotin Valley. Hanceville, B.C. or Ski Travel Centre, 1271 Howe St., Vancouver, B.C. V6Z 1R3.

Tabor Mountain — Hickory Wing Trails
Location: From Prince George east 22.5 km (14 mi.) on Hwy. 16.
Length: 3 loop trails of 15.5 km in total. Travel time 30 min. to 3 hr.

Well laid out trail system maintained by the members of the Hickory Wing Ski Club. Partially logged 15 to 25 years ago. High brush with scattered conifers. Downhill facilities at Tabor Mountain Ski Resort. Day lodge, cafeteria. Rentals. Accommodation at nearby Purden Lake Resort or at Prince George. Map at area. Site of many competitions.

Crooked River Provincial Park
Location: From Prince George, north 64 km (40 mi.) on Hwy. 97.
Length: About 20 km in total. Travel time 30 min. to one hour and 45 min.

Beginners may ski on Bear Lake Trail, 400 m on wooded, flat terrain and on all campground roads, about 6.5 km. Intermediate skiers have the choice between Crooked River Trail, 5 km through wooded hilly terrain, and Squaw Lake Trail, 8 km on flat land. Caution must be exercised when travelling on frozen lake surfaces. Wildlife in area includes moose, lynx and whisky-jacks. Children's toboggan run, winter picknicking, ice rink. Accommodation in Prince George. Free maps available at the park. For information, phone Bear Lake District Park Headquarters at 562-8288 or Crooked River Park at 972-4492, or contact B.C. Parks Branch, Department of Recreation and Conservation, Box 2045, Prince George, B.C. V2N 2J6.

Eastern Mountains

Fernie Area Trails
Location: Three trails start either from town of Fernie or from nearby Fernie Snow Valley ski resort.
Length: 2, 30 and 50 km trails.

Cross-country skiers in this southeastern

British Columbia town have a choice ranging from short to very long trails. Fernie, a turn of the century coal mining town which still has some of its original brick and stone buildings, lies on Hwy. 3 just west of the Crowsnest Pass. It is in the Macdonald Range of the Rockies. Skiing here starts about late November and continues until May.

About 5 km (3 mi.) from town the Snow Valley downhill resort, set against a high mountain ridge with 7,000 ft. peaks, is the starting point for two cross-country trails. A 2 km loop maintained by the ski school travels through gently rolling wooded areas below the lodge. Also at the lodge advanced skiers can start out on a 30 km trip to Island L. and back. This trail follows old logging roads and ski roads with some open areas. Part of this trail is maintained by the ski school but the last section can have deep snow if no skiers or snowmobiles have passed that way since the last snowfall.

At Island L. skiers will find a large, empty cabin which makes a handy spot for a lunch break or can be used as an overnight stop if the party plans to explore the surrounding mountain country. At the start of both these trails there is a ski lodge, shop, rentals, instruction, cafeteria and bar. Lodging is in town. The third trail, from Fernie up Coal Creek and down Morrissey Creek back to town mostly follows old logging roads and does not have difficult grades. However, deep snow which has not been packed by skiers or snowmobiles may slow travel to the point where the whole trip is not practical. It is necessary to get a detailed description of the trail from skiers in the area and maps of the area may be obtained from a local government agent. For more information on skiing in the area contact Fernie Snow Valley Ski Ltd., Box 788, Fernie, B.C.

Kimberley Ski Resort

Location: Southeastern corner of the province. 2.5 km (1.5 mi.) from downtown Kimberley. Trails start at south end of ski hill parking lot.

Length: 3 loop trails of about 20 km in total. Travel time 15 to 40 min.

Trails located in mountainous wooded area. Suitable for beginner through advanced. Three-metre wide trails groomed by local cross-country ski club and Kimberley Ski Resort. Used for running in the summer. Rentals, instruction. Maps available at resort. Kimberley is a major downhill ski

Winter campers find complete solitude in the deep snows of the Diamond Head region in Garibaldi Provincial Park, north of Vancouver.

resort in British Columbia. It has North America's longest lit run for night skiing. Lodge with dining, lounge and cabaret facilities. Ski shop. Snowmobiling, snowshoeing.

The growing interest in cross-country skiing has encouraged the resort to add cross-country options to what were exclusively downhill ski week packages. Cross-country package includes a guide-instructor for two hours each day. Accommodation at resort or at winter campground, The Happy Hans Kampground, located about 1 km from the lifts or at Kimberley.

Through a gigantic community effort, Kimberley has become the Bavarian city of the Rockies. Citizens have transformed their shop fronts to authentic Bavarian look and turned downtown core into a park-like platzl (mall) with high country trees, bubbling brook, flowers, benches and Alpine huts. Annual Winterfest with cross-country races held second weekend in February. Organized by Kimberley Bavarian Society, Box 63, Kimberley, B.C. For information write Kimberley Bavarian Society or Kimberley Ski Resort, Box 33, Kimberley, B.C.

Kootenay National Park

This long, narrow park, lying along the western edge of the Continental Divide in the Rocky Mountains, offers many attractive trails for cross-country skiers. The Banff-Radium Highway, which bisects the 530-square-mile park, provides easy access to all routes. The parks service alone has marked and maintains about 70 km of routes suitable for day trips and there are additional trails, many of them following the paths of summer hikers. Kootenay is part of a chain of national and provincial parks which straddle the Alberta-British Columbia border and provide an immense reserve for outdoors enthusiasts. To the north it is bounded by Yoho and to the east by Banff and by Mount Assiniboine parks.

The northern section of Kootenay, lying between the divide on the east and the Vermilion Range or Rockwall as it is sometimes known on the west, is particularly rugged. It is an area for scenic trips and wilderness camping for the hardy and experienced. The parks service asks all skiers to register. Those using the park-maintained trails can fill in forms at self-registration boxes which are checked regularly by park officials. Skiers heading out on other trails or planning overnight trips are asked to register directly with the warden service.

The wardens and alpine specialists are excellent sources of information. They keep track of such crucial details as the avalanche hazard and the probabilities of severe weather. In addition, they can provide interesting details such as where to find good lookouts or to watch for mountain goats. Many of the trails in the Vermilion and Kootenay River valleys are on gentle, rolling terrain suitable for light cross-country equipment. More daring trips into mountain country should only be attempted by well equipped, experienced and properly guided parties.

Tumbling Glacier Trail
Location: From Marble Canyon warden station on Banff-Radium Highway.
Length: 15 km one way.

Tumbling Glacier, literally falling down the face of a steep mountain, is one of the most spectacular sights in Kootenay Park. This is an experts' trip because there is severe avalanche hazard through valleys with high mountains on either side. Skiers should check with park officials about slide conditions before starting out.

The trail begins along the Vermillion R.

and travels through a forest of spruce, lodgepole pine and Douglas fir. Then it commences a long climb beside Tumbling Cr., past a waterfall, then up a series of switchbacks. There is a beautiful view of the glacier and the Rockwall of the Vermilion Mountains from larch-dotted meadows. This massive barrier of Cambrian limestone and dolomite, at points rising a sheer 2,500 ft. from the meadows, forms the western boundary of the park for 25 miles. From the glacier, hardy skiers and campers can bear south through Numa Pass as far as Floe L., before turning back to the highway.

Floe Lake
Location: Start from Banff-Radium Highway across the road from the Hawk Creek highway maintenance camp and follow summer hiking trail sign.
Length: 10 km one way.

The trip, through mountain terrain, provides one of the most rewarding sights in the park — a small lake backed by a massive wall of rock. Trail starts by the Vermilion R. and joins the creek draining Floe L. Skiers will pass through a forest of lodgepole pine, spruce and Douglas fir and into open areas bared by avalanches. These serve as a warning that you should check slide conditions with the park wardens before starting and should be prepared for travel in avalanche country. There are some switchbacks on the trail, particularly on the last haul up to the lake itself.

Floe L. takes its name from the ice floes which tumble from a small glacier along its shores. This ice mass huddles at the foot of a sheer rockface which rises from the edge of the lake. In addition, there are excellent views of mountain tops in the area and as far away as the Wenkchemna Peaks in Banff. From the lake there is an optional trip north through Numa Pass. Near Floe L. there is a partly demolished log cabin which gives good shelter if you have a tarpaulin to make it a bit more windproof.

Kaufmann Lake Trip
Location: From Marble Canyon on Banff-Radium Highway via Tokumm Cr.
Length: About 15 km one way.

This is another expert trip because it passes through rugged terrain with a high avalanche risk. Again skiers should check with the parks service before setting out. The trail starts along the west side of the creek and in fact is a parallel route to the Boom Lake trip east across the Continental

Divide in Banff National Park. Skiers will follow Tokumm Cr. through a heavy forest of pine, spruce and fir and at times come to open meadows where the route is ill-defined. Here it will be navigation by map, compass and possibly by instinct.

Along the way the route passes below the Fay Hut of the Alpine Club of Canada. This shelter, perched higher in the mountains, might be difficult to reach. If skiers plan to stay in it, they should get permission from the ACC in Banff. The trip ends at Kaufmann L., a long narrow body of water nestled between mountains on the west slope of the Divide. All around and in the distance are views of peaks, many of them capped by glaciers.

Park Maintained Trails

The parks service lists 11 maintained and marked ski trails totalling 70 km along the Banff-Radium Highway. They range from little jaunts of about 2.5 km to day trips of 15 km. These are all one-way trails so skiers must make allowance for return travel time or arrange to have a second car parked along the highway in some cases. For maps and more information contact park warden or write: Superintendent, Kootenay National Park, Radium, B.C. V0A 1M0.

Yoho National Park

Though small (500 square miles) on the scale of national parks in the Rockies, Yoho compensates with excellent scenery and ready access to good skiing areas. The Trans-Canada Highway from the Lake Louise area cuts through the Kicking Horse Pass and from there traverses the park. Skiers can head north or south into nearby valley systems. Yoho, a Cree expression of surprise, has rugged and spectacular views, including the western side of the Continental Divide and a 1,248 ft. waterfall that spills from the mountains.

The eastern edge of the park abuts Banff and lies just over the mountains from some popular skiing areas in that park.

There are two major regions used by cross-country skiers in Yoho. To the south is L. O'Hara and a network of trails, while to the north is the Yoho Valley and Emerald L. There is a good overall topographical map of the park available: Yoho Park. Information about the park may be obtained from the Superintendent, Yoho National Park, Field, B.C. V0A 1G0. The park has not as yet specifically marked ski trails but wardens can provide advice on the good ski areas, on

lodging and on the avalanche hazard in each area at various times. Registration with the wardens or at the self-registration boxes is required as a safety measure.

Sherbrooke Lake Trail

Location: Start from Wapta Lake Picnic area on Trans-Canada Highway (Hwy. 1) about 6 km (4 mi.) west of park border with Banff.

Length: About 3 km one way.

This is a very short but pleasant trip to a lake tucked away in a spruce and fir forest just over a kilometre from the main highway. Starting from the north side of the road follow a summer hiking trail to the long, narrow lake. Looking back you will see a panorama of mountains behind including Vanguard Peak, Cathedral Mountain, Cathedral Crags and Mount Stephen rising in a solid mass of Cambrian rock. The trail continues from the north end of the lake but ends at the Daly and Niles glaciers, in another kilometre. These glaciers, which feed their slowly melting waters to the mountain lake, are generally tackled only by mountaineers.

Lake O'Hara Region

Location: Access via Lake O'Hara Fire Road. This road heads south from the Trans-Canada Highway (Hwy. 1) about 3 km (2 mi.) west of the park border with Banff.

Length: 13 km. to lake. Numerous side trips from L. O'Hara.

The L. O'Hara area is one of the more attractive to skiers in the western parks. The trip in is an easy uphill for beginners and often skiers will find the trail already packed by snowmobiles. Many parties simply make the trip in for lunch, wander around the immediate lake area, then ski out in the afternoon. Others come in and stay for a few days at one of the large log cabins and make excursions into surrounding valleys. Mountain lakes are often the goal and many skiers end up scraping ice from their skis after discovering that springs have spread water on the ice surface but just beneath the layer of snow. The lake region first attracted attention in the 1890s when CPR surveyors and a Lieut.-Col. Robert O'Hara visited and were charmed by its beauty.

Early in this century the Alpine Club of Canada began summer camps there and still has a hut by the lake. In addition to the Elizabeth Parker hut there is a lodge and warden's cabin, visited occasionally in winter by park officials. Accommodation should

A group of young skiers spurts away from the starting area in a race in the Revelstoke area of B.C.

be reserved with Parks Canada at Field or with the Alpine Club in Banff. After so many years of exploration there is an extensive summer trail system and this is being partially adopted by skiers who stay in the cabins or winter camp in the meadow.

Among the options for ski parties staying at L. O'Hara are:

Base of Mount Odaray — This 10,175 ft. mountain is one of the peaks which towers over the L. O'Hara campground. The base begins only a few hundred metres from the huts but if avalanche conditions are safe, skiers can climb farther and higher to get impressive views of the surrounding mountain area.

McArthur Pass and Lake McArthur — This is a trip of up to 3 km south from the camp area, across the meadow then up the pass. The full trip goes west around the base of Mount Schaffer and keeps climbing to the lake, perched high in a cirque. Parts of the route are steep and exposed to avalanches from the nearby slopes so caution must be used.

Lake Oesa and Abbot Pass — The trip to L. Oesa runs for about 3 km east from L. O'Hara and up the creek connecting the two bodies of water. Skiers will cross a moraine before reaching the barren, sub-alpine environment of the lake. L. Oesa is a cold little lake and is free from ice only for a short period during the summer. From the east end of the lake skiers with a bit of the alpinist in them might try to ski and climb the steep route to Abbot Pass between Wiwaxy Peaks on the left and Mount Lefroy on the right. This is a major alpine route over the Continental Divide to the Lake Louise area. High in the pass at 9,598 ft. is the Abbot Hut of the Alpine Club of Canada. Skiers wishing to use it should make arrangements with the club in Banff.

Opabin Plateau and Pass — Just southeast of L. O'Hara there is a short, steep rise, marking the boundary of the Opabin Plateau. Atop this level surface skiers can roam among the small lakes which dot the surface or can push further southeast toward Opabin Pass. This gap in the mountains, hugging the western slope of the Continental Divide, should be attempted only if avalanche conditions on the steep slopes above are safe.

Yoho Valleys

Location: Access via summer road running north from Trans-Canada Highway (Hwy. 1) about 3 km (2 mi.) east of Field.

This is a highly skiable area with two valleys, numerous trails and permanent shelter. In winter, skiers must park in a plowed area not far from the highway and ski about 15 km up a roadway beside the Yoho R. to a summer picnic area with a shelter and a summer ranger station. From there you can ski about 8 km up the Yoho Valley to the start of the Yoho Glacier, an offshoot of the massive Wapta Icefield.

To the right of this north-south valley are the ice-capped peaks of the Continental Divide, while to the left are two openings in the President Range. The first, located below the shelter area, is the Yoho Pass, leading to the popular Emerald L. area. Above that is the Little Yoho Valley, leading into the centre of the President Range. Up this valley one finds the Stanley Mitchell Hut of the Alpine Club of Canada at the 7,000 ft. level. Reservations for this hut must be made with the club in Banff and wardens at Field should be asked about other lodging in the area.

Emerald Lake Area

Location: Access from summer road leading north from Trans-Canada Highway (Hwy. 1) just west of Field.

Like the Yoho Valley area just to the east, Emerald provides the skier with numerous opportunities for long and short trips into valleys around the President Range. There is about a 6 km trip up the access road to Emerald L. itself, set in the middle of a wide, forested valley with the President peaks to the north, Mount Wapta to the east and Mount Burgess to the south. At the lake there is a small chalet. For information about its use, contact the parks service in Field.

Numerous possibilities exist for such trips as a visit to the Emerald Basin to the north, the Burgess Pass area to the south or a trip through the Yoho Pass to the Yoho Valley. Another possibility for winter campers is a long trek up the valley of the Amiskwi R., which penetrates deep into the moutains to the north.

Glacier National Park

Taking its name from the masses of ice and firn snow in névés which dominate its mountains, Glacier is rugged and beautiful and offers some of the most interesting ski touring on the continent. The 520-square-mile park lies in the heart of the Selkirk Mountain Range and many of the routes are steep and short. In the middle of the park is the famous Rogers Pass, home of avalanche research in Canada. Looking at the

map it is easy to see why. Above the avalanche research station lies infamous Avalanche Mountain, which has been long noted for sending massive slides from high on its 9,000 ft. altitude.

The area so impressed early travellers and particularly railwaymen that they had cartographers add Avalanche Glacier, Avalanche Crest and Avalanche Cr. to the maps. The Canadian Pacific Railway lost so much track to the snow slides there that it finally built the five-mile-long Connaught Tunnel under Mount Macdonald and Avalanche Mountain. When the Trans-Canada Highway pushed through the same pass, road traffic faced similar problems. The answer in this case has been the research station headed by Fred Schleiss and an impressive crew to control the slides. This includes not only wardens who warn drivers of hazards and batteries of snowplows to clear away the results of slides, but artillery crews who trigger small slides to prevent big ones from developing.

Obviously the artillery fire, the snow slides, the big snowfalls and deep accumulations create heavy touring conditions and many areas are suitable only for mountain touring equipment. Several areas are closed permanently to skiers for safety reasons. These include artillery target zones, regions which often produce sympathetic avalanche releases in response to nearby shell concussions and several ''snow plots'' which are crucial for observing snow settlement to help predict avalanche conditions.

Despite the hazards in some areas, there are relatively safe ski zones or at least areas which are safe when the snow is stable. The parks service provides information about the avalanche risk and demands that all skiers register as a safety measure. There is a warden station in Rogers Pass and information may be obtained from: Superintendent, Glacier-Revelstoke National Parks, Revelstoke, B.C. V0E 2S0. There is a good general topographic map in the national parks series titled Glacier Park. Obviously, when skiers start out from the highway, parking is a problem and even more so in this high snow area where plows sweep through with great frequency. Plowed parking areas have been provided so skiers won't stop in artillery posts or on shoulders. If you find a red card on your windshield after returning from a tour it means the road has been temporarily closed due to avalanche conditions and you must wait for the warden to pass by notifying you when it is open again.

Beaver River Area

Location: South from Trans-Canada Highway (Hwy. 1) 14 km (8.5 mi.) east of Rogers Pass summit and about 300 m east of Beaver R. bridge. Park beside gravel storage shed but do not block access.

Length: About 50 km one way in trails.

These are routes which follow summer hiking routes South along the river valley between the Selkirk Range on the west and the Purcell Range on the east. Wardens note the snow is deep and skiers may find the going heavy. The grade is gentle with a few sections where there is some climbing. The trail passes through forest of fir, hemlock, cedar and engelmann spruce, giving occasional glimpses of the surrounding peaks and glaciers.

As an option, about 6 km from the start you can branch to the left up Grizzly Cr. for about 3 km, then bear right up Copperstain Cr. to the Bald Hills. At the 7,000 ft. level you break out of heavy timber and can ski for 13 km along a wide, open expanse atop the ridge. From here you have a grand panorama of nearby peaks and the Selkirks to the west, capped by the glacier forming Illecillewaet and Deville Névés.

Bostock Creek Trail

Location: From Rogers Pass west about 20 km (12 mi.) on Trans-Canada Highway (Hwy. 1) and park at Flat Creek parking area about 500 m west of access. Bostock Creek runs north from highway.

Length: About 8 km one way.

Trail heads along creek through dense forest of spruce, cedar, fir and some white birch and hemlock. Along the way there are several potential slide paths but they are not the critical type. At Bostock Pass skiers should turn back unless they have received permission from the wardens to continue into the Casualty Cr. area. The valley has steep walls with frequent avalanches.

Asulkan-Illecillewaet Areas

Location: South side of Trans-Canada Highway beside hotel grounds gun position. Climb to old railway grade behind Illecillewaet summer campground to avoid slide path from Avalanche Crest.

From the campground area there are numerous possibilities in the Valley. Among these is the steep switchback trail to Marion L. for excellent views of mountains and valley lands. There is considerable slide danger above the lake. Another option is the Asulkan Trail along the west side of the valley to the Asulkan Glacier. Along the way you ski across a foot bridge, providing an opening through the forest to see the mountains. Higher up the tree cover is less dense. The glacier carved the classic, U-shaped valley and for most of this century has been retreating.

Further to the east one can ski up an easy slope along the Illecillewaet R. toward the glacier that feeds it. Even further to the east is another steep trail which skirts the high avalanche area to touch on Avalanche Crest. This leads out of timber and allows good views of the avalanche areas and glaciers.

Mount Revelstoke National Park

About 30 miles west of Glacier National Park, lies its twin, Mount Revelstoke, at 100 square miles the smallest of the national parks in the mountains. It nestles in the angle of the Illecillewaet and Columbia Rivers, on the western edge of the Selkirk Mountains. The park is centred around the Clachnacudainn Range and a massive snowfield of the same name. In this case there is no easy route to the interior as the Trans-Canada Highway traverses the southern border of the park and travel is by ski or by foot to all but one area.

Skiing in the area, except for two cross-country trails, is rugged and tends more to touring equipment or even mountain skis. Though this is not the wild avalanche country of Glacier Park, there is still considerable hazard along the steep slopes and skiers should check with the parks service in Revelstoke for avalanche information.

Registration with the wardens or at self-registration booths is required as a safety measure in case search and rescue is necessary. A national parks series map, Mount Revelstoke National Park, is available. More detailed information can be obtained from the Superintendent, Mount Revelstoke and Glacier National Parks, Revelstoke, B.C., V0E 2S0.

Mount Revelstoke Summit Road

Location: Northeast of city. Access from Trans-Canada Highway (Hwy. 1), 5 km (3 mi.) west of city.

Length: 25 km one way.

This trail follows a highly popular summer road leading the viewpoint atop Mount Revelstoke, in the 5,800 ft. region. From here one has beautiful views of the Selkirk Range to the east of the Monashees to the West, with the Columbia R. dividing the two

Among the winter activities skiers may see is dog-team racing, still popular in an era when the snowmobile has almost replaced canine power for the working trapper.

mountain systems. This trail is used by snowmobiles and some skiers compromise by getting a tow to the top of the mountain, then enjoy the long glide down. There are shelters located at the 8, 20 and 24 km points along the trail.

Nels Neilson Ski Area
Location: Ski hut along Trans-Canada Highway (Hwy. 1), about 5 km (3 mi.) west of Revelstoke.
Length: 2 km loop.

This trail for cross-country skiers is maintained by the Revelstoke Ski Club near the start of the road up Mount Revelstoke. It is an intermediate route through a wooded area and there is registration out at the starting point. The trail is usually open by Dec. 1.

Berg Lake-Mt. Robson
Location: From Yellowhead Highway (Hwy 16) about 60 km (40 mi.) west of Alberta-B.C. border to Nature House visitor centre on north side of road.
Length: About 20 km.

This potentially hazardous trip near the tip of Jasper National Park offers the skier spectacular views of Mount Robson, 12,-

972 ft., the highest peak in the Canadian Rockies. Trail follows a dirt road up the Robson R. through a miniature rain forest of Douglas fir, cedar, spruce and hemlock created by the weather effects of Mt. Robson. This massive upthrust of Cambrian rock creates a micro-climate more typical of the B.C. coast by blocking passing rainstorms and causing them to fall on the area. In the area of Kinney L. one becomes acutely aware of the avalanche hazard posed by the massive mountain. In the spring of 1968 a slide swept down the western slopes, shearing the tops from huge cedar trees. Along the western edge of the mountain the trail traverses the Valley of a Thousand Falls before reaching Berg L., where Berg Glacier feeds thousands of tons of ice at a chunk into the lake.

Ranch of the Vikings
Location: Off Yellowhead Highway 16, 6.5 km (4 mi.) west of McBride, 166 km (104 mi.) west of Jasper, 203 km (127 mi.) east of Prince George.
Length: Over 90 km of trails.

All trails loop from the Viking Lodge parking lot. Wide variety of trails for all levels of ability, ranging from 2.5 to 25 km in length. Trails pass through tall timber area and some wander on to alpine meadows. Located in the peaceful Robson Valley. Beautiful views of the snow-capped Cariboo Range on the south side and the McGregor Mountain Range of the Rockies on the north side. Very moderate weather, no avalanche hazard. Abundant wildlife in the 4 to 8-mile wide valley.

The Robson Valley is ideal ski country and it is here that Canada's National Ski Team has done most of its training during the mid-1970s. This development is one of the major cross-country centres on the continent. Lessons, lectures and coaching are provided at the Ranch. Equipment may be bought or rented. There is a vast undeveloped potential for alpine skiing in the area. Bell Mountain Resort Ltd. is in the initial stages of development on Little and Big Bell Mountains.

Winter season starts on November 1 and ends on May 15. Summer skiing is also possible in the snow fields on the surrounding mountains, accessible only by four wheel drive vehicles or trucks. Shelters, cookout. Cafeteria with home cooked meals. Sauna, sport shop. Summer activities include hiking and jogging, riding, soccer, hunting and fishing, camping facilities, running track. Accommodation for 25 people at the ranch and in town of McBride. Maps posted in the Lodge. All trails are groomed, set and marked. Site of annual Race of the Vikings in January-February.

Ranch is operated by Bjorger and Anita Pettersen, two of Canada's top cross-country skiers. Bjorger Pettersen has been Canada's Head Coach for cross-country skiing, our National Ski Team Coach, the developer of the first ski racing team in the Northwest Territories and Canada's representative at the International Ski Federation. Anita Pettersen was for a number of years a member of Canada's National Cross-Country Ski Team and has been both Canada Winter Games Champion and U.S. Champion. For information write The Ranch of the Vikings, Box 487, McBride, B.C.

Raven Lake Recreational Area
Location: About 115 km (70 mi.) east of Prince George on Hwy. 16. Take Hungary Cr. Rd. and start from south side either at mile 8 or mile 9.6. Alternate access from Hwy. 16 is via Bowron Access Rd., then Tumuch Rd. to mile 13.6.
Length: Three trails totalling 19 km.

Trails in forested mountain country. The 5 km route from mile 8 to the Grizzly Den cabin is the only one suitable for beginners. Trail from Tumuch Rd. passes through terrain with some avalanche hazard. Weather can be unpredictable. There are two heated cabins on the land and they will each sleep about 20 persons. The trails and cabins were built and maintained by Northwood Pulp and Timber Ltd. of Prince George. Skiers may use the cabins free of charge or can find lodging at Purden Lake resort, 32 km (20 mi.) west of the skiing area. Maps available from government office in Prince George or from timber company at Box 9000, Prince George, B.C. Sons of Norway Ski Club, Box 772, Prince George, B.C., hold special events on the trails.

Cariboo Mountain Wilderness
Location: From Prince George east 150 km (90 mi.) on Hwy. 16.
Length: Wilderness skiing with more than 150 km of skyline skiing. No marked trails.

This is wild mountain country with the possibility for expert touring groups to explore alpine regions at the 5,000 to 7,000 ft. level. There are no shelters or even marked trails so skiers should be prepared to navigate and make camp in the wilderness. For specific information on access contact Sons of Norway Ski Club, Box 772, Prince George, B.C. or Northwood Pulp and Timber Ltd., Box 9000, Prince George. The ski club regularly organizes an Easter trip to the region.

Alberta

An uphill trek near Sunshine Village in Banff National Park. There are vast skiing possibilities in the national parks region of Alberta.

With its wide variety of terrain, Alberta actually has three types of skiing requiring at least two different types of equipment for most skiers. On one side of this 255,285 square mile province are the flatlands, forested lake and river country in the north and prairie in the south. On the other side are the Rocky Mountains with the foothills in between. While cross-country skis are highly suitable for the flat and rolling areas, their use in mountain terrain becomes a matter of judgment and experience.

There is no problem in many of the mountain valleys or on trails across the gentle slopes and plateaus in many areas. It is when one starts skiing untracked snow or close to the steep sides of the mountains themselves that care must be exercised in the choice and use of equipment.

While experts have trekked across glaciers with heavy packs using only light touring skis, this is not recommended for most skiers and the National Parks Service, which administers much of the mountain region in Alberta, urges caution. For skiers not capable of handling the light equipment expertly in deep snow the wardens suggest mountain touring gear: heavier boots, wider and heavier skis and heavier bindings, either cable or of a downhill design with a heel lift feature.

The service also demands that all skiers using anything but well-marked trails close to towns register out and back in to prevent long and costly searches in the wrong part of the park. Mountain skiing and winter camping are ever more popular pastimes for the skilled and adventurous. Many cross-country skiers take advantage of alpine cabins once used by summer hikers or skiers who plodded in on alpine skis. Anyone travelling in the mountain regions should, of course, carry at least a day pack and if travelling in avalanche areas should be familiar with signs of danger. Parks personnel can usually outline safe routes and give evaluations of relative avalanche hazard. Some skiers buy their own avalanche beacon radios or rent them so other members of a party can locate them under the snow in case of a slide.

Even more than in other parts of the country, newcomers to the sport are well advised to team up with experienced skiers, either through friends or clubs, or to hire qualified guides for at least the first few trips into mountain country.

Skiing in western Alberta has a well established history, dating back at least to the ski trains of the 1930s which used to bring touring parties to Lake Louise. From there they would make what was often a two-day trip to Skoki Lodge, then make excursions into the surrounding mountains from that base. Since ski lifts were invented, much of the emphasis was switched to downhill and the big airline promotions of the past few years have largely been aimed at that sector. Now the picture is changing as more and more residents and visitors look for the quiet excitement of cross-country adventure in this spectacular mountain country. There are endless kilometres of abandoned logging roads, seismic line cuts, muskeg and meadows in the foothills plus many more days, even weeks of travel on mountain hiking routes. Recently the parks service and ski clubs have started marking specific cross-country routes, particularly around such ski centres as Banff and Jasper. Even big cities like Edmonton, which is cut by the North Saskatchewan River valley, have their own ski trail networks.

One type of skiing adjunct deserves mention because of its uniqueness: the helicopter. Heli-skiing, as it is called, was actually an offshoot of alpine ski touring in which skiers climbed for hours on heavy downhill equipment to reach a high point, then enjoyed a brief but thrilling descent to a base camp. When Hans Gmoser introduced the copter to eliminate the long climbs and pack in much more downhill, it became an international success and drew visitors from all over the world. Skiers like Prime Minister Pierre Trudeau added glamor to the new sport.

This is a special type of skiing, requiring at least high intermediate skill on skis, particularly in deep snow, and a great deal of stamina. You are literally perched on the top of a mountain and have to follow a guide and copter load of skiers down the slopes, glaciers, old avalanche paths and forest trails that lead to the pickup point. It is fast paced skiing, packed with thrills and if conditions are right you will get a crack at the best powder skiing in the world. Anyone contemplating this kind of skiing should first take some deep powder lessons at a western ski resort and should be in top physical shape. You should also be ready to lay down at least sixty dollars a day (and up to $1,000 a week if you stay in a remote mountain lodge) for the experience. The main copter ski operators are based in the town of Banff, but most of the skiing is in British Columbia because the government forbids such operations in the parks and they cover most of the Alberta mountains.

In addition to providing a very special treat for the skier who is proficient on downhill equipment, the helicopter has been discovered by the cross-country skier who wants to reach remote terrain. Now ski parties can be ferried to remote mountain cabins which might otherwise be inaccessible or reached only by long and arduous journeys with heavy packs of equipment. In addition, ski parties can travel from one point to another and be picked up without having to ski all the way back. Obviously such trips have to be planned with great care and many safeguards.

Skiing in Alberta can be a half-year long affair on the deep and heavy snows that fall each winter. The season usually starts in November and lasts until May and snow accumulations range from around 650 cm (250 in.) to 1,000 cm (400 in.). The latter is the equivalent of a three-storey building. On the glaciers and icefields skiing can go on year-round though conditions are not always ideal. There is a tremendous variety of winter weather ranging from bitter cold and severe storms to warm Chinook winds from the southwest which can raise the temperature by as much as forty-five degrees Celsuis (eighty degrees Fahrenheit) in a day. In the mountains the weather is virtually unpredictable except for major storm fronts. The tremendous network of valleys creates a series of micro-weather systems that can put a storm in one valley and blazing sunshine in the next.

For this and other reasons persons going even for one-day trips usually carry warm clothing and some survival gear in their packs.

Alberta is well-known as Canada's major source of fossil fuels and as a producer of some of the best steaks. Another treat awaiting many visitors to Alberta restaurants is the occasional buffalo steak from animals culled out of the captive herds. The province has a population of over 1.7 million and this includes the most northerly major city in the country: Edmonton. In addition, settlement is scattered to the west in the beautiful Peace River country and also to the north. With the continuing boom in oil and natural gas development this is a growing permanent population and the interest in skiing is ever increasing the stream of winter visitors.

As a result of its concentration of national and provincial parks, Alberta has some of the best wild animal viewing opportunities in Canada. Since hunting is banned and development limited, many of the wild animals have virtually lost their fear of man and some even move in for a closer look. It is not unusual to look up from your dinner in the Banff Springs Hotel and see deer nibbling on bread thrown into the courtyard on the other side of the window.

Along the highway it is common to see Bighorn Sheep posing majestically on nearby snowbanks and when skiing in the woods you may glimpse a herd of elk. Even the normally shy coyote will trot along a frozen river with virtual disdain for the passing traffic and if you listen on a still night you can hear a pack of them answering the train whistle with their high-pitched cries.

Among the ski events held in Alberta is the Telemark Race, which draws hundreds of entrants to Lake Louise each year. This is usually held in mid-March and is organized by the Alpine Club of Canada. For information write the club at Box

1995, Calgary, Alta. T2P 2M2.

The Alpine Club, which in the past has been more involved with mountain climbing and mountain ski touring than cross-country, also is responsible for a number of mountain cabins which can be used by ski parties. The club may be contacted in Calgary or at Box 1026, Banff. Also in Banff are four helicopter skiing outfits. Gmoser's operation, which includes a strictly cross-country ski division run by guide Walter Batzhuber, is Canadian Mountain Holidays, Box 1660. The other copter ski outfits are Banff Helicopter Skiing, Box 895; Cariboo Helicopter Skiing, Box 1824; and Golden Heli-Skiing, Box 543. The postal code for Banff is T0L 0C0.

Also in Banff are the Association of Canadian Mountain Guides, Box 1537, and the Banff/Lake Louise Chamber of Commerce, Box 1298. Of course the headquarters for Banff National Park is located here and is a major source of travel and avalanche information. A similar headquarters is located in Jasper for that park. The regional office for Parks Canada is located at 134 – 11 Ave. S. E., Calgary, Alta., T2G 0X5. In Banff the parks service offers a winter interpretive program of slides, films and speakers on sports, wildlife and recreation in national parks. Information on skiing and lodging can be obtained from the provincial government. Write Travel Alberta, 10255 – 104 St., Edmonton, Alta., T5J 1B1. One of the most active cross-country clubs in the west is the Foothills Nordic Ski Club which regularly organizes trips into the mountains of Alberta and B.C. The latest contact was Ken Rathje, 10 Varbrook Pl. N.W., Calgary.

		Mean Temperature In Celsius (Fahrenheit)		Snowfall In Mean Centimetres
		Min	Max	(Inches)
Edmonton	Dec	-17.8 (- 0.1)	- 6.8 (19.7)	20.6 (13.4)
	Jan	-22.0 (- 7.6)	-10.6 (12.9)	24.9 (14.0)
	Feb	-17.9 (- 0.3)	- 6.2 (20.8)	21.1 (11.7)
	Mar	-13.3 (8.1)	- 1.3 (29.7)	17.5 (9.1)
Calgary	Dec	-13.4 (7.9)	- 1.7 (28.9)	17.0 (6.7)
	Jan	-16.7 (2.0)	- 5.3 (22.5)	19.1 (7.5)
	Feb	-13.3 (8.0)	- 1.6 (29.1)	21.3 (8.4)
	Mar	- 9.8 (14.3)	1.3 (34.3)	21.6 (8.5)
Banff	Dec	-13.1 (8.5)	- 4.4 (24.0)	34.0 (13.4)
	Jan	-16.3 (2.6)	- 6.1 (21.1)	35.6 (14.0)
	Feb	-12.9 (8.8)	- 0.7 (30.7)	29.7 (11.7)
	Mar	-10.1 (13.9)	2.5 (36.5)	23.1 (9.1)
Jasper	Dec	-13.6 (7.6)	- 4.6 (23.7)	28.7 (11.3)
	Jan	-17.3 (0.9)	- 7.1 (19.3)	31.0 (12.2)
	Feb	-12.7 (9.2)	- 0.4 (31.2)	23.1 (9.1)
	Mar	- 8.9 (15.9)	3.5 (38.3)	11.9 (4.7)
Peace River	Dec	-20.2 (- 4.3)	-10.2 (13.6)	26.7 (10.5)
	Jan	-25.9 (-14.7)	-15.7 (3.8)	22.4 (8.8)
	Feb	-19.6 (- 3.2)	- 8.1 (17.4)	24.4 (9.6)
	Mar	-14.9 (5.2)	- 2.3 (27.9)	21.1 (8.3)

Wood Buffalo

Athabasca R.

○ Peace River

Athabasca Falls

Willmore Wilderness

North Saskatchewan R.

■ **Elk Island**

Rocky Mountains Forest Reserve

Yellowhead Pass ○ ○ Edmonton

Jasper

White Goat

Siffleur

②

Lake Louise

Banff

○ Calgary

Kananaskis Lakes

Bow R. 🍁

Pincher Creek

○ Lethbridge

Medicine Hat

Waterton Lakes

▓ **National Park**

▒ **Provincial Park**

░ **Wilderness and Forest Reserves**

--🍁-- **Trans Canada Highway**

------ **Provincial Highways**

Alberta Trails

Rocky Mountains

Waterton Lakes National Park

This 200-square-mile park, tucked in the southwest corner of Alberta, has four trails, totalling 30 km, for cross-country skiing. The park shares its southern boundary with Glacier National Park in Montana and together they made the world's first international peace park in 1932. Waterton is in a highly scenic area where the vast expanse of open prairie suddenly stops at a fortress-like barrier of sedimentary mountains, thousands of feet high. The lakes are at the 4,200-foot level and nearby mountains tower in the 8,000 to 9,000-foot-plus range.

The sudden transition from prairie through foothills to mountains provides a variety of grasslands through some deciduous trees such as aspen, cottonwood and maple into evergreens like fir, spruce and pine. There is considerable wildlife, including bighorn sheep, mountain goats, moose, coyote and cougar. Hundreds of elk and mule deer winter in the parkland belt and prairie grass-lands. Overhead a skier may see a falcon, hawk or eagle soaring. The park is highly popular in summer and has more than 150 km of good hiking trails, most of them easy to walk and climb.

In winter the park is quieter with a few skiers, winter campers and snowmobilers. Most skiing is between January and March. Registration is necessary for most winter activities. Park gate manned weekends. Warden in townsite. Maps there, from Superintendent, Waterton Lakes National Park, Waterton Park, Alta. T0K 2M0, or from federal map offices. Following are ski trail descriptions.

Twin Lake Trail

Location: End of Red Rock Canyon Rd. Follows summer road and hiking trail to Twin Lakes at edge of park.

Length: 11 km one way. Average return travel time is 8 hr. This is a day-long trip for skiers of intermediate ability, though beginners could handle the first 5 km. The trail heads northwest, then west from parking lot at Red Rock Canyon, following a summer road in the valley of Bauerman Cr. to Twin

Lakes Cabin picnic ground. From there it swings south to follow the Twin Lakes hiking trail to Twin Lakes.

This is a scenic trip with good possibility of sighting wildlife and is suitable for winter camping. Skiers should be fit if they plan to make the whole trip in one day. The area is remote and one has to be on the lookout for weather changes and possibility of ava-lanches. On the east-facing mountains at the end of the trail there is high avalanche danger and skiers should be cautious about approaching these slopes. For trail information contact warden in Waterton Park town-site.

Blakiston Valley Trail

Location: Same as Twin Lake Trail.
Length: 10 km one way. Average return time 6 hr.

Another day-long trip from the Red Rock Canyon parking lot. In summer this is known as the South Kootenay Pass hiking trail. To take this trail, head southwest along the Blakiston and Lone Creek valleys with 8,230-foot Lost Mountain to your right. This is a wooded trail for intermediate skiers and is in remote mountain country. There is excellent scenery and the chance to spot wildlife. There are hazards of severe weather changes and possible avalanches, especially at the east slopes of the moun-tains at end of trail. For trail information con-tact park warden in Waterton Park townsite.

Lakeshore Trail

Location: Trail starts in Waterton Park townsite just below Cameron Falls bridge.
Length: 8 km one way. Average return time 5 hr.

An old hiking trail, this route heads due south along the west shore of Upper Water-ton L. to the United States border. This is wooded area with contrasting scenery of the long, narrow lake and the surrounding mountains.

Some skiers make it a two-day camping trip as the trail ends at Boundary Bay camp-site. There are good chances of seeing wild-life along the route. This is mountain country with avalanche hazard and the possibility of severe weather changes. Trail information from warden in townsite.

Crandell Lake Trail

Location: From Waterton Park 13 km (8 mi.) up Red Rock Canyon Rd.

Length: 1.5 km one way. Return trip time about 1 ½ hr.

This is a good half-day trip to visit little Crandell L., nestled in a valley between Mount Crandell and Ruby Ridge. Trail is for intermediate skiers, passes through wooded terrain. There is some hazard from avalanches and severe weather changes. Scenery is good and there are chances of spotting wildlife. Some skiers use this area for camping. For information on trail conditions check with warden in Waterton Park townsite.

Syncline Ski Trails

Location: Southwest Alberta. From Pincher Creek southwest about 32 km (20 mi.) to ski trails on West Castle R. in Rocky Mountains Forest Reserve.

Length: Three interconnecting loops of 5, 10 and 15 km.

This ski area, about 13 km (8 mi.) northeast of Castle Mountain Resort, was originally constructed for the 1975 Canada Winter Games. Trails pass through undulating, forested area, of valley bottom land in the foothills of the Rockies and has beautiful mountain scenery. Suitable trails for all levels of skiers marked and maintained by Alberta Forest Service. Emergency phone at site. One section may be reserved by organized groups who contact Forest Superintendent, Box 3310, Stn. B, Calgary, Alta. T2M 4L8.

Ribbon Creek Youth Hostel

Location: Kananaskis Valley, 90 km (56 mi.) southwest of Calgary. From Trans-Canada Highway (Hwy. 1) south at Kananaskis interchange and along Kananaskis Forestry Trunk Rd. about 25 km (15 mi.), then west at government campground road.

Length: More than 55 km.

This Canadian Youth Hostels camp is located along the beautiful valley of the Kananaskis R. at the former Ribbon Creek coal mining camp. There is an extensive network of cross-country trails ranging from beginner runs of just over a kilometre to longer runs which are steep enough to challenge an expert skier. Good powder skiing in Marmot Basin and excellent views from some of the slopes surrounding the camp. This hostel is ideal for youth groups as it has dormitories for 44 persons and areas for cooking and eating.

The geological history of the area is visible on the rock slopes surrounding the hostel. About 60 million years ago during mountain building large sections of rock were lifted and folded upward, leaving layers of rock exposed. The highest peak in the area, Mt. Bogart, 10,300 ft. lies directly west of hostel. Tree cover in the region includes lodgepole pine, white spruce, trembling aspen, alpine larch, and firs. Elk can be seen in the forests and Rocky Mountain sheep on Mt. Allan. For more information about the hostel and ski area contact the Canadian Youth Hostels Assn. in Calgary.

Fortress Mountain

Location: Kananaskis Valley, 115 km (70 mi.) west of Calgary. West on Trans-Canada Highway (Hwy. 1), then South on Kananaskis Rd. (Hwy. 940) to ski resort road.

Length: About 3 km of marked trails plus extensive skiing in valley and along mountain slopes.

A small series of loop trails is located at the foot of the recently reopened Fortress Mountain Ski Resort, a downhill area once known as Snowridge. The resort is located in a spectacularly scenic area of the river valley where the Kananaskis Mountains, including one peak shaped like a turreted fortress, tower over the landscape. This region is in the Bow Lake Forest, just east of the Continental Divide.

The resort, located at the 6,700-foot level, has snow from mid-November until May. There is a 140-bed lodge with a three-storey-high copper-clad fireplace. Resort has instruction, rentals and babysitting. There is even hang-gliding for the more daring skiers.

Banff National Park

To many people Banff is synonymous with Western Canada. It is the towering Rockies, rolling alpine meadows and jewel-like lakes set in high cirques, the amphitheatres nature has carved from massive rock. Banff is better known than its sister parks in the west because it is the path of the Trans-Canada Highway and the original Canadian Pacific Railway route through the mountains. It is a major summer resort, drawing visitors from around the world, and in recent years has become one of Canada's principal winter resort areas.

Late in the 1960s the decision to open the famous Banff Springs Hotel for skiers signalled the real start of the western ski boom. Special airline ski packages suddenly began filling up the 3,000 spaces available for winter visitors. Most of these skiers were headed for the three famous downhill resorts: Mount Norquay, Sunshine and Lake Louise.

During this period westerners both local and from such centres as Calgary were discovering the pleasures of cross-country skis and were busily scouting trails for the new sport. They followed some of the old routes of alpine ski tourers, such as the famous trails to Assiniboine and Skoki lodges and blazed new routes through the rolling, forested country of the lower mountain regions. Some moutaineers challenged the high country with the new equipment and proved to doubters that experts could skim some of the glacier regions with light, waxed skis rather than just slog along on alpine skis, clad with sealskins.

The opportunities for cross-country skiing within the park are staggering. Banff stretches for more than 150 miles along the eastern slope of the Continental Divide and covers more than 2,500 square miles. It is a land of dozens of major mountain peaks, myriad passes, streams, rivers and lakes· and vegetation ranging from heavy forest to sparse, sub-Arctic ground cover. Much of the interior has barely been seen by humans on foot and part of the park boundary has not even been surveyed. There are places where you will find larch which have been standing for as long as 6,000 years and naturalists are continually urging campers not to cut these trees, which often appear dead in winter.

In the past few years a few groups and individuals have been particularly active in mapping routes for cross-country. One of these is Walter Batzhuber, a licenced mountain guide. Batzhuber, who operates out of his ski shop on the main street of Banff, has produced a unique map of 71 cross-country ski trails in the park. The trails are marked for length and graded for ability of skier. The map, a useful tool for locating routes, is available at the shop, or by mail for $1.50 (early 1976 price) from CMH, Cross-country Division, Box 316, Banff, Alta., T0L 0C0.

Another source of information is a flyer produced by Parks Canada with a list of relatively easy routes in the vicinity of Banff and Lake Louise townsites. This can be had from park officials or by writing the Park Warden, Administration Building, Banff National Park, Banff, Alta. T0L 0C0.

If you are skiing in the park, and hundreds more are trying it every year, registration

with the parks service is mandatory for remote or overnight trips as a safety precaution. You can do it in person or at one of the self-registration boxes located in the park. That way the rescue squad knows where to start looking for you if you don't return within a reasonable time.

It's a good idea to get in touch with the parks people in any case if you are tackling some of the trails around the mountains. The experts can advise you on good routes for different times of the year and about the relative avalanche hazard of any route at a given time.

Banff and Lake Louise Townsite Trails

In recent years the swelling popularity of cross-country skiing among native westerners and many winter visitors has prompted the parks service to mark more than 80 km of routes in 16 trails around the two resort towns. Many of these trails emanate from the back doors of hotels or local parking lots and there are a few from the Trans-Canada Highway between the townsites. The trails are popular with ski instructors teaching new students and with skiers who want half-day or leisurely full day trips.

Registration with park officials for these trails in low elevation country is voluntary but recommended for inexperienced or lone skiers travelling even a bit off the beaten path. Trails are marked with orange tape and trail heads with skier symbol signs. Detailed information and map of the general area available from warden offices in Banff and Lake Louise, Banff East Gate, Sunshine and Temple avalanche research stations and Mount Norquay. Banff warden is at 762-3600.

The trails around Banff vary from the simple to the technicaily easy but tiring. For starters, most learners in the area have at least made one trip to.the famous Banff Springs Hotel golf course along the shores of the Bow R.

Other possibilities are unplowed fire and summer access roads, riverbanks and hiking trails. Some skiers get an introduction to the rigors of winter camping by making a safe trip to some area nearby or even try an arduous climb up one of the local mountains to get just a taste of mountaineering. Many summer hiking trails are suitable for cross-country skiing. In the case of Carrot Creek, skiers have the advantage of a smooth blanket of ice and snow over what is a rough and wet summer walking route. These and other small trails are listed in the flyer available from the parks service.

Skiers who want a map with details should obtain the Banff Park map in the federal series on national parks. It gives decent topographical coverage of the whole park area. For finer shadings of the mountains and valleys you can get the 1:50,000 scale maps.

Sunshine Area

Sunshine Village, about 25 km (15 mi.) southwest of Banff, has long been one of Canada's top downhill and alpine touring ski areas. More recently, cross-country skiers have discovered the pleasures of high country travel through mountain passes and between the peaks of this beautiful region. The resort and Parks Canada co-operate to keep open a few short trails for trips in the one to three hour range, but most of the skiing is of the more strenuous mountain type. For this, skiers will need touring equipment and outfits. If skiers are not familiar with the area, they should have a guide or leader who knows the region, since navigation can get a bit tricky at times and weather can sock in suddenly and totally.

The lodge is a nice place to visit or to stay, since it has 180 beds and an alpine ambience. All cars must be parked at the Bourgeau parking lot on Healy Cr., about 5 km down a winding mountain road from the resort. From there a shuttle bus brings most skiers to the starting point, though eager beavers on cross-country skis may opt for the trip up with climbing wax. The resort now offers cross-country ski weeks with instruction and trips into the surrounding countryside. There is a day lodge, rentals, and a guide service. During the Christmas season, the resort holds special activities such as torchlight parades, ski races and cookouts.

Sunshine is known for its good snow conditions. The base lodge is located at the 7,200 foot level so snowfalls tend to be heavy and the total averages 900 cm (350 inches) a year. The ski season runs from early November to late May – about half a year. The National Parks series of Banff Park gives a good overall look at the area but the 1:50,000 scale topographic sheets of Banff East and Banff West provide better detail.

Citadel Pass

Location: Sunshine area.
Length: About 10 km one way.

This is a relatively easy trip for a party of intermediate skiers. The quick way to start is to take the two chairlifts up the Great Divide route, then begin the trek southeast across alpine meadows and easy slopes. Keep to the eastern flank of Quartz Hill, about halfway along the trip, and bear southeast to the pass. The pass is between Citadel Peak, 8,556 ft., on the right, and Fatigue Mountain, 9,707, on the left. From here you can make it back to Sunshine in one day trip or this can be the halfway point for an overnight trip to Mount Assiniboine.

Though the trip from Sunshine to the pass is not far, remember that it's mostly downhill on the way out and a gradual but long uphill trip back, so save some energy. There is little avalanche hazard to the pass but it is high country and if you are caught in a whiteout you may have to make an emergency shelter. Check with the warden station at Sunshine and keep an eye on weather conditions.

Sunshine to Assiniboine

Location: Sunshine area and southeast.
Length: 30 km one way.

This is a popular trip for experienced skiers led by qualified guides and it passes through one of the most beautiful areas of the Rockies. Mount Assiniboine, 11,870 ft., has a shape similar to the famous Matterhorn of Switzerland. The start of the trip in winter is generally made from Sunshine and is the same as for Citadel Pass. From there a party would make a 1,300 ft. descent to the Golden Valley and the Simpson R. This is often a camping area during a two-day trip, but great care must be taken because there are many avalanche paths. Some park officials recommend that trips be made in April or early May just to avoid the avalanche hazard.

From the Golden Valley the route follows the foot of the Great Divide through forests of spruce and pine to the Valley of the Rocks and to Og L. The last leg of the route follows the shore of L. Magog and south to Assiniboine Lodge, which is open in the winter. Arrangements for lodging must be made in advance or skiers can camp in area.

Once at Assiniboine the main mountain lies to the south and there are many possible side trips in the area. This is actually a British Columbia provincial park since skiers have crossed the border at Citadel Pass. The area was settled by the Assiniboine (Stoney) Indian tribe. In 1921 the Alpine Club of Canada urged the B.C. government to make the region a provincial park and by now 150 square miles has been set aside. It is an area

For the daring, athletic and experienced skier, kite-flying is a new kind of thrill. With these parabolic wings and downhill skis, you can soar over the snow like some great snow bird.

of jagged peaks, glaciers, lakes, rivers and alpine meadows. There is a range of forest including boreal varieties such as spruce, alpine fir and lodgepole pine. Some high country stands of alpine larch are as much as 5,000 to 6,000 years old. Along the mountain streams there are even dense thickets of low willows and bog birch. The park is home for such animals as Rocky Mountain elk, mule deer, moose, mountain goats and bighorn sheep. Wolverine, wolf, marten, coyote, porcupine and snowshoe hare inhabit the park but the skier is more likely to see only their tracks. With luck he may see a golden eagle or broadwinged hawk soaring overhead. For more detailed information on the park write: District Super-intendent, Provincial Park Branch, Box 118, Wasa, B.C., V0B 2K0. Detailed maps are available through: Map Production Division, British Columbia Lands Service, Parliament Buildings, Victoria B.C. V8V 1T7.

Rock Isle Lake and Larix Lake
Location: Sunshine.
Length: About 2.5 km one way.
This is a nice little morning or afternoon jaunt for an intermediate skier heading out from Sunshine Village. Skier can take the lifts up from base lodge or ski up the hills, then loop back around the two small lakes and possibly by Grizzly L. to the side.

Sunshine to Quartz Hill
Location: Sunshine and south.
Length: About 6 km. one way.
Another morning or afternoon outing for intermediate skiers starting from the lodge. A steady climb will take you to the top of Quartz Hill at 8,464 ft. and provide a good view point. To the north is Lookout Mountain and the top of the Sunshine ski lifts, while far to the south Mount Assiniboine glistens like a great white tooth in the sky. The run from the top of Quartz is a pure delight when the powder is good and there are slopes for beginner to expert skiers on cross-country equipment.

Sunshine to Simpson Pass
Location: From Sunshine west and behind the lodge.
Length: About 5 km one way.
This is a favorite trip at the end of the day for skiers making their way back to the Bour-geau parking lot and then on to lodging else-where. However, there is some tricky skiing and it is rated for expert skiers. There is a

steep ledge to descend through the trees and navigation can be a bit tricky if the leader does not keep his bearings. While this trail can lead back to the lodge, many skiers bear northeast down Healy Cr. which leads right past the parking lot.

Trips to Egypt Lake
Location: Northwest of Sunshine resort about 8 km by air.

Egypt L. with its two shelter cabins is a very popular goal for skiers in the Sunshine area since it allows an overnight trip with the possibility of numerous side trips to neighboring lakes and slopes. There are two major approaches. The first, from Sunshine, actually has two possible starting points. Skiers can leave from the Bourgeau parking lot and work their way up Healy Cr. or they can start from the lodge and make the trip through Simpson Pass. To the left is The Monarch, a 9,528 ft. peak, and Monarch Ramparts, a wall of rock along the Great Divide.

The trails merge below Healy Pass. This pass should be taken high on the left side to give both an outstanding view of the landscape ahead and behind, and to get a long gentle downhill run through a few trees to Egypt L. This makes about a 10 to 12 km trip. The alternative is an easy but long 15 km trip up Redearth Cr. from Hwy. 1. The trip begins on a summer road then bears south along Pharaoh Cr. to the Egypt area. The route, gentle and lined with trees, is a good foul weather exit. There are two cabins at Egypt but arrangements to use them should be made ahead of time with the parks service in Banff. Campers should carry gas stoves rather than count on firewood.

Egypt Lake Excursions
Once at Egypt there are many possibilities for touring in this area of Middle Eastern names. Some skiers settle for peaceful excursions around the base of Pharaoh Peaks while others try near suicidal runs from areas like Scarab L., a few hundred feet above the camps. There is a warden's cabin at Egypt L. and skiers can get information there about some of the side trips and advice about the relative avalanche hazard.

Popular trips lead to the nearby series of small lakes. For example, starting at the Egypt L. cabin you can find a trail in the woods and bushwhack up to Scarab L. and a good view of the Healy Pass. Keep an eye

on the ridge for possible avalanche hazard. From Scarab you can continue on up to Mummy L. and possibly on to Natalko L. if conditions are favorable. Here you are skiing right along the Great Divide and the Alberta-British Columbia border.

Another option from Egypt is northwest through the larch uplands of Whistling Valley with Pharaoh Peaks on your right and Haiduk Peak on your left. From this high pass there is a good view to the north with Haiduk L. in the foreground and behind it Mount Ball, 10,865 ft., and Storm Mountain, 10,372 ft.

You can ski down the valley to Haiduk L. or stay high on the slopes to the right and follow a small pass around to tiny Sphinx L. The creek will lead you to Black Rock L., named for the high, stony wall to one side, then on to the cabin. You will pass the spectacular twin peaks of Pharaoh, both close to 9,000 ft. high. Back at the cabin you can usually get a drink of very fresh water from a brook which manages to stay open most of the winter.

Bourgeau Lake
Location: Start from Trans-Canada Hwy. (Hwy. 1) at Wolverine Creek picnic area 3.2 km (2 mi.) west of Sunshine access road and follow hiking trail.
Length: About 8 km one way.

From parking lot it will be necessary to cut back about 300 m to the east to reach the start of the trail. The route begins through lodgepole pine and spruce and winds its way up Wolverine Cr. About three-quarters of the way up, you hit steep switchbacks and the going will be tough for a short stretch as you mount beside what is a series of cascades in the summer. The last haul is fairly flat land leading to the lake in a great amphitheatre of mountains.

On the left is Mount Bourgeau, 9,615 ft. and to the right Mount Brett, 9,760 ft. The lake is surrounded on three sides by massive limestone walls. During avalanche season great care should be taken in the immediate lake area, as slides often come crashing down the couloirs and can sweep across the lake itself.

Twin and Shadow Lakes
Location: Northwest of Egypt L. area and south of Eisenhower Junction on Hwy. 1.
Length: Trips range from about 15 km one way to 35 km in and out trips.

Three sub-alpine lakes at the foot of the Continental Divide are the objectives for trips starting either from Redearth Cr. or the Eisenhower Jct. farther up the highways. To take the first route, start at the Trans-Canada Highway (Hwy. 1) and follow the Redearth Cr. fire road uphill. At the warden's cabin keep going straight until you arrive at Shadow L., literally in the shadow of the massive cliffs of Mount Ball, at 10,865 ft. the highest peak in the Ball Group. This 2 km-long lake is large for a sub-alpine body of water.

From here you can head either south and east to the Egypt L. region or return to Brewster Cabin, then head northwest through Gibbon Pass to Twin Lakes. These frozen lakes sit at the base of Storm Mountain, a massive collection of rifted rockfaces which guard snow in nooks and crannies even through the summer. For overnight stays, check with the parks service in Banff about use of cabins.

The alternate approach is up the hiking trail from the Eisenhower Jct. at Mount Eisenhower (Castle Mountain). This is a direct, southwest route to Twin Lakes, starting up through a forest of lodgepole pine and white spruce and along a moderate to steep grade. In this case the higher you get the larger the trees become, because you are leaving an old forest fire region and entering a climax spruce forest. Farther up the trail, this tapers off into open stands of spruce and alpine fir before becoming alpine meadowland in the last leg to Twin Lakes. These two approach routes can be interchanged and the round trip from one point on the Trans-Canada Highway to the other, using the two routes, is about 35 km.

Bow Glacier
Location: From Num-ti-jah Lodge on Banff-Jasper Highway (Hwy. 93) southeast around the end of Bow L.
Length: 5 km one way

This is a short trip but is rated for experts because of the stiff climb toward the glacier and the avalanche hazard in the area. From a flat area through spruce forest, in the shadow of Crowfoot Mountain, 9,975 ft., the route begins rising steeply through a narrow but spectacular gorge. Along this gorge the skier will see to one side a natural bridge of a 20-foot-long limestone block which tumbled into the gap in the rock sometime in the past and rests between the canyon walls. Above is the Bow Glacier and beyond that the Wapta Icefields; but travel there on cross-country skis can be difficult and the avalanche hazard quite high.

Experienced skiers with good weather conditions can make exciting overnight trips along the Continental Divide at this point. They reserve use of the Alpine Club of Canada's Balfour Hut at the 8,100-foot-level and spend one night there in the Balfour Pass. They finish the travel over ice-fields at the Banff-Radium Highway near Sherbroke L., just west of Kicking Horse Pass.

Dolomite Pass and Lake Helen
Location: Access from area of Crowfoot Glacier viewpoint on Banff-Jasper Highway south of Bow L. Trip to north.
Length: 6 to 9 km one way trips.

Both points are accessible from the same starting point but are of varying difficulty. The trip to L. Helen is 6 km but steep and passes through areas of both snow and rock slides. The route to Dolomite Pass is longer and gentler and therefore suitable for intermediate skiers. This is a very scenic area.

Leaving the Bow Valley you move northward with the castellate cliffs of 9,828 ft. Dolomite Peak visible on your right through the spruce and fir. The trail mounts and takes you into the area of L. Katherine.

This is the point to look back. To the southeast is 11,135 ft. Mount Hector, towering over the highway, and if the day is clear you will see the peak of 11,870 ft. Mount Assiniboine more than 100 km away. The pass was named by nineteenth century mountaineers who found the light grey mid-Cambrian limestone was similar in appearance to the Swiss Dolomites.

Mosquito Creek to Molar Pass
Location: From Mosquito Creek Campground on Banff-Jasper Highway beside Bow Peak head north.
Length: About 11 km one way.

This is a major summer hiking trail and in the winter is a nice intermediate trip into the back country. It is very scenic and offers the possibility of side trips to nearby valleys. The trail leads into a huge, open bowl between Dolomite, Devon and Molar mountains. This route can be greatly extended by winter campers who make a trek south through the Molar Pass right down to the Pipestone River valley and head back to the highway at Lake Louise. That is a trip of about 40 km.

Rockbound Lake
Location: From area of ranger station at Eisenhower Jct. to lake behind Mount Eisenhower.

Length: About 8 km one way.

This is a rather steep trail with an elevation gain of 2,400 feet but can be skied by intermediates and is worthwhile for the excellent views. The route climbs out of the Bow Valley, following a stream from the lake across the southern flank of Mount Eisenhower. This mountain, one of the most striking in the park, is a classic example of a castellate formation and its original name, still frequently used, is Castle Mountain.

As you mount the base of this rock mass, the Bow Valley stretches out behind and a few kilometres away stand the peak of Pilot Mountain and the pyramidal shape of Copper Mountain, both more than 9,000 ft. high. There is an excellent view of the Sawback Range, a series of serrated peaks formed by erosion. The trail winds behind Eisenhower and into a narrow valley, which cuts right into this massive mountain. Within you will first find Tower L., then Rockbound, enclosed by a high cirque.

Pipestone River from Lake Louise
Location: Start at Lake Louise on east side of highway and head up river.
Length: About 20 km one way.

This ski route follows a main horse trail into the park interior as it heads up the wide valley of the Pipestone. This can become the corollary of the Molar trail and a ski party could head north up Molar Pass or could push straight up the river towards Cataract Peak and further into the mountains. The usual turnaround point is at the warden's cabin at Little Pipestone Cr.

Boom Lake
Location: North from Banff-Radium Highway (Hwy. 93) about 8 km (5 mi.) southwest of Eisenhower Jct.
Length: About 5 km one way.

This is a popular beginners' trip since it follows a well-cleared trail for most of its length, narrowing only near the lake itself for a quick taste of skiing between the trees. There is little avalanche danger except at the foot of the high mountains at the lake, but skiers should check with the parks service in any case.

After you pass through the forest of white spruce, lodgepole pine and Douglas fir it is worth skiing to the end of the narrow lake to look back at the splendid view of mountains rising from the lake's edge. A 2,000 ft. wall of grey limestone guards the southern shore while to the west is a glacier-capped mountain more than 10,000 ft. high. Here are the

Skier pauses for a break during day-long ski trip. Heavily forested areas provide protection from wind while clearings seem to gather the sun.

icy spires of Mount Quadra and the twin peaks of Bident Mountain, shaped like a pair of teeth. Skiers who picnic at the lake often end up sharing their lunches with the noisy Canada Jays which inhabit the forests and sweep in at the first sight of crumbs. On the north side of the lake there is a gentle slope for downhill runs.

Taylor Lake
Location: West of Banff-Jasper Highway, just north of Eisenhower Jct. Access from Taylor Creek picnic area.
Length: About 6 km one way.

This is somewhat similar to the Boom L. trip but the climb is a bit more demanding and this is usually rated as intermediate terrain. It entails a slogging, 1,900 ft. climb through a fire succession forest of lodgepole pine and spruce along a winding fire road track, but the view at the top is worth the effort. Taylor L. is set in a cirque overlooking the Bow Valley and Mount Eisenhower across the river. The twin spires of Bident Mountain rise sharply from the south side of the lake as do the rock walls of Mount Bell.

Skiers can continue from the end of the lake west up a small pass (Taylor Pass) and look back for an even more splendid view or they could opt to keep on going into Consolation Valley. If weather and avalanche conditions were safe they could even cut through Consolation Pass and hit Boom L. However the run back down the fire road used for entry is pleasant and speedy and most skiers will exit this way.

Skoki Area

Location: From Lake Louise townsite northeast.

Length: Trip to Skoki Lodge from Mount Temple Ski Lodge about 11 km one way. Many possible variations.

Skoki is one of the most popular ski trips in western Canada and the area is steeped in the ski history of this part of the country. The large and attractive log building was constructed in the 1930s when there was a single sport of skiing. Downhill lifts were just being invented and skiers trekked everywhere on what would now be considered mountain skis — boards considerably heavier than cross-country equipment. They enjoyed the flat sections through scenic country and climbed nearby slopes for exciting runs. At the time, skiers took the Canadian Pacific Railway to Lake Louise, then skied in, usually stopping the first night at a halfway hut. There are even tales that ghosts of skiers lost in avalanches on the surrounding peaks haunt the valleys by night — tales with a cautioning message to those who find the route easy and would ignore the normal mountain precautions.

Now the trip has been abbreviated a bit by a shuttle bus for the first 5 km from Lake Louise townsite to Mt. Temple Ski Lodge. From the lodge skiers often make a simple day trip of about 5 km one way as far as the halfway hut at Boulder Pass, then ski back out and down the road to town. The full trip is an 11 km jaunt to Skoki Lodge itself and a stay in a dorm or one of the private rooms. Accommodation at Skoki or in the halfway hut should be arranged through the Post Hotel in Lake Louise. Of course you can always try winter camping with the knowledge there is permanent emergency shelter nearby.

The start of the trip from Temple is a gentle uphill through sub-alpine forest of spruce, fir and some Lyall's larch. Near Boulder Pass the trail enters open meadowland and views of some of the rugged peaks in the 90-square-mile Slate Range, including 10,-

125-ft. Mount Richardson to the north and just east of that Ptarmigan Peak at 10,036 ft. Looking back across the Bow R. you see Mount Temple, 11,626 ft., the second highest peak in Banff National Park, and the dominant feature of the mountainscape. The log halfway hut near the head of Corral Cr. is at the entry to Boulder Pass and Ptarmigan L. This is at the timber line and the country flattens out, making the trip a bit easier. Day trippers may make some side excursions here before turning back, but for the Skoki bound this is the halfway point.

The highest point in the trip comes at 8,000 ft. in Deception Pass and from there on it is a beautiful downhill run to the lodge at the foot of Mount Skoki. The trail is now groomed by snowmobiles so it is not too difficult for intermediate skiers to make a run to the lodge, have lunch and head back to Lake Louise before dark. Ideally a skier would spend at least a couple of days at Skoki and make side trips into the beautiful and peaceful mountain country, exploring the numerous valleys and lakes tucked between mountain peaks. Skiers will find rentals and instruction at Lake Louise and can make reservations for food and lodging there. For more information write Village Lake Louise Ltd., Box 5, Lake Louise, Alta.

Lake Louise Teahouse

Location: From Chateau Lake Louise follow hiking trail to Plain-of-Six-Glaciers Teahouse.

Length: About 5 km one way.

A nice outing for intermediate skiers, this route leads across L. Louise from the big hotel and starts up the lower reaches of surrounding mountains through a forest of spruce and Douglas fir. After a couple of kilometres, the trail enters a barren area influenced by the Victoria Glacier, which feeds L. Louise. The teahouse, crowded in summer but closed and silent in winter, is the terminal of the trip. Here you can sit on the balcony and enjoy a spendid view of the lake, surrounded by mountains, and see the trails of the Lake Louise downhill resort in the distance.

Though it is tempting to continue onto the glacier area in front and go to the left of the trail, only skiers experienced around crevasses should tackle this area. Another tempting option is the summer hiking trail to L. Agnes, behind The Beehive rock formation. This, too, should be avoided because the trail becomes progressively narrower and is exposed to avalanches. It is better to make Agnes a separate trip from the hotels going via Mirror L.

Mount Temple Area
Location: Valleys on both sides of the mountain, accessible from Chateau Lake Louise.
Length: 10 to 15 km range one way.

Mount Temple, 11,636 ft. high and the highest peak in the southern Rockies, dominates this part of the park and valleys on either side of the majestic hunk of granite provide interesting and attractive day trips for skiers of intermediate ability. In addition, there is a short but interesting trek for expert skiers to the Saddleback area between Mount Fairview and the "horn" of Saddle Peak. This 4 km excursion heads up a moderate to steep grade through a forest of spruce and Douglas fir. This is avalanche area and should be treated with great respect. From a high viewpoint you can get one of the most dramatic views of Mount Temple across a chasm. There are panoramic views all around, including an excellent view of the Bow Valley.

Longer but less hazardous is the Paradise Valley route between a collection of mountain peaks on your right and Mount Temple on your left. You can make an 8 km trip up to Lake Annette or continue another 8 km to Horseshoe Glacier at the head of the valley.

On the south side of Mount Temple is the Valley of Ten Peaks, which obviously provides outstanding views of the mountain country. The less interesting side of the trip is an 11 km trek up a plowed but chained-off access road to Moraine L. Once at the lake there are numerous options for trips into the nearby passes and to small lakes. Sentinel Pass is good for scenery as it provides a viewpoint back over the Valley of the Ten Peaks and a close look at the impressive sides of Mount Temple. Another trip will take you northwest to Eiffel L., lying in the shadow of a peak of the same name. The tip of this peak bore enough resemblance to the famous tower in Paris to inspire the name.

Whistlers Campground Loop
Location: From Jasper townsite south 5 km (3 mi.) on Icefields Parkway, then right into winter camping area. Use plowed parking lot.
Length: 4.5 km.

This trail, on level terrain along summer campground road, is ideal for beginners or for more advanced skiers looking for a conditioning track. Entry to trail at sign at north end of parking lot. Evening skiing some nights under campground lights on abbreviated section of trail. Main trail marked with yellow tape, night trail with blue and yellow flagging. Trail maintained and patrolled by parks service.

Pyramid Bench Trail
Location: From Jasper townsite north 4 km (2.5 mi.) on Pyramid Lake Rd., then right into plowed parking lot at Pyramid Lake Riding Stable.
Length: 4.7 km.

An intermediate loop trail from east end of parking lot through gentle, sloping terrain along edge of a bench overlooking Athabasca River valley. To the northwest are the mountains of the Victoria Cross Ranges behind Pyramid and Patricia Lakes. Area is covered with moderately dense forest of lodgepole pine, aspen and Douglas fir. There are many unmarked hiking trails in this area so skiers should keep to the route marked with red flagging tape. Trail maintained and patrolled by parks service.

Jasper National Park
The largest of the mountain parks, Jasper has 4,200 square miles of magnificent mountain scenery and most of the area is wilderness, accessible only to travellers on foot or skis. The park lies on the eastern slope of the Rockies and the Continental Divide and is bounded on the south by Banff National Park. This forms part of a massive block of federal and provincial parkland along the Rockies.

There are hundreds of kilometres of trails in Jasper. Near the park headquarters at Jasper townsite three trails have been marked for beginner, intermediate and advanced skiers. In addition, about 300 square miles of valley bottom land and mountain passes in the 3,500 to 6,500 foot level offer more than 100 km of trails near the townsite. These trails are through gently rolling country with magnificent scenery. Beyond this are about 1,000 km of high country and remote routes which require heavy touring or mountain skis, equipment and clothing. This is rugged country where weather can unpredictably change from brilliant sunshine to whiteout and where one must be on the lookout for avalanche conditions.

Registration is required for travel on all but the three marked trails and park officials can

Wind and blowing snow combine to form fantastical snow sculptures as convoluted and complex as anything we can imagine. The best time to camera hunt is after a blizzard or a strong windstorm.

provide skiers with trail and avalanche information. It is wise to check with the warden for route details and they can provide maps or help update your topographic sheets. There is a good overall topographic map, Jasper National Park, available from federal map offices and the more detailed 1:50,-000 scale sheets may be obtained for specific routes. For information on the park write: Superintendent, Jasper National Park, Box 10, Jasper, Alta. T0E 1E0. See the Chief Park Warden at headquarters on Connaught Dr. in the town or phone 852-4583. Major downhill ski area at Marmot Basin near townsite.

Patricia Lake Circle
Location: Same as Pyramid Bench Trail.
Length: 5.9 km.

This loop trail for advanced skiers starts on the opposite side of the Pyramid Lake Rd. from parking lot and cuts through moderately steep terrain. Best taken in clockwise direction. Forest cover changes frequently with most common trees Douglas fir, aspen and pine. Skiers pass through clearings which give excellent view of mountain ranges to south. Marked with blue tape. Trail maintained and patrolled by parks service.

Cavell-Tonquin-Eremite Routes
Location: South of Jasper, starting from road to Mount Edith Cavell and in valleys facing The Ramparts.
Length: About 30 km into Tonquin Valley from Hwy. 93A with further options.

The Tonquin and nearby valleys are one of the most beautiful regions in the Rockies with a combination of impressive mountain walls and peaks, small lakes and rolling alpine meadows. There are extensive ski-touring possibilities for the winter camper. Skiers will have to tent out or arrange with Alpine Club of Canada in Banff for use of the Wates-Gibson hut.

This area has been used by hikers for many years and is now becoming popular with both cross-country and alpine touring skiers, who use heavier equipment. For example, Canadian Mountain Holidays, better known for helicopter ski trips, operates a camp out of the ACC hut each spring and skiers make trips into the Eremite Valley. Access to the region is from Hwy. 93A. If you ski up the summer road, you may be able to camp in the Youth Hostel if you make arrangements in Jasper.

There is a short side trip to the Angel Glacier lookout and one to the Edith Cavell Teahouse, closed in winter. Some skiers avoid the climb up the road by making arrangements with local snowmobilers for rides to the teahouse area. With an early start and good conditions, they can make the 20 km run through spruce and fir, then across meadows to the ACC hut in one day. From the hut area you can ski the Amethyst Lakes area with its spectacular views of rugged mountain peaks to the east and The Ramparts to the west. The Ramparts is a wall of mountain peaks, partially along the Great Divide. To the south is the Eremite Valley, an area of glaciers and small lakes. The highest peak is Mount Erebus, 10,234 ft.

Athabaska Falls-Whirlpool River
Location: From Hwy. 93A south of Jasper at Athabasca Falls.
Length: Trips in the 35 to 50 km range possible.

This is sometimes used as an alternate entry point for the Tonquin Valley, Amethyst Lakes area or for separate trips into nearby valleys. It avoids the climb up the Edith Cavell Rd. Starting from the falls skiers are following the old fur trade route and the first main route across the Canadian Rockies. There is a hiking trail up the Whirlpool R. and skiers often cut north through Verdant Pass to join the main trail into the Wates-Gibson hut.

Skyline Trail
Location: In Maligne Mountain Range southeast from the edge of Jasper townsite.

In summer there is a series of hiking trails through this high and scenic range with trips up to 50 km. However in winter these 8,000 and 9,000 ft. peaks can be cold and inhospitable as the wind sweeps through them creating whiteout conditions and avalanches sweep down their sides. There are safe areas for skiing, but anyone planning trips in the area should check with the park warden's office for information on snow conditions and should have prepared a detailed route with skiers who know the safe sections.

Jacques Lake
Location: Start from Maligne Rd., east of Jasper townsite and follow mountain passes to north, west and north.
Length: About 12 km.

This is a nice trip through impressive mountain country. As you start the trip from the north end of Medicine L., the jagged grey limestone walls of the Queen Elizabeth

Range are on the right and the Colin Range guards the left. Trail starts on an old fire road, then follows a summer hiking path. You pass through spruce, lodgepole pine and cottonwood around a series of small lakes before traversing a dense forest and arriving at Jacques L. From there you can see the Jacques Range to the north.

Athabasca Falls-Fryatt Creek
Location: Same starting point as previous trail. From falls head southeast along west bank of Athabasca R., then skiers cut southwest up the valley of the Fryatt Cr.
Length: about 20 km one way.

This is a highly scenic trip up the Fryatt Valley. The start is a 7 km flat stretch along the westerly shore of the Athabasca R. This may be avoided if skiers can make arrangements with parks personnel to use cable car across river near Fryatt Cr. Entrance to valley is between the towering peaks of Mount Fryatt, 11,026 ft., on your right and Mount Christie, 10,108 ft., and behind it Brussels Peak, 10,370 ft., on the left.

Trail follows the creek, then begins climbing across the spruce and fir-clad western slopes of Mount Christie. Continue along Fryatt L. and enjoy the views of mountain peaks on both sides. From the lake continue to end of valley and climb the headwall to a plateau where you will find the Sidney Vallance Hut of the Alpine Club of Canada at the 6,200 ft. level. Arrangements for use of hut must be made in advance with club in Banff.

Terratima Ski Hostel
Location: Southwest of Rocky Mountain House 21 km (16 mi.). From Hwy. 11 east of town south on Hwy. 922 for 10 km (6 mi.) then west 8 km (5 mi.) to access road and south to hostel. South of Strubel L.
Length: Trail network allows trips of half day duration.

Terratima is based in an old, two-storey ranch house at the edge of the Rocky Mountains Forest Reserve. Skiing is on a series of loops ranging through field and forest area inhabited by considerable wildlife. Skiers may see tracks of rabbits, moose, lynx, deer and fox. Trails cross Prairie and Swan Creeks.

Skiers often bring food and bedroll and stay in the ranch house, two nearby cabins or a very old log house about 1.6 km from the hostel. Log sauna house heated Saturday nights. Guided moonlight tours to cabin for hot drinks and singsong. Cooking on

A sunny day and a nicely packed trail over rolling terrain form the ideal combination for a skier with light equipment trying to make good time.

wood stove in main building. For map, information and reservations write Terratima, Box 1636, Rocky Mountain House, Alta. T0M 1T0.

Blue Lake Centre (not public)
Location: Northwest of Hinton.

Though the Blue Lake Centre is not public it is of interest to skiers. It is a provincial government training area for leaders, instructors and coaches in outdoor activities such as cross-country skiing. There are nine levels of training for persons who want to become ski instructors, tour leaders and examiners. Skiing on about 10 km of trails in area plus extensive forest, meadow and muskeg areas in the foothills area. For more information contact: Centre Manager, Blue Lake Centre, Box 850, Hinton, Alta. T0E 1B0.

Edmonton Area

Edmonton — North Saskatchewan River Valley

Edmonton skiers have the advantage of a major river valley slicing through the heart of their city and providing a greenbelt where they can find good trails close to home. The city parks and recreation department notes there are at least several thousand cross-country skiers in the population of 446,000 to take advantage of the trails. In recent years the department and a local newspaper have had thousands register for learn-to-ski programs in the parks. The city lists eight primary areas for skiing along the river valley and many of these can be skied in sequence, providing extensive touring pos-. sibilities.

Terwillegar Park:

Located in southwest section of river valley opposite the Edmonton Country Club. Access from junction of 45 Ave. and 156 St. This is rated as an advanced 2.5 km trail with some beginner and intermediate skiing nearby.

Victoria Golf Course:

Golf course at 99 Ave. and 121 St. has no marked trails but opportunities for family touring in beginner to intermediate categories. Skiers asked to stay off greens.

Kinsmen Park:

Located at bottom of Walterdale Hill near 105 St. Bridge. Trail starts opposite south rink and from west of field house. Advanced

5 km trail with some easy skiing and steep sections, a long, downhill run and stiff climbs. Some parts of trail suitable for intermediate and even beginners.

Buena Vista Flats:

Downstream from Laurier Park and Valley Zoo. Access from 81 Ave. at entrance of Edmonton Rowing Club for 6 km beginner trail and 2.5 km intermediate trail. Access for intermediate trail also at west end of McKenzie Ravine on 145 St. near 94 Ave. Intermediate trail gives a pleasant, easy run up ravine by tall spruce, poplar and some birch on river banks. Fire pit. Beginner route similar, along river, avoids steep terrain.

Forest Heights Park:

Located opposite Riverside Golf Course south of Dawson Bridge and Rowland Rd. A 2.5 km intermediate trail running from parking lot through protected area of birch, poplar and spruce. Steep climb to hill which gives spectacular views of city and river valley. Sharp turns on descents.

Riverside Golf Course:

At Rowland Rd. and 84 St. on south side of Dawson Bridge, this is the site of annual cross-country ski learning program. Series of beginner and intermediate trails of 2 to 5 km. Trails groomed. As in Victoria, skiers asked to keep off greens.

Kinnaird Ravine:

A 2 km intermediate trail starts at Community League property at corner of 82 St. and 111 Ave. Skiing in peaceful ravine of tall spruce leading to hill to Jasper Ave. Skier can run trail both directions or cut off toward Dawson Bridge and 10 km tour of trails at Riverside and Forest Heights.

Rundle Park:

Park beside Clover Bar Bridge near 111 Ave. and 30 St. has no marked trails but excellent area for beginner to intermediate skiing. An old cart trail along river bank leads past signs of beavers which have inhabited area for some time. Skiers asked to avoid small golf course.

More information about the trails and about special events can be obtained from Parks and Recreation Dept., Outdoor Recreation Division, 10th Floor, CN Tower, Edmonton, Alta.

One of the best collections of detailed information on 143 skiing, snowshoeing and hiking trails and areas in the city has been documented by a local physical education teacher. *Edmonton Trails For All Seasons* by Ben Buss is a $2.95 paperback published by Whistler Publishing, Box 8693, Stn. L, Edmonton, Alta. It contains information on 115 km of trails and provides descriptions on access points, character of each area and routing and marking of trails. There are maps of each section. Mr. Buss is an expert cross-country skier and won the coveted Gold Coureur de Bois award at the Canadian Ski Marathon.

Elk Island National Park
Location: East of Edmonton about 25 km (15 mi.) on Hwy. 16.
Length: 27 km.
   This 75-square-mile park just east of Alberta's capital has a network of four trails north from the freeway. Trails circle Tawayik L. and range north through lake and river country to southeast edge of Astolin L. The routes are from 5 to 16 km long and form a series of loops. To the east of Astolin L. there are three snowshoeing trails. Firepits. This park is the home of the Plains Buffalo, which makes it a particularly interesting place to visit on skis. Map from Parks Canada.

Willow Canyon Ski Hill
Location: 1.6 km (1 mi.) north of Donalda in central Alberta.
Length: 3.5 km.
   Two cross-country ski trail loops were laid out recently by members of a downhill ski club who wanted a change of pace. The trails are in and beside a 125-foot deep coulee which is about one-third wooded. Located near a tributary of the Battle R. Chalet with snack bar open weekends and holidays. Lodging in Donalda.

Saskatchewan

A group of Saskatchewan cross-country skiers takes delight in proving the province is not all flat and treeless wheat fields.

Located in the midst of Canada's breadbasket, Saskatchewan is an almost rectangular area of 251,700 square miles, most of them skiable. In the southern region skiers are busy exploring forested parklands and river valleys between the thirteen million acres of wheat farms. In the middle of the province parklands replace open fields while the northern one-third of Saskatchewan lies in the Precambrian Shield. There are few trails cut there as yet, but there is great potential for wilderness skiing in this lake and forest region. Some camps are starting to cater to cross-country skiers who want to explore the area during the winter and other groups are organizing guided trips into the north country.

Until the introduction of cross-country skiing, Saskatchewan residents had to work hard for their skiing. For example, one of their major feats was the creation of Mount Blackstrap in 1970 by piling 800,000 cubic yards of earth to double the 150 ft. natural vertical rise southeast of Saskatoon. The flatland skiers have taken off in all directions however and their numbers are growing rapidly in this province of almost one million residents thanks both to the nation-wide interest in the sport and to the efforts of an active ski association. Some skiers have trails almost at their front doors. In the heart of Regina there is a unique park area call Wascana Centre. This 2,300-acre region contains the Legislative Building, the University of Regina and extensive parklands around a small lake. There is skiing, skating, hockey, tobogganing, music and bonfires. At the end of February it is the site of the Waskimo Winter Carnival.

The cross-country division of the Saskatchewan Ski Association is busy organizing an extensive series of competitions and plans to hold an annual provincial marathon. For information on skiing in the province contact the association at 106 Wilson Cr., Saskatoon. In addition, the provincial government publishes tourist information and a booklet on lodging. Write: Travel Information, Department of Tourism and Renewable Resources, Box 7105, Regina, S4P 3N2.

		Mean Temperature In Celsius (Fahrenheit)		Snowfall In Mean Centimetres (Inches)
		Min	Max	
Regina	Dec	-18.0 (- 0.4)	- 7.8 (17.9)	18.5 (9.2)
	Jan	-22.6 (- 8.6)	-12.0 (10.4)	19.6 (7.7)
	Feb	-19.9 (- 3.9)	- 8.8 (16.1)	18.0 (7.1)
	Mar	-13.7 (7.3)	- 2.9 (26.7)	18.0 (7.1)
Saskatoon	Dec	-18.9 (- 2.1)	- 9.1 (15.6)	19.1 (7.5)
	Jan	-23.9 (-11.1)	-13.5 (7.7)	19.6 (7.7)
	Feb	-20.7 (- 5.3)	- 9.5 (14.9)	18.8 (7.4)
	Mar	-14.2 (6.4)	- 3.2 (26.2)	16.8 (6.6)
Prince Albert	Dec	-21.7 (- 7.1)	-11.0 (12.2)	23.4 (9.2)
	Jan	-26.9 (-16.5)	-15.1 (4.8)	17.8 (7.0)
	Feb	-23.6 (-10.4)	-10.3 (13.5)	17.5 (6.9)
	Mar	-17.2 (1.0)	- 3.7 (25.4)	18.8 (7.4)
Estevan	Dec	-16.4 (2.5)	- 6.6 (20.1)	19.8 (7.8)
	Jan	-20.9 (- 5.6)	-10.8 (12.5)	20.6 (8.1)
	Feb	-18.0 (- 0.4)	- 7.3 (18.9)	16.8 (6.6)
	Mar	-11.6 (11.2)	- 1.2 (29.9)	15.0 (5.9)

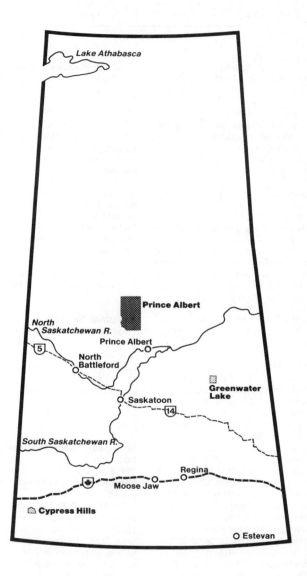

Lake Athabasca

Prince Albert

North Saskatchewan R.

⑤

Prince Albert

North Battleford

Saskatoon

Greenwater Lake

⑭

South Saskatchewan R.

Regina

Moose Jaw

 **Cypress Hills**

O Estevan

	National Park
	Provincial Park
--🍁--	Trans Canada Highway
------	Provincial Highways

Saskatchewan Trails

Prince Albert Area

Prince Albert Municipal Golf Course
Location: Prince Albert, 22nd Street and 8th Avenue.
Length: 2 loop trails of 5 km total.
Well maintained and well marked trails for beginner to intermediate level. Rentals, instruction available. Food. Central warming shelter and trail shelter. For information phone 764-1488.

Prince Albert National Park
Location: North of Prince Albert.
Prince Albert National Park with about 1,400 square miles, is the largest public park in Saskatchewan. It's the gateway to Saskatchewan's northland, where the rolling plains of southern Saskatchewan gradually change into the province's parkland area. It has 5 marked trails for cross-country skiing: Lee Ski Trail, Fisher Ski Trail, Wapiti Ski Trail, Spruce Ski Trail and Trappers Ski Trail. Two nature trails can be used also: Boundary Bog and Mud Creek. Information at east gate entrance, main office.

Whelan Bay Resort
Location: About 100 km (60 mi.) northeast of Prince Albert on Whiteswan Lake.
Length: Main trail of about 16 km plus numerous bush routes such as traplines.
Whiteswan Lodge is located at Whelan Bay on Whiteswan Lake in a heavily wooded area and skiers can use a trail that circles the lake. There is skiing through the area on logging roads, meadows and traplines. The lodge is open in the winter and has a licensed dining room, accommodation for up to 50 persons in cottages or cabins. Ice fishing, snowmobiling. Exploration of area possible with light aircraft at lodge. For information contact The Warren Leiperts, Box 83, Meath Park, Sask. Phone contact through Sasktel Long Distance Operator, Northern Radio Service, No. X0Z 859, Whelan Bay.

Adanac Ski Valley
Location: From Prince Albert east 1.6 km (1 mi.).
Length: 5 km.
Adanac Ski Valley is situated in a scenic area overlooking the North Saskatchewan River. Privately owned and operated. Cross-country trail close to downhill facilities with vertical rise of 200 feet. Chalet, cafeteria. For information, write Adanac Ski Valley, Box 68, Prince Albert, Sask.

Little Red River Park Ski Area
Location: From Prince Albert 5 km (3 mi.) east on Hwy. 55.
Length: about 13 km.
The ski area is situated in an attractive, forested setting. Little Red River Park is owned by the City of Prince Albert and the ski facilities are owned and operated by the Prince Albert Ski Club. Downhill runs. Instruction available through Prince Albert Ski Club. Two toboggan runs. Lodge. For information, phone Cosmopolitan Lodge at 764-5464, or write Prince Albert Ski Club, 701-3rd St. East, Prince Albert, Sask. S6V 0H7.

Minatinas Ski Resort
Location: From Prince Albert south 48 km (30 mi.) on Hwy. 2 to town of Domremy, then west 8 km (5 mi.).
Length: 8 km.
Located in the pleasant wooded surroundings of the Wakaw Lake Regional Park. Ski resort operated by three local people. Marked trail. Downhill facilities. Chalet, cafeteria, pro shop, two toboggan runs.

Greenwater Lake Provincial Park
Location: Southeast of Prince Albert. From Chelan, 16 km (10 mi.) south on Hwy. 38.
Length: Loop trail of 8 km. Travel time 2.5 to 3 hr.
The terrain is slightly hilly going through poplar stands scattered with some spruce. This trail is designed for the intermediate skier. Trail is groomed. Snowshoeing, ice fishing, snowmobiling. Accommodation, gas and food available at park. A private outfitter has both motel rooms and cabins for rent. Write: Fisherman's Cove, Greenwater Lake, Sask. Accommodation also at Kelvington, 41.6 km (26 mi.) south of Greenwater Lake. Trail is marked. For information, contact Greenwater Lake Provincial Park, Box 430, Porcupine Plain, Sask.

Nisbet Provincial Forest — Eb's Trail
Location: South of Prince Albert. From Duck Lake north 16 km (10 mi.) on Hwy. 11. Trail starts on west side of highway.
Length: Network of 4 loop trails, from 2 to 5 km. Travel time 30 to 60 min.

Trails go through wooded rolling hills with some open areas. Groves of spruce, jack pine and poplar. Small animals. Sharp turns at bottom of some hills, intermediate skills necessary. Accommodation at Duck Lake and at Prince Albert. Free sketch map available at Eb's Boat and Ski Shop, 1640 Saskatchewan Ave., Saskatoon, Sask.

Central Saskatchewan

City of Saskatoon

Within the city limits there are 6 areas suitable for cross-country skiing: Kinsmen Park, River Bank East Trail, River Bank West Trail, Forestry Farm, Wildwood Golf Course, Holiday Park Golf Course. Trails range from 1 to 5 km long. Travel time about 15 to 45 min. Trails mostly flat and sheltered from wind. Can be skied by all levels. Most trails follow the South Saskatchewan River. Night skiing available on the Kinsmen Park trail and the River Bank West trail. Instruction and ski rentals from downtown ski shops. Some shops have sketch maps of trails.

Beaver Creek
Location: 16 km (10 mi.) south of Saskatoon on Lorne access road to Pheasant Farm.
Length: 1 trail of 5 km plus alternate routes around hills.

Marked trail, patrolled in the afternoon, for beginner to intermediate skiers. Instruction available. Shelter cabins at beginning and end of trail. Heated lodge and coffee for members of Nordic Ski Club. For information phone 374-0004 or 652-7900.

Blackstrap Provincial Park
Location: From Saskatoon south 37 km (23 mi.) on Hwy. 11 to Dundurn, then east 11 km (7 mi.) on Hwy. 211.
Length: Loop trail of 5 km. Travel time about 30 min. Recommended to be skied clockwise. Trail starts behind pro shop.

Half the trail is sheltered by native deciduous shrubs and trees. About 2 km of it is very exposed above valley floor. Trail is challenging and suitable for advanced beginners and intermediate skers. Adjacent to downhill resort. Mount Blackstrap, Sas-

katchewan's "man-made" mountain is situated in Blackstrap Lake Recreation Site. Built in 1970, the "man-made" part of the mountain is composed of 800,000 cubic yards of earth fill which rises 150 feet above the natural vertical elevation of 150 feet. Day lodge, food, toboggan slide, small rink lighted for night skating. Trail patrolled by snowmobiles every evening. Annual race organized by Saskatoon Nordic Club. For information on Park, write Department of Tourism and Renewable Resources, 311 - 21st St. E., Saskatoon, Sask.

Manitou Regional Park
Location: Southeast of Saskatoon. Just north of Watrous on Little Manitou L.

Area for cross-country skiing located near downhill ski area with vertical rise of 125 feet. Clubhouse, parking, paved access road.

Twin Towers Ski Area
Location: Southwest of Saskatoon. From Stranraer, south 3 km (2 mi.) on Hwy. 31.
Length: One loop trail of 5 km.

Double T Ski Club operated by Regional Park Committee. Marked trail suitable for beginners. Limited rentals. Central warming shelter. Downhill facilities. For information phone 932-2163.

Finlayson Island
Location: On Saskatchewan River, between Battleford and North Battleford.
Length: 8 km with several cutbacks.

Densely wooded level terrain with shelters and fire pits. Variety of wildlife including deer, lynx, rabbit, weasel and mink. Suitable for all levels of skiers. Accommodation in North Battleford. For information write Parks and Recreation Dept., North Battleford, Sask.

Table Mountain Regional Park
Location: From Battleford, west 19 km (12 mi.) on Hwy. 40, then 5 km (3 mi.) north and 5 km (3 mi.) west on all-weather access road.
Length: Loop trails of 3, 5 and 10 km.

Novice Trail of 3 km and Expert Trail of 5 km wind through Drumming Creek Valley. Expert Trail climbs three-quarters of the way up 400-foot high Table Mountain. The Gorge Trail of 10 km climbs one side of Table Mountain and descends on the other side through a picturesque gorge. All trails are well protected from wind. Table Mountain has heavy tree cover for the Prairies.

Wascana Centre, in the heart of Regina, is a unique area. Skiers are within sight of the legislative and university buildings.

The area has considerable wildlife including many deer and small animals. On the Gorge Trail skiers pass through acres of beautiful birch. Adjacent to downhill facilities. Chalet, cafeteria, pro shop. Accommodation in The Battlefords. Contact Chamber of Commerce, Tourist Bureau, North Battleford, Sask. Battlefords Ski Club Cross-country Race, sanctioned by the Saskatchewan Ski Assn. For information on maps and trails, write The Battlefords Ski Club, Box 430, North Battleford, Sask.

Kamsack Ski Area
Location: Eastern edge of province. From Kamsack east 21 km (13 mi.) on Hwy. 57.
Length: 3 trails of 3 km total.

The Kamsack Ski Area is located in the scenic woodland of Duck Mountain Provincial Park. Skiing on golf course. Marked trails, intermediate level, rentals, shelter. Downhill facilities. Clubhouse. Coffee and hot dog concession operated by Kamsack Ski Club on Sundays. Pro shop. Toboggan run. For information, write Mike Sass, 233 Nicholas St., Kamsack, Sask.

Duck Mountain Provincial Park
Location: Eastern edge of Saskatchewan. From Kamsack east 21 km (13 mi.) on Hwy. 57.
Length: Four trails totalling 23 km.

The provincial government maintains a network of ski trails on the south side of Madge Lake in the centre of the park. Skiing on trails ranging from 4.8 to 6.4 km in length over rolling, scenic spruce and poplar woodland. This is in the province's major snowbelt and receives about 180 cm (70 in.) per winter. Shelters on trails. Snowmobiling and snowshoeing in separate areas. Small downhill area nearby. Maps at park administration office, open 8 a.m. to 5 p.m., weekdays. Cross-country lessons available in park. Lodging in Kamsack. Information from Dept. of Tourism and Renewable Resources, Box 39, Kamsack, Sask. Phone 542-3482.

Outfitting Groups
At least two outfitters in central Saskatchewan will arrange tours in little-travelled areas. The Outfitters Group at the Ski

Cross-country skiers like to pause and share information on trail conditions or simply to chat before setting out on the next leg of the trip.

Haus in Saskatoon has cross-country ski packages at Whelan Bay Resort, Whiteswan Lake. There is opportunity for ice fishing at the lake. The lodge has a cocktail lounge and dining room. In addition the Outfitters Group or Ken and Nancy Loewen, Box 38, Prince Albert, Sask., can arrange weekend tours to Little Bear Lake. This area is in The Cub Hills northeast of Prince Albert and north of Nipawin Provincial Park. Another contact is Jacobson Bay Outfitters, Warren Leiperts, Box 83, Meath Park. Skiing is at Anglin L.

Nordic Ski Club

One of the most active groups in the Saskatoon area is the Nordic Ski Club, which arranges trips to a number of trails around the province. Contact is Al Ritchie at 374-0004.

Southern Prairies

Wascana Centre

Location: In the heart of Regina. Trail starts from the Totem Pole located north of Lakeshore Drive in Wascana Centre.
Length: 6.5 km loop winding around the shoreline of Wascana Lake and crossing the lake at each end. Travel time about 45 min.

An easy trail through wooded areas with gentle slopes emerging into open lake crossings. Warning signs are posted if ice is considered unsafe. For further information regarding ice conditions contact the Wascana Centre Public Relations Office. Wascana Centre, a 2,500-acre urban park, prepares its winter recreation facilities as early as weather conditions allow. These include a four mile cross-country ski trail, a sheltered skating area, a winding shoreline promenade for lake skating, hockey and shinny surfaces and a toboggan slide.

The Wascana Centre Authority in conjunction with the City Parks and Recreation Department and local radio stations offer Sunday lake parties, a special holiday program and the Waskimo Winter Carnival. For Sunday lake parties, bonfires are maintained in the major activity areas with picnic tables and benches nearby.

Carnival held on the last weekend in February. Special events include: cross-country ski instruction with equipment provided, figure skating shows, speed skating demonstrations, skating races, broomball, ice fishing, snow golf, snow sculpture, hayrides. The Centre is administered by the provincial and city governments and the University of Regina. It contains many historic items including the Museum of Natural History, reputed to be one of the finest in North America and the Norman Mackenzie Art Gallery associated with the University of Regina. Wascana Centre Authority will forward brochures, free of charge, upon request. Write to Wascana Centre Authority, Public Relations Department, C-21, University of Regina, Regina, Sask. S4S 0A2.

Torr Hill Ski Area

Location: From Regina east 6.5 km (4 mi.) on Trans-Canada Highway (Hwy. 1), then north and east on access roads.

Torr Hill Ski Area is located in city owned King's Park. Mostly for family recreational skiing. Cross-country on area surrounding small downhill facilities. Shelter.

Snoasis Ski Resort

Location: From Regina north 29 km (18 mi.) on Hwy. 6.

Length: Up to 6.5 km.

Resort is owned by SNOasis Properties Limited, a private company formed by Regina skiers. Located on the slope of a scenic, narrow offshoot of the Qu'Appelle Valley. Marked trails, through trees, intermediate level. Cross-country skiing on area surrounding downhill facilities. Day lodge with cafeteria, nursery and club lounge. Pro shop. For information, write SNOasis Properties Limited, 2939 College Ave., Regina, Sask.

Last Oak Park

Location: East of Regina. From Broadview east 3 km (2 mi.) on Trans-Canada Highway (Hwy. 1), then 22.5 km (14 mi.) north on all weather road.

Length: Loop trail of 6.5 km.

Scenic area for cross-country skiing. Trail runs on south side of Qu'Appelle Valley, which is about 600 feet deep and 1 to 1.5 mi. wide. Trail on valley floor and climbs the slopes at several points. Beginner through advanced. Abundant wildlife in the area. Located near downhill ski resort with the highest natural elevation of all ski resorts in the province, 450 feet. Day lodge, food services, cabin rentals available, pro shop. The park is situated on Indian lands and is being developed by the Indian-owned Corporation with financing from federal and provincial governments. Accommodation at Broadview and Grayson. For information write David Acoose, Manager, Last Oak Park, Box 190, Broadview, Sask.

White Track Winter Resort

Location: From Moose Jaw northeast 35 km (22 mi.) on Hwy. 2 and 202.

Length: 3.6 km.

Saskatchewan's oldest established major ski resort, White Track was developed on the slopes of the scenic Qu'Appelle Valley in Buffalo Pound Provincial Park. Owned and operated by Saskatchewan Department of Tourism and Renewable Resources. Marked trail good for intermediate skiers. Shelter at halfway point. Very beautiful, quite hilly countryside. Adjacent to downhill facilities. Upper Chalet with cafeteria, lunch room. Lower chalet with canteen. Pro shop. Toboggan slope, small skating rink. For information, write Department of Tourism and Renewable Resources, 313-1st Avenue N.W., Moose Jaw, Sask.

Shell River

Location: West of Regina. From Shellbrook west 8 km (5 mi.).

Length: 5 km.

Series of marked trails suitable for beginners, in pine tree area. Trails through the bush, some hills. Rentals, instruction can be arranged, shelter. Open weekends. For information phone 763-3465.

Moose Mountain Provincial Park

Location: Southeastern corner of the province. From Whitewood south 57.5 km (36 mi.) on Hwy. 9.

Length: 13 km plus golf course and Seismic Trails.

Marked trail, in excellent area, suitable for beginners. Trail shelter. For information write Department of Tourism and Renewable Resources, Administration Building, Regina, Sask., S4S 0B1.

Cypress Hills Provincial Park

Location: Southwest Saskatchewan. From Maple Creek south 30 km (19 mi.) on Hwy. 21.

Length: Travel time up to one hr.

Intermediate trail traverses hilly, wooded terrain near downhill runs. Abundant wildlife. Located in the pine-clad highlands of Cypress Hills it is one of Saskatchewan's most beautiful provincial parks. Accommodation in Maple Creek. Maps available at park office. For information write Norman Roy, Box 277, Maple Creek, Sask.

Estevan

Length: 2.5 km.

Operated by Estevan Cross-Country Ski Club. Marked trail for average skiers in heavily used Souris River Valley. Central warming shelter and trail shelter. For information phone 634-3587.

Elwood Golf Course, Swift Current

Good trails for average skiers along creek on golf course.

Manitoba

Breaking trail in fresh snow. Much of Manitoba is forest and lake country with end-less possibilities for wilderness skiing.

Though skiing in Manitoba has a history going back at least forty years to the time some Winnipeggers started a club, cross-country skiing is fairly new. For years skiing was mostly of the climb up and slide down variety on solid wood boards, then small downhill resorts were developed on the Prairie lands. Recently cross-country skis were introduced in number and the flatland residents have found them ideally suited to the terrain and long winters. Many of the parks have started catering to cross-country skiers by providing such facilities as campsites and firepits in addition to marked trails. A number of the downhill resorts are also marking ski trails out from the bases of their developments. Beyond that there are great expanses of prairie dotted with woodlands in the south and endless miles of forest to the north. Logging roads in many parts of the province provide ready-made routes.

This province of just over one million people spreads over 251,000 square miles. There are wheatfields and farmlands in the south, massive lakes in the middle and Precambrian Shield and forest over more than half the territory. The land is generally flat with the highest point, 2727 ft. high. Manitoba's climate has continental extremes of heat and cold. Winters can be long and bitter with the mercury often seeing the lower side of minus forty degrees. Though the snowfall is generally lighter than that of either the east or west, the cold temperatures, particularly in the northern latitudes, allow skiing into May.

It is not suprising then that one of the more active centres of skiing is in Thompson, a city built on nickel mining, 800 km (500 mi.) north of Winnipeg. What started as an International Nickel Co. tent camp in 1956 has grown into the third largest city in the province. Cross-country skiing was only introduced in the early 1970s but it was explosively popular with the ski contingent growing from a dozen to about 700 in about three years.

As befits a boom town, Thompson puts on a winter carnival each February with such events as snowmobile and dogsled races, native contests and, of course,

		Mean Temperature In Celsius (Fahrenheit)		Snowfall In Mean Centimetres (Inches)
		Min	Max	
Winnipeg	Dec	-18.2 (- 0.7)	- 9.2 (15.4)	25.4 (9.4)
	Jan	-23.2 (- 9.8)	-13.4 (7.9)	25.9 (9.8)
	Feb	-21.1 (- 6.0)	-10.4 (13.3)	18.8 (7.8)
	Mar	-13.3 (8.0)	- 2.9 (26.8)	16.8 (8.3)
Brandon	Dec	-18.9 (- 2.0)	- 8.7 (16.4)	21.6 (8.5)
	Jan	-23.7 (-10.7)	-13.3 (8.1)	21.6 (8.5)
	Feb	-21.4 (- 6.5)	- 9.2 (15.5)	20.1 (7.9)
	Mar	-14.7 (5.6)	- 3.1 (26.5)	21.8 (8.6)
Flin Flon	Dec	-21.3 (- 6.4)	-14.0 (6.8)	22.9 (9.0)
	Jan	-25.9 (-14.7)	-17.6 (0.3)	20.6 (8.1)
	Feb	-22.7 (- 8.9)	-12.6 (9.3)	19.8 (7.8)
	Mar	-16.2 (2.9)	- 4.6 (23.7)	22.9 (9.0)
Churchill	Dec	-25.8 (-14.5)	-17.7 (0.1)	20.8 (8.2)
	Jan	-31.4 (-24.6)	-23.7 (-10.7)	15.2 (6.0)
	Feb	-30.8 (-23.4)	-22.5 (- 8.5)	13.7 (5.4)
	Mar	-25.0 (-13.0)	-15.6 (4.0)	17.5 (6.9)

cross-country ski races. Other northern towns are following a similar pattern. A bit to the south at The Pas there is the Northern Manitoba Trapper's Festival, the major winter carnival and site of the World Championship Dog Sled Derby and competition for the title of King Trapper.

Information about tourism in Manitoba and a booklet on accommodation are available from the Department of Tourism, Recreation and Cultural Affairs, 200 Vaughan St., Winnipeg, Man. R3C 1T5.

In the heat of competition ski poles whip in a blur of activity. A well prepared track provides an easy route for the touring skier out for a smooth run and a target for the skier ready for a bit of racing.

National Park

Provincial Park

Wilderness and
Forest Reserves

Trans Canada Highway

Provincial Highways

Manitoba Trails

Winnipeg Region

Sunny Harbour Resorts
Location: From Perimeter Highway at western edge of Winnipeg, west 11 km (7 mi.) on Trans-Canada Highway (Hwy. 1), then turn south at statue of white horse.

Cross-country, snowshoeing, skating, snowmobiling, snack bar. Skiers can park trailers at resort for winter use. Open seven days a week. For information, write Sunny Harbour Resorts, Box 89, Headingley, Man. R0H 0J0.

Whitemouth Cross-country Ski Trail
Location: From Winnipeg east 101 km (63 mi.) on Trans-Canada Hwy. (Hwy. 1) and 1.6 km (1 mi.) south of Hadashville.
Length: Loop trail of about 6.5 km.

The trail follows and loops along the Whitemouth River, in mostly wooded area. Terrain is flat with a few rolling hills, black spruce forest and meadow. Suitable for novice to average skiers. Accommodation in Hadashville. Maps available at start of trail or from Parks Branch Office, Falcon Lake, Man. R0E 0N0.

Sandilands Provincial Park
Location: Southeast of Winnipeg near Steinback. From Trans-Canada Highway (Hwy. 1) south on Hwy. 12 to Provincial Rd. 210, then southeast on 210 to Marchand Wayside at intersection with Provincial Rd. 404.
Length: Loop trails of 5, 9, 10 and 16 km.

Trail passes through mostly wooded terrain, flat with some moderate hills. Good for average skiers, not a novice trail. Snowshoeing and tobogganing. The escarpment in the park was formed during the period when Glacial Lake Agassiz covered most of Manitoba, about 10,000 years ago. Winds blowing across this great prehistoric lake created waves which caused sand particles to be continually deposited on the lake shore. Large sand beaches were formed as a result of this wave action. Man probably emigrated into this area between 8,000 and 10,000 years ago. Native people used the prehistoric lake shore for setting up their hunting camps. The bones of ancient bison and elk and woodland caribou have been uncovered here. Accommodation in Steinback and Marchand. Maps available at all parking lots and from Parks Branch Office, Falcon Lake, Man. R0E 0N0.

Whiteshell Provincial Park
Location: From Winnipeg east 144 km (90 mi.) on Trans-Canada Highway (Hwy. 1) to town of Falcon Lake. Trail starts at Falcon Ski Resort 11 km (7 mi.) on South Shore Rd. and at West Hawk Lake, off P.T.H. 44.
Length: Loop trail of 12 km. Travel time about 4 hr.

Trail crosses east end of Falcon Lake for 2.5 km, then through mostly wooded area on a rough and hilly terrain. Not a novice trail. Falcon Ski Resort offers downhill facilities. Ski rentals, lunch bar, skating rink and shelter, snowmobile trails and tobogganing. Town of West Hawk Lake has 3 lodges, restaurant and beverage room, service station. Maps available at start of trail or from Parks Branch Offices in West Hawk Lake and Falcon Lake.

Whiteshell Provincial Park — Falcon Lake
Location: From Winnipeg east 144 km (90 mi.) on Trans-Canada Highway (Hwy. 1) to town of Falcon Lake. Trail starts at southerly edge of golf course.
Length: About 14.5 km. Travel time 4 to 5 hr.

Through mostly wooded area, on flat terrain. Novice trail. Picnic site. Falcon Lake has 2 motels with licenced restaurants and service station. Also accommodation in 2 lodges nearby. Maps available at start of trail or from Parks Branch Office, Falcon Lake, Man. R0E 0N0.

Whiteshell Provincial Park — High Lake Ski Trail
Location: From Winnipeg, east 144 km (90 mi.) on Trans-Canada Highway (Hwy. 1) to town of Falcon Lake. Trail starts at Falcon Ski Resort 11 km (7 mi.) on South Shore Rd.
Length: 5 km. Travel time about 2.5 hr.

The trail goes through wooded, rough and hilly terrain and across eastern side of High Lake. Suitable mostly for expert skiers. Downhill facilities. Ski rentals, lunch bar, skating rink and shelter, snowmobile trails

Skiers sprint into an uphill start. Friendly, local races are a growing part of the sport as more and more people seek to test their new-found skills.

and toboggan slide. Accommodation at Falcon Lake: two motels with licenced restaurants, one service station, and in two lodges nearby. Maps available at start of trail and from Parks Branch Office, Falcon Lake, Man. R0E 0N0.

Holiday Mountain Ski Resort
Location: From Winnipeg, southwest on Hwy. 3, 176 km (110 mi.) to Village of La Riviere, near North Dakota border. Ski resort 800 m west of village.
Length: 5 km. Travel time about 1 hr.

Competition trail, through mostly wooded area, that was chosen as the site of the 1970 Canadian Junior Nordic Championships. Open daily 9 A.M. to 4.30 P.M. Holiday Mountain, tucked away in the Pembina Valley, is a major centre for downhill skiing. Snowmobiling, skating, curling and tobogganning. Chalet with licenced dining room, lounge, snack bar. Accommodation at resort and in area. Lodging in private homes available in town of La Riviere. Skiers wishing accommodation can make reservations at Holiday Mountain. The fifty metre jump at the Holiday Mountain ski resort has been the site of the Manitoba Championships and the La Riviere International Jumping Tourna-ment for many years. Friday and Saturday night dances.

Brandon and North

Spruce Woods Provincial Park
Location: From Brandon east 48 km (30 mi.) on Trans-Canada Hwy. (Hwy. 1), south on Provincial Rd. 258.
Length: 2 loop trails of about 8 km total.

Spruce Woods Provincial Park is one of Manitoba's newest provincial parks. Covering 90 square miles, Spruce Woods, a Manitoba Centennial project, lies mostly in the beautiful valley of the Assiniboine River. Part of its 57,000 acres is on shifting sand dunes, while most of the area is covered with aspen and spruce. Park is the eastern segment of Spruce Woods Provincial Forest. Wildlife thrives in the park.

Naturalists may follow the trails of Ernest Thompson Seton, world renowned naturalist, artist and writer. Born in England, educated in Ontario and Europe. In 1882 he joined his brother on a homestead near Carberry and began to keep scientific records. The nearby hills later became the setting of some of his most famous stories, including

Half-way house at Mystery Mountain ski area near Thompson. Rustic cabins like this provide a welcome shelter for the skier who wants to rest, warm up, eat or change wax.

"The Trail of the Sandhill Stag," and parts of "Wild animals I have known." Appointed Naturalist to Manitoba Government in 1890. Moved to the United States. Founded Woodcraft League. Became first Chief of Boy Scouts of America and founded Seton Institute in 1930.

Snowshoeing. Snowmobiling. Lodging and food in Carberry and Glenboro.

Leaf Rapids Ski Club
Location: Leaf Rapids
Length: About 10 km of loop trails.

Series of trails located on east side of village with access from collector road or Hwy. 391 which runs northwest to Lynn Lake and southeast to Thompson. Trails cut through woods or follow fire road. Fairly narrow but scenic. Skiing began in the community in the early 1970s and a group of citizens cut a series of trails. Ski equipment donated by a local bank and rented for a nominal fee from town gym. During annual winter carnival ski races held on nearby lake.

Westbran Ski Trail, Brandon
Location: In Brandon.
Length: 6.5 km.

Westbran Trail follows partially forested bank of Assiniboine River and golf course circuit. Some wildlife along riverbank. Topographic map, Brandon 1:50,000. Occasional local race, informal night trips.

Glenorkey Ski Trail
Location: From Brandon west 16 km (10 mi.) along Grand Valley Road.
Length: 13 km.

Near Assiniboine River. Rolling terrain, river banks and valley, partially forested, oak, beech, etc. Considerable wildlife including white tail deer. Chalet with ski rental, food, downhill and toboggan facilities, instruction. Accommodation in Brandon. For information contact Chamber of Commerce, Brandon, Man. Topographic map, Brandon 1:50,000.

Brandon Hills Ski Trails
Location: From Brandon south 13 km (8 mi.) on Hwy. 10.
Length: 16 km.

Forested rolling terrain. Moraines can be seen in the area. Considerable wildlife including white tail deer. Accommodation in Brandon. For information contact Chamber of Commerce, Brandon, Man. Topographic map, Brandon 1:50,000.

Shilo Wildlife and Forest Reserve
Location: From Brandon east 24 km (15 mi.) on Hwys. 451 and 340.

Length: 16 km.

Area of sand dunes covered with coniferous and deciduous trees. Abundant wildlife including white tail deer, elk, moose, wolves and coyotes. Accommodation in Brandon. For information contact Chamber of Commerce, Brandon, Man. Topographic map, Shilo 1:50,000.

Pioneer Bay, Clearwater Lake Park

Location: From the Pas north 19 km (12 mi.) on Hwy. 10, then 21 km (13 mi.) on Provincial Rd. 287.

Length: Network of trails from 3 to 18 km.

Trails go through varying types of forests and are suitable for beginners to average skiers. Camp for overnight use at halfway point of 18 km trail. Tracks set mechanically. Accommodation at Clearwater Lodge, Lot 17, Clearwater Lake, The Pas, and in town. Trails marked and maps posted along the routes. Hugo Bay Tour annually and other special events. For information, contact The Pas Cross-Country Ski Club, Box 1950, The Pas, Man. R9A 1L6.

Mystery Mountain

Location: From Thompson north on Hwy. 391, turn right 3.2 km (2 mi.) past the Burntwood River Bridge on road leading to Golf Course, follow this road for 16 km (10 mi.) to the ski hill.

Length: Main trails about 10 km each, with good possibility to vary tours. Many short runs for beginners. All trails start and end at Ski Chalet.

Mostly wooded, gently rolling terrain. During January and beginning of February the temperatures are so low they may be hazardous. Please register at the Ski Shop before starting on the trails and return by 4:30 P.M., as there is no phone at Chalet nor bus service after 4:30. Burntwood River and banks, surrounding lakes and a countless number of cut grid-lines and old winter roads may be used for cross-country skiing, although these are not as yet maintained as trails. Thompson Ski Club plans expansion of marked trails in the area. Lots of tracks can be seen along the trails and sometimes even the animals such as ptarmigans, rabbits, lynx, moose, wolverine, fisher, etc. Ski area situated on a trapline. Downhill skiing. Lunch counter, ski shop renting, selling and servicing ski equipment. Trails groomed. Instruction.

Two log cabins on the trails serve as halfway houses. Mystery Mountain Ski Complex is owned and operated by the members of the Thompson Ski Club. It operates on weekends and holidays from 9 A.M. to 5 P.M. in Thompson and Sasaui Rapids. Further information may be obtained from the Ski Club members at the Chalet or call Mystery Mountain Ski Shop (204) 677-4729. Thompson Winter Carnival usually during the first weekend of February, arranged by the Kinsmen service club. The annual Ski-A-Thon in March ''skis in'' proceeds to a new centre (Kindergarten and adult workshop) for C.A.M.R.

Ontario

A peacefully snowbound log cabin in the Ontario countryside makes an ideal retreat for the cross-country skier.

The rolling, often forested countryside of Ontario has been favorably compared with the classic ski terrain of the Nordic countries which developed cross-country skiing. For many years this fact was ignored by all but a handful of devotees. Though records show that Lord Frederick Hamilton, a British aide-de-camp to the Governor-General, skied near Ottawa in 1887, relatively few residents of the province followed in his tracks.

It was not really until the early 1970s that the sport caught hold in this province. There was already a substantial corps of downhill skiers and considerable interest in the sport of skiing generally when what is called the cross-country boom began. In the space of a few years tens of thousands of residents had taken up the sport. With a population of 8.2 million, Ontario is a region with tremendous potential for development. At first the new skiers had a limited selection of trails, but that picture is changing rapidly. Downhill ski resort operators, for example, were quick to respond and most have by now blazed at least a couple of trails from their base lodges.

Ski clubs, especially those with a Nordic bent, also became more active and they are responsible for many of the free trails which have been cut across public and private lands. These provide some of the best touring in the province. Since they often cross private property it is essential skiers show the utmost respect for the land and avoid leaving any garbage, cutting wood or setting fires unless there are specific fire areas officially marked. Otherwise the trails may be closed.

The third major source of trails is the hiking clubs such as the Bruce Trail Association and its younger sisters, which have trails suitable for skiing. One cannot automatically assume he can ski any hiking trail for these routes sometimes make precipitous climbs not feasible on skis or even on foot in the winter, but there are usually skiable sections of trails. Finding them requires personal research or information from the trail club.

Ontario's ski trail system is still at a relatively early stage of development. Though there are thousands of kilometres of marked or mapped routes, this province has not quite reached the sophisticated stage of, for example, the Laurentians in Québec, where trail systems connect to allow extensive trips. Ontario skiers must usually return to their starting point or camp out overnight, but there are indications that trail systems will start meeting and linking such points as hotels and overnight shelters in a region.

Government agencies have thousands of square miles of potentially skiable land under their jurisdiction but relatively little of it has been cut and marked for such travel. The agencies seem to be responding to the ever-growing public demand for trails with a steady increase in marked routes and in other cases are aiding private ski clubs which are laying out trail systems on public land. The recently formed Ontario Trails Council is expected to make recommendations to the provincial government on a ski trail development policy.

In Northern Ontario winter ski camps, many of them based at summer canoe lodges, are starting to draw skiers seeking weekend or week-long snow adventures. Groups make day trips from rustic hotels or overnight outings with tents and sleeping bags.

With an area of 412,582 square miles, Ontario is the second largest province and with 8.2 million residents by far the most heavily populated. The northern section of the province, an area of endless miles of lakes, rivers and boreal forest on the Precambrian Shield, is a sparsely populated region but has fantastic skiing potential. There are thousands of miles of trails that follow logging, mining and summer cottage access roads.

By contrast the small southern section, ranging from Shield land to hardwood forests and rolling farm land, is densely populated. A large portion of it falls within a rich agricultural area of intensive mixed farming, fruit orchards and livestock grazing land. Where the fields end the subdivisions begin in many parts of the region, which helps to explain why many of the trail systems are so short. They are often located on woodlots or forest reserves intended for preservation of timber and for recreation.

Generally skiers in Southern Ontario can count on a season starting in December, usually around Christmas, and lasting until late March or early April. Even within the south the season may vary by a month, as Toronto skiers who drive north to the Muskoka region realize. In the north the season is even longer. Local weather patterns and temperatures tend to vary widely because of the moderating effect of winds passing over the Great Lakes and creating localized storms along the shorelines.

As befits a province with a burgeoning ski population, Ontario has some big ski events each year. There are three main ski races, which are open to all.

Muskoka Loppet — Started in the early 1970s this race has become one of the biggest in Canada and draws a couple of thousand entries each year. It is usually held in early January and run over a 30 km course from Hidden Valley, east of Huntsville, to Port Sydney on Mary Lake. While racers may finish the course in half a day, skiers usually take most of the daylight hours to make the trip through Muskoka countryside. For those seeking a shorter test of their skills there are 7.5 and 15 km courses laid out from Port Sydney. Scandinavian immigrants or descendants have added such Nordic touches to the event as pine garlands and blueberry soup. For information write Muskoka Loppet, Box 1239, Huntsville, Ont.

Silver Spoon Grand Prix — This started as a local race in Deep River in 1973 but now draws entrants, including racers preparing for the Canadian Marathon, from Quebec and from Ontario points as far away as Sault Ste. Marie and Toronto. The event is part of festivities on the second weekend of February, with competitions Saturday and tours in the nearby Petawawa Forest Experiment Station on Sunday.

The race has an interesting history. In the fall of 1972 two Deep River skiers, Aston Eikrem and Henry Hollo, were clearing a ski trail near the town and trying to think of a name for it when Aston's two-year-old son, Andreas, found a silver spoon lying in some bushes. That spoon gave the trail its name and became the symbol of a regular ski race. Now the fastest man over a 15 km course and the fastest woman over a 10 km course win silver spoons as trophies. For information write: Mike Watson, Box 770, Deep River, Ont., R0J 1P0.

Kawartha Ski Tour — Also preceding the Marathon is the Peterborough area tour which offers a challenge to all levels of skier. The trail starts at the village of Apsley, 50 km (30 mi.) north of Peterborough on Hwy. 28. From there it follows the course of Eel's Creek south to the hamlet of Haultain, then bears west through rugged country near the Burleigh Ridge and across Long Marshland. This is a wilderness trail with a great variety of skiing. The event is usually held in the middle of February and is organized in sections so skiers of all levels can find a route that matches their abilities. While racers may cover the 60 km course in a day, less seasoned skiers may opt to do it over the weekend or to ski one section only. Busing is arranged to shuttle skiers to and from their cars. In the past registration has been limited to the first 400 skiers. For information write: Kawartha Tourist Assn., Box 802, Peterborough, Ont.

In addition to these and a growing number of similar races, loppets and marathons there are other winter events which often interest skiers visiting or living in a given region. For example, there is a growing number of winter carnivals, often with ski races as part of the festivities.

The provincial government has a comprehensive winter information program

		Mean Temperature In Celsius (Fahrenheit)			Snowfall In Mean Centimetres (Inches)	
		Min		Max		
Toronto	Dec	- 7.3 (18.8)	.3	(32.6)	27.9	(11.0)
	Jan	-10.5 (13.1)	- 2.2	(28.1)	35.1	(13.8)
	Feb	-10.3 (13.5)	- 1.4	(29.5)	30.0	(11.8)
	Mar	- 5.2 (22.6)	3.3	(38.0)	22.1	(8.7)
Ottawa	Dec	-11.6 (11.1)	- 3.7	(25.3)	51.6	(20.3)
	Jan	-15.6 (4.0)	- 6.4	(20.5)	48.5	(19.1)
	Feb	14.4 (6.1)	- 4.7	(23.5)	47.8	(18.8)
	Mar	- 7.5 (18.5)	1.3	(34.4)	35.1	(13.8)
North Bay	Dec	-13.1 (8.4)	- 4.1	(24.7)	51.3	(20.2)
	Jan	-17.9 (- 0.2)	- 6.7	(20.0)	51.1	(20.1)
	Feb	-16.3 (2.6)	- 4.4	(24.0)	41.9	(16.5)
	Mar	-10.1 (13.9)	1.6	(34.9)	29.0	(11.4)
Sault Ste Marie	Dec	-11.1 (12.0)	- 2.9	(26.8)	55.4	(21.8)
	Jan	-14.3 (6.3)	- 4.7	(23.6)	65.0	(25.6)
	Feb	-14.3 (6.2)	- 4.4	(24.0)	51.3	(20.2)
	Mar	- 9.9 (14.1)	.5	(32.9)	38.1	(15.0)
Huntsville	Dec	-11.5 (11.3)	- 2.3	(27.9)	71.6	(28.2)
	Jan	-15.3 (4.4)	- 4.6	(23.8)	71.6	(28.2)
	Feb	-14.3 (6.3)	- 2.7	(27.1)	55.4	(21.8)
	Mar	- 9.4 (15.0)	2.1	(35.8)	42.9	(16.9)
London	Dec	- 7.2 (19.1)	0.0	(32.0)	47.2	(18.6)
	Jan	- 9.9 (14.2)	- 2.2	(28.0)	49.0	(19.3)
	Feb	- 9.7 (14.5)	- 1.6	(29.2)	40.9	(16.1)
	Mar	- 5.0 (23.0)	3.4	(38.2)	26.9	(10.6)
Thunder Bay	Dec	-15.9 (3.4)	- 5.6	(21.9)	45.5	(17.9)
	Jan	-20.7 (- 5.2)	- 8.9	(16.0)	51.6	(20.3)
	Feb	-19.7 (- 3.5)	- 6.2	(20.8)	31.0	(12.2)
	Mar	-12.3 (9.9)	0.0	(32.0)	35.3	(13.9)
Peterborough	Dec	- 9.9 (14.2)	- 1.6	(29.2)	34.0	(13.4)
	Jan	-13.4 (7.9)	- 3.7	(25.3)	39.9	(15.7)
	Feb	-12.6 (9.3)	- 2.4	(27.7)	37.3	(14.7)
	Mar	- 6.9 (19.5)	2.9	(37.3)	21.1	(8.3)
Collingwood	Dec	- 7.3 (18.8)	- 0.3	(31.5)	69.1	(27.2)
	Jan	-10.3 (13.5)	- 2.3	(27.8)	68.6	(27.0)
	Feb	-10.3 (13.5)	- 1.9	(28.6)	43.4	(17.1)
	Mar	- 6.0 (21.2)	2.9	(36.7)	31.8	(12.5)

which provides skiers with snow reports. This is located at the Barrie Travel Centre (705) 726-0932 or 728-5851. Skiers in Toronto can call toll free at 364-4722. In addition most newspapers and radio stations and a number of television stations carry snow reports. Information on driving conditions during the winter can be obtained from (416) 248-3561 in Toronto.

Booklets giving lists of downhill and cross-country ski resorts, snowmobile areas and winter parks as well as a Winter Events booklet are published each year and are available from the Ministry of Industry and Tourism, Queen's Park, Toronto, Ont. The Ministry of Natural Resources, Information Office, Queen's Park, also has a useful booklet called Winter Recreation on Public Lands, which simply indicates places such as parks, public forests and conservation areas where cross-country skiing can be practiced. Lodging information is often available through ski resorts or chambers of commerce in particular towns or regions but a province-wide handbook is Accommodations Ontario, also from the Ministry of Industry and Tourism.

Southern Ontario Trails

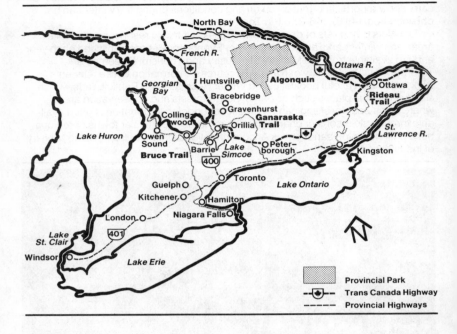

Provincial Park
Trans Canada Highway
Provincial Highways

Southwestern Ontario

The Bruce Trail

Location: From Queenston, on Niagara R., north to Tobermory at the tip of the Bruce Peninsula.

Length: About 700 km.

The Bruce is the mother lode of hiking in Ontario and one of Canada's major trails. Much of it traverses rolling farm and woodlands typical of Southern Ontario and is very suitable for cross-country skiing. As this 1.5 metre wide footpath winds across the landscape, it traverses some of the most scenic parts of this region. In many places it crosses or passes close to ski resorts or public parklands with cross-country trails and is commonly adopted into trail networks. For example, it passes the major ski resort developments in the Collingwood - Thornbury belt and in the Beaver Valley.

Though much of trail is skiable, anyone planning an outing would be wise to do some research on the terrain crossed before setting out. Parts of the trail pass through some of the wildest and most rugged countryside in Southern Ontario and are either unskiable or suitable only for experts. Unless you know or get direct knowledge of the suitability of any section, it would be wise to obtain a copy of *The Bruce Trail Guide Book,* which has text and topographical maps of the entire route.

The trail is generally easy to follow, using the two by six-inch white blazes painted on trees. Side trails are marked in blue. The only problems might arise in areas, like the Bruce Peninsula, where blazes are painted on rocks and might be snow-covered. In any case, it is wise to carry a compass and topographic maps. The Bruce section, particularly near the tip, is extremely rugged as it passes along the edge of the escarpment and sometimes winds down the rocks to the shoreline. Anyone tackling an area like that should travel in a party with experienced skiers and get detailed information about the condition of the trail.

Geologically the trail passes over a variety of land. The escarpment is formed of dolomite limestone and the softer shale. In places, erosion over the millenia has left the harder dolomite overhanging the base of shale and created precipitous ledges and such unique formations as the free-standing "flowerpots." As well, the dolomite has split in many places, creating fascinating caves.

Historically, the Bruce trail was originated in 1959 and finished in 1967. It is maintained by local clubs and largely traverses private land and travellers should respect the fact. For information write: Bruce Trail Assn., 33 Hardale Cr., Hamilton, Ont. L8T 1X7.

Cyprus Lake Provincial Park

Location: About 10 km. (6 mi.) south of Tobermory at the tip of the Bruce Peninsula.

This 1,600-acre park runs northeast from near Hwy. 6 to the north shore of the Bruce Peninsula overlooking Georgian Bay. The Bruce Trail runs along the top of the Niagara Escarpment at this point and the trail club describes a section of just over one kilometre here as "beyond any doubt the most spectacular part of the entire (700 km) Bruce Trail." For example, it includes Overhanging Point, a precipice projecting several hundred feet high over the bay and many caves, at least one with an underwater connection to the bay. The Bruce here is at its wildest and most rugged and especially in the winter is a lonely and beautiful place.

Skiers wanting to explore the region can follow park roads to many areas without much trouble, but the Bruce Trail tends to be winding and rugged in many places. Care is obviously necessary along the high cliffs and around cave areas. Anyone wanting to bushwhack should carry a good pack of equipment, including climbing rope, compass and maps. This area is chopped by the edges of three topographic sheets of the 1:50,000 series, including Dorcas Bay, Dyer Bay and the west sheet of Flowerpot I. in the 41 H map region.

Rankin Ski Trails

Location: Red Bay area north of Sauble Beach and west of Wiarton in Bruce Peninsula. Access points at western edge of Red Lake and west side of road running south to Oliphant.

Length: 17 km. Sections of 8 and 9 km with small loops.

Trails are located on scenic land owned privately and by the Sauble Valley Conservation Authority. Trails managed by the Ministry of Natural Resources. Cross-country skiing is just becoming popular in the Bruce Peninsula area and as of 1976 this was one of the few marked trails there. The area is very popular as a summer resort and winter sports are starting to bring people back for that season.

The trails pass over largely forested, rolling countryside with some short, steep hills and ridges. Mature hardwood bush, small meadows, cedar swamp and small inland lakes. Trail runs from Spry L. in south to Beattie L. in north. Variety of winter birds and wildlife includes deer, rabbit, fox, skunk and the occasional brush wolf, which is extremely shy of humans and rarely seen.

The 9 km northern section of the trail is more rugged and has some steep sections. A short side trip from this trail leads to Tower Hill, the highest point in the area, and gives a view of some of the finest scenery on the western edge of the peninsula. The 8 km southern section also has some steep pitches and areas where the trail wanders through heavy brush. A good afternoon outing would be the loop around North Hodgins L. Most areas demand intermediate ability. No camping, fires or motorized vehicles. Trails marked with red blazes. Compass useful.

For maps and brochures contact Sauble Valley Conservation Authority, 330 Tenth St. W., Owen Sound, Ont., N4K 3R5 or Ministry of Natural Resources office in Owen Sound. Some Red Bay area lodges open in winter. For information write: Bruce Peninsula Tourism Association, Barbara Gibbons, 307 Berford St., Wiarton, Ont.

Sucker Creek Conservation Area

Location: On the shore of L. Huron north of Sauble Beach. Located on Sucker Cr. between Pike Bay and Howdenvale.

This conservation property of about 300 acres is centred around a large creek and swamp area just inland from the rugged shoreline in a sparseley inhabited area. There is some snowmobiling and plenty of opportunity for bushwhacking on strong skis. Lakeshore area is beautiful, but on days when the wind sweeps across more than 100 km of open lake the skiing is warmer in the dense bush of deciduous and coniferous growth.

Skinner Bluffs Conservation Area

Location: East of Wiarton overlooking Colpoy Bay. From hamlet of Lake Charles inland go north about 5 km (3 mi.) on local road which crosses escarpment before heading toward North Keppel.

This is a highly scenic lookout and at

places the limestone cliffs have been spectacularly eroded and are perilously overhanging the valley more than 100 feet below. From places you can see White Cloud and Griffith Islands at the mouth of Colpoy Bay and you can look out over Georgian Bay. The Bruce Trail follows the Niagara Escarpment at this point, wandering through pasture and by farm fields before plunging into stands of tall maples. Conservation area of about 600 acres. Locating site is difficult and requires detailed maps of area such as Bruce County road map. Managed by Sauble Valley Conservation Authority, 330 Tenth St. W., Owen Sound, Ont.

Keppel Escarpment Conservation Area
Location: North of Owen Sound about 16 km (10 mi.). Follow county roads 1 and 17 to cliffs of Niagara Escarpment.
Length: 13 km.
Skiing is on a 2,900-acre conservation area based on the Niagara Escarpment. Area is highly scenic with good views over surrounding countryside. The Bruce Trail passes through this region.

Harrison Park
Location: In south end of Owen Sound off Second Ave. E.
Length: 4 km.
This attractive park, located along the Sydenham R., combines wooded hillsides and rolling lands near the river in the valley which encloses much of the city. Trails wind through both heavily and lightly wooded areas and there are opportunities for downhill runs between the trees for the more daring. A small downhill ski hill is located nearby and area is also used for tobogganing. Snack bar.

West Rocks
Location: Owen Sound, atop west hill and on southern edge of development at Niagara Escarpment.
This conservation area is located on rugged cliff area and includes a section of the Bruce Trail. It is used by many local residents for short ski outings.

Bay Motor Inn Ski Village
Location: South of Owen Sound. From Chatsworth south on Hwy. 10, then east and north on local roads following signs for about 5 km (3 mi.) to entrance.
Length: 5 km.
The Ski Village is a product of the Georgas brothers of Owen Sound, an active

group of skiers who were among the first in the area to treat cross-country skiing seriously. Originally this resort was known mainly for downhill skiing and for jumping competitions, but cross-country skiing through the rolling countryside of fields and forests has developed in recent years. The area has a full range of facilities, including instruction, sales, rentals, food, liquor and lodging nearby. From this area skiers can link up with the Bruce Trail to the northeast.

Saugeen Bluffs
Location: From Paisley North on County Rd. 3 about 5 km (3 mi.), then west on marked access road.
This 350-acre conservation area overlooks the Saugeen, one of the largest rivers in Western Ontario, from the high, clay bluffs. Area is generally mixed agricultural with farm and pasture land, but along the river there are many treed spots remaining. Skiers have a choice of relatively flat table lands atop the banks or the sometimes steep slopes of the riverbank. More level areas are found along the shore of the river itself. Ice should be tested before use.

Saugeen Highlands
Location: Centred around Saugeen River, crossing Hwy. 4 between Flesherton and Durham.
Length: About 200 km.
The trail system has been created by a group of resorts in the Durham area. They wander over rolling agricultural land cleared for crops and pasture, and through woodlot sections. At several points they cross the frozen Saugeen R. or wander along the cut it has made in the soft soil.

Mount Forest Conservation Area (Angus Smith)
Location: 1 km south of Mount Forest on Hwy. 6, then west on Arthur Sideroad.
Cross-country skiing on about 10 acres, near Saugeen River.

Pike Lake Lodge
Location: From Mount Forest 6.5 km (4 mi.) west on Hwy. 89.
Mixed farm and wood area near Saugeen R. Night skiing, skating, snack bar. Accommodation at the lodge.

Stonehills Sun 'N' Snow Park
Location: From Durham, east 11 km (7 mi.) on Hwy. 4, then south 4.8 km (3 mi.) on County Rd. 23 (Dromore Rd.)

Length: 10 km

Situated in the Saugeen Highlands. Varied terrain, rolling hills, woods and some open spaces. Suitable for all levels of ability. Skating, tobogganing and night skiing. Accommodation on premises or write Grey-Bruce Tourist Council, RR 4, Owen Sound, Ont.

The Homestead Resort

Location: From Durham south 8 km (5 mi.) on Hwy. 6, then west 4.8 km (3 mi.) on Wilder Lake Rd.

Length: 10 km.

The Homestead is in the heart of the beautiful Saugeen Highlands. The property consists of 750 acres of rolling terrain, approximately 250 acres cleared for a golf course, with the balance in its natural state, bush and streams, a 96-acre lake, cottages, lodge, restaurant, snack bar. Groomed trails for all levels of ability. Rentals, ski instruction, tour guide, tobogganing and night skiing. 2-way radio patrol on trails. Bus transportation to and from the resort. Accommodation at resort or contact Grey-Bruce Tourist Council, RR 4, Owen Sound, Ont.

El Ron Inn Resort

Location: From Flesherton 1.6 km (1 mi.) north on Hwy. 10.

Length: 10 km.

Near scenic Beaver Valley area. Suitable for all levels of skiers. Night skiing. Dining room. Accommodation at the resort.

Happy Valley Ski Resort

Location: Off Hwy. 4 about 16 km (10 mi.) west of Walkerton.

Several local trails in connection with a downhill resort. Trails pass through woods and open fields in a farming area. Chalet, snack bar, rentals, downhill skiing, lodging in Walkerton. Contact resort at Box 306, Walkerton, Ont. N0G 2V0

Thames Valley Trail

Location: Trail begins at Byron Bridge in London's Springbank Park and runs upstream along the Thames River to the town of St. Marys.

Length: Full distance is 62 km but there is 20 km loop running to Fanshawe Lake and back.

This is basically a hiking trail and some sections are on city streets and not suitable for skiing. In country the trail runs along the river valley with some steep sections along hillsides and some fence crossovers using stiles. Snow conditions can vary widely and skiers should check with federal government weather office in London. There is no trail grooming. Much of the trail is on private land and users are asked to respect that fact. Trail is marked with arrowhead blazes. The trail is maintained by the Thames Valley Trail Assn., 403 Lansing Ave., London, Ont. N6K 2J2. Maps and membership applications available.

Minto Glen Ski Club

Location: From east side of Harriston north on Hwy. 89, then follow County Rd. 2. Total of 5 km (3 mi.) from town.

Length: 4 km.

Minto Glen was originally a downhill resort but added groomed cross-country trails on its 97-acre property. Rentals, snack bar, cookout shelter. Resort open weekends and holidays.

Conestogo Conservation Area

Location: North of Waterloo. Conestogo Dam at Conestogo L. 800 m (½ mi.) southwest of Drayton.

Length: Loop trail of 35 km.

The trail passes through hardwood bushes, plantations, agricultural and recreational lands. Accommodation in the Kitchener-Waterloo area or in Listowel. Trail groomed and marked.

Elora Gorge

Location: North of Guelph. From Elora south on Elora Rd. 2 km (1.2 mi.).

The Elora Gorge, located in a 250-acre conservation area, is one of the major natural land features in Southern Ontario. The Grand R. passes between steep, rock walls and provides exceptional scenery. Most skiing is on about 8 km of hiking trails that range through the conservation lands and the area is obviously a place to bring a camera on a sunny day.

Longwoods Road Conservation Area

Location: From London west 26 km (16 mi.) on Hwy. 2. Proceed on Hwy. 2 about 3.2 km (2 mi.) west of village of Delaware and follow signs.

Length: About 11 km.

Both wooded and open areas. Some steep trails. Suitable for beginners and intermediate skiers. Trail passes by Ska Nah Doht Indian Village, reconstructed Neutral Indian Village. The area has a wide range of small wildlife and good scenery. Accommodation in London. Maps available by writing

to: Lower Thames Valley Conservation
Authority, 41 Fourth St., Chatham, Ont.
N7M 2G3.

Trillium Woods Nature Trail
Location: Southwest of Woodstock. From
Sweaburg exit on Hwy. 401, follow County
Rd. 12 south of Sweaburg. Continue 1.6 km
(1 mi.) to first intersection beyond village
and turn right for 8 km (5 mi.).
Length: 1 km.
25 acres of wooded, gently rolling terrain.
Trail passes through undisturbed area
known for trilliums in the spring. For accom-
modation, contact Chamber of Commerce,
Woodstock.

Woodstock Ski Club
Location: From Woodstock 13 km (8 mi.)
north on Hwy. 59.
Length: 5 km.
A cross-country and downhill ski centre
located on 30 acres of rolling, wooded land.
Trails groomed, rentals, snack bar, shelter.
Downhill skiing closed some days.

Chicopee
Location: South of Kitchener with access
off Hwy. 8 via Freeport and Morrison Roads.
Length: About 4 km.
Skiing on more than 100 acres including
conservation area lands and near the downhill resort first established in the hilly countryside. Grooming, rentals, lessons, snack bar.

Blandford Woods
Location: Oxford Outdoor Education
Centre on northeastern outskirts of Wood-
stock.
Length: 1 km.
240 acres of gentle to rolling terrain with
low lying swampy areas. Trail goes through
pine plantations, mixed hardwood forest.
For accommodation, contact Chamber of
Commerce, Woodstock.

Hullet Wildlife Management Area
Location: From Clinton northeast 6 km (4
mi.) on Hwy. 4.
This is a 4,600-acre parkland area in
Western Ontario countryside with some trails
and extensive possibilities for exploration.

Hullett Cross-country Ski Trail
Location: From Clinton, north 2 km (1.2
mi.) on Hwy. 4. Turn east on Hullett Conc. II
for 4.4 km (2.7 mi.). Located on north side
of road.
Length: 2 loop trails of 8.8 km.

The trail, groomed once a week, passes
through mainly rolling grassland but also
encounters some swampy areas.

Falconer Cross-Country Ski Trail
Location: From Teeswater south 4 km (2.5
mi.) on Hwy. 4. Turn left on Culross Concession Rd. II and proceed for 5.5 km (3.5 mi.).
Located on south side of the road.
Length: Loop trails of about 5.2 km.
A very scenic trail, groomed once a week,
winding through a spruce-pine plantation,
then a swamp and hardwood bush. Rolling
terrain that provides some challenge for the
skier.

Pinery Provincial Park
Location: From Grand Bend south 8 km. (5
mi.) on Hwy. 21.
Length: Trail network of over 20 km with
loops and individual circuits for different levels of expertise.
The full trail traverses the entire topographic range of Pinery's 6,000 acres of
Natural Environment park. Pinery's dune
topography offers many "ups and downs"
for the cross-country skier through close
pine and oak forested areas. Downhill ski
run on weekends. Heated chalet, tobogganing, skating rink. 130 electrical outlets at
campsites, heated washrooms and refreshment facilities. Pinery Park is one of the largest provincial parks in the southern part of
Ontario and offers splendid possibilities for
all types of winter recreation.

Parkhill
Location: Near Village of Parkhill near Lake
Huron shoreline in Western Ontario.
There is skiing on 1,885 acres of park
land, with about 6 km of trails at Parkhill
Conservation area east of village and on the
Saddler Tract, 5 km (3 mi.) west of the vil-
lage on Hwy. 7.

Pine Valley Golf Club
Location: From Simcoe west 11 km (7 mi.)
on Hwy. 24 to golf club.
Length: A network of trails ranging from
about 1 km to 10 km.
Area about half wooded and rolling coun-
tryside beside Turkey Point Provincial Park.
Trails pass through Spooky Hollow Nature
Sanctuary. Washrooms and rest area at Nor-
mandale Provincial Fish Hatchery along Red
Trail. Map at starting point. Trail maintained
by Norfolk Cross-Country Skiers and Hikers.
Accommodation information from Simcoe

An abandoned farm returning to nature can be a place to explore for skiers who get off the beaten track.

Chamber of Commerce, Simcoe, Ont. Rentals, instruction and ski clinics.

Rondeau Provincial Park
Location: From Chatham 40 km (25 mi.) south on Hwys. 40, 3 and 51.
Length: 16 km of marked trails.

Any part of Rondeau Park is "fair game" for the cross-country skier. Since snow conditions are often very limited it would be best to inquire at the park office in order to locate the best skiing opportunity. Rondeau is a flat sandspit formation on Lake Erie shoreline that is heavily wooded by rare vegetation types. Roads and walking trails wind through an immense hardwood forest, the largest remaining forest in Southwestern Ontario.

Skiers should be careful about venturing onto Rondeau Bay in the wintertime. The Bay does partly freeze over but is generally unsafe for winter activities. Many species of birds, wildlife and rare vegetation are found at the park. An interpretive program has been established to aid the visitor in discovering more about some of Rondeau's unique features. A campground with a limited number of electrical sites is operated in the winter with heated washrooms, trailer dumping facilities, etc. Hotels are located within

16 km of the park. For information contact the Park Superintendant, Rondeau Provincial Park, RR 1, Morpeth, Ont.

Iroquois Beach Provincial Park
Location: Eastern edge of Port Burwell on Hwy. 19.

This 350-acre park on the Lake Erie shoreline is used for cross-country skiing. Snowmobiling allowed on park roads.

Fisher Conservation Area
Location: From Port Ryerse in Long Point region west 6 km (4 mi.) on Hwy. 24 to Fisher's Glen.

This is 122-acre conservation area on the L. Erie shoreline. Some cross-country trails.

Luther Marsh
Location: West of Orangeville. Marked access points from Hwys. 9 and 89.
Length: 35 km.

The Luther Marsh Wildlife Management Area is one of the major wildlife and waterfowl refuges in Southern Ontario. The trail wanders through a variety of uplands and wetlands, forest plantations and agricultural land. It passes nearby the Egerton Esker, a leatherleaf bog and Luther L. A rich variety of birds and mammals may be observed in this area. Trail is groomed. Accommodation in Arthur, Orangeville, Fergus and Mount Forest, all about 25 to 32 km from Luther. Trails marked.

Hockley Hills Resort

Location: From Orangeville, north of Hwys. 10 and 24, then east on Hockley Rd. for a total of 6.4 km (4 mi.).

Length: Small trails for instruction, skiing on Bruce Trail.

Situated in Hockley Valley, with flat sections and gently rolling hills. Instruction, rentals, pro shop, floodlit downhill skiing, snowmobiling. Closed Mondays. Hotel with swimming pool, sauna, dining room, cafeteria, lounge with nightly entertainment and dancing. Basically a downhill resort. Maps available.

Cedar Springs Ski Club, Orangeville

Location: North from Orangeville on Hwy. 10, then east 10 km (6 mi.) on Hockley Valley Rd.

Length: 2 km.

This is one of six small ski resorts located in the Hockley Valley of the Nottawasaga R. Both cross-country and downhill skiing at this development. Great variety of terrain as the land is cut up with several streams and the river, creating a highly varied valley pattern.

Hockley Valley Winter Park

Location: From Orangeville north on Hwy. 10, then east about 10 km (6 mi.) on Hockley Valley Rd.

Length: 9 km.

Another of the six resorts in this part of the Nottawasaga Valley, the winter park is located on 150-foot-high slopes. The valley is a highly scenic area with broad bottom lands and complicated contours on the hillsides. Downhill resort open weekends with snack bar.

Golden Horseshoe Region

Metro Toronto Area

Many skiers in this massive urban area first tested their new equipment and learned to kick and glide on parts of the 10,000 acres of parkland. There is a wide variety of terrain, ranging from flat fields to very scenic ravines and river valleys. While some parks are suitable only for a quick dash through a fresh fall of snow, others are extensive enough to permit an afternoon's excursion.

A few have trails marked for skiers and offer such services as waxing huts, lessons, barbecues and even chalets. Most still only have walking or bicycle trails which can be used for skiing.

Some skiers set their own tracks in little used areas and return for daily exercise or race training sessions. After storms, a number of skiers are even seen gliding their merry way along unplowed sidewalks while pedestrians slip and slide at each painful step.

Toronto is not known for its heavy snow cover during most of the winter, but some of the parks are so well groomed one can ski on a dusting of snow. The only problem arises when an area has heavy pedestrian traffic and the snow there becomes packed and rough. The best skiing is just after a snowfall or on routes little used for walking.

As the jurisdiction over parkland is fragmented between such bodies as the Metro government, six area municipalities, the Metro Zoo and the Metro Toronto and Region Conservation Authority, it sometimes takes research to locate parks and find out how each is developed. One way is to get a road map which has parkland marked clearly in a color such as green, then start visiting. Another way is to phone parks authorities at the following numbers: Metro- 367-8186; City of Toronto- 367-7251; East York- 461-9451; Etobicoke- 626-4557; North York- 225-4611; Scarborough- 438-7411; York- 653-2700; Conservation authority- 661-6600; Zoo- 284-8181.

Finch East Park

Location: North York. Straddles Finch Ave. E. between Bayview Ave. and Leslie St.

This parkland along the east branch of the Don R. is quite hilly and rugged with thick stands of trees and considerable wildlife. Skiing is of the bushwhacking type and travellers pick their own routes over fields and through the trees.

Don Valley Parks

Location: From York Mills Rd. and Bayview Ave. in north, south and east to Victoria Park Ave. north of Danforth Ave.

Length: Chain of parks stretches almost uninterrupted for more than 10 km.

In the north you can start at Windfields Park and ski behind some of the most exclusive estates in Metro. There is a short stretch of private land before the parkland picks up again with Edward's Garden at Lawrence Ave. Here there is a series of paths both beside Wilket Cr. and along the well-treed high ground to the west. The parkland then branches out into Wilket Creek, Sunnybrook and Serena Gundy parks. It also reaches northwest along the west branch of the Don R. to Glendon College campus.

South from this cluster of parks the greenbelt continues under Eglinton Ave. and past the Ontario Science Centre at Ernest Thompson Seton Park. There is a break at the Don Valley Parkway, then Taylor Creek Park stretches along a valley as far as Victoria Park Ave. There is another break for a golf course, then parkland picks up with Byng Park.

Scarborough Parks
Location: Especially along the Highland Creek.
Length: A chain of parks runs along creek for about 10 km.

Scarborough is the Metro municipality with the most undeveloped land and in the northern regions, particularly around the new Metro Zoo, there are many acres of open fields. In the more populated section there are a number of parks along a creek providing scenic trips. Thomson Memorial Park, which runs southeast from Ellesmere Ave. to near McCowan Rd., south of the Civic Centre, has several small trails. Bendale, Hague, McCowan Road, Knob Hill and Cedar Brook form a chain of parks as far as Scarboro Golf and Country Club. Then the large Morningside Park fans out around the creek. Highland Cr. continues through Scarborough College campus and into Colonel Danforth Park on the east side before emptying into L. Ontario.

Humber Region
Location: Western section of Metro from northern boundary at Steeles Ave. to L. Ontario along Humber R.
Length: More than 20 km.

The Humber R. forms a spine for the major series of parks in the western part of the city. In a chain that is broken in places, the system starts with the 232-acre Rowntree Mills Park in the north, then the system wends its way south through Summerlea and The Elms. South of Hwy. 401 it picks up with Cruickshank and Raymore, then broadens out in a 150-acre region known as Eglinton Flats. Scarlett Mills, Smythe and Lambton Woods, then a small gap for the Canadian Pacific rail line.

To the south again, in Magwood Park, there are lessons and trails reaching south along the river. Below Bloor street, the river widens and deepens and trails wander through heavy bush. Further south still is an area known as the Humber Marshes. It is full of wildlife, but the swampy nature of much of the land makes skiing an exercise in bushwhacking. For easier skiing in the region there is the 340-acre High Park, with rolling, wooded hills beside Grenadier Pond, to the east. Centennial Park, with 4 of its 200 acres reserved for cross-country skiing, is to the west of Eglinton Ave., west of Hwy. 427.

North York Ski Centre
Location: Earl Bales Park, east side of Bathurst St., south of Sheppard Ave.

The Borough of North York has developed a public ski centre for cross-country and downhill skiers in a new park on the former York Downs Golf Course. The 160 acres are a mixture of fields and woods with a large ravine along the west branch of the Don River. This provides a modest hill for the downhill runs and interesting terrain for cross-country skiers on an afternoon outing. The centre has a full ski program including pre-season exercises, ski school, pro shop, rentals, club house and snack bar. For information phone 638-5315.

Ski Woodnewton
Location: From Claremont follow Brock Rd. north 8 km (5 mi.) to Coppins Corners, turn east on Durham Rd. 21 1.6 km (1 mi.), north on 6th Con. of Uxbridge Twp. 1.6 km (1 mi.).
Length: 10 km of interlocking trails in 3 loops.

Scenic wooded trails utilizing a ridge of hills 150 ft. high. Trails graded easy, intermediate and expert. Rentals, snack bar, trail grooming, cookout. Open daylight hours daily, except Monday and Tuesday. Accommodation available at Whitby, Oshawa, Toronto. Maps posted on trails, sheet maps available.

Terra Cotta Conservation Area
Location: 1.6 km (1 mi.) north of Village of Terra Cotta on Conc. 11, Halton Hills Twp.
Length: 5 km.

Conservation area of 310 acres is open daily. Trails wind through wooded areas and meadows with some hilly areas. Partly on Bruce Trail. Skirts highly scenic river valley. Area for cookouts and small lake with skat-

Winter touring in the Toronto area can hold some surprises when it is conducted in the Metro Zoo. Two trails are marked for cross-country skiers.

ing. Operated by Credit Valley Conservation Authority. Trails are not groomed.

Metro Toronto Zoo
Location: Northeast corner of Metro Toronto. From Exit 61A on Hwy. 401 north 1.6 km (1 mi.)
Length: 3 and 5 km trails.

The Metro Zoo is one of the newest and finest in the world. The 3 km, Eurasian trail starts near zoo entrance and passes Eurasian and Polar regions before ending at restaurant. Passes Bactrian (two-humped) camels, Siberian tigers, Chinese leopards, dromedaries, yaks, Barbary apes and Polar bears. African trail of 5 km skirts rim of Rouge River valley giving good view of Canadian Animal Domain. Free maps at ticket booth, regular zoo admission, closed Monday, Tuesday in winter until March 31. Call 284-0123 for snow report. Hours: 10 A.M. to 4:30 P.M. Last admission, 3:30. Zoo has thousands of animals and plants on 710-acre site in Scarborough.

Mountsberg Wildlife Centre
Location: From Hwy. 401 interchange 38, south on Guleph Line to Campbellville, west on No. 5 Sideroad 6.5 km (4 mi.), north on Town Line 1.6 km (1 mi.).
Length: 4 trails from 1.5 to 6.5 km. Maximum trip time 2 hr.

This area is a wildlife preserve and nature interpretive centre. There are 1,300 acres of natural landscape including a 500-acre reservoir; creeks, wooded areas, some old farm land, open fields, some reforestation along gently rolling terrain. The area is noted for a wide range of wildlife: white tailed deer, many small animals and birds. Open weekends. Films, interpretive displays, horse drawn sleigh rides, native animal displays, skating, snowshoeing. Rentals, snack bar, trail grooming, guide services. Accommodation: contact the Milton Chamber of Commerce, Main St. Milton, Ont. or Mohawk Inn, Campbellville. Maps in brochure available at Centre.

The Albion Hills Conservation Area
Location: From Bolton 8 km (5 mi.) north on Hwy. 50.
Length: Loop trails of 1.7, 2.6, 2.7, 5.8, 7.6 km. Graded beginner to intermediate.

Undulating terrain typical of the Oak Ridges moraine area, both open and wooded areas in natural and reforestation plots. Scenery and opportunity for wildlife viewing evident on the trails. Open seven days a week. Trail grooming. Refreshment booth with quick service food and chalet type shelter available on weekends only. Skating, downhill skiing, tobogganing and snowshoeing areas adjacent to the ski trails.

Rental service available and interpretive hikes scheduled on weekends. Motel accommodation at Bolton, but area within a forty mile drive from Metropolitan Toronto. Free maps available at area. Holds regular ski events. Fees. Palgrave Forest, 3.2 km (2 mi.) north, has some trails free.

The Cold Creek Conservation Area
Location: From Bolton 3.2 km (2 mi.) east or west from Nobleton on the King sideroad.
Length: Loop trails of 9.6 km primarily for novices.

Undulating terrain with mostly open areas and some natural bush. Trails open daily, groomed on weekends. Food concession and shelter building. Accommodation available within easy driving distance. Free maps available at the area.

Claireville Conservation Area
Location: Northwest edge of Metro Toronto. Main access south off Hwy. 7 west of Hwy. 50.

Claireville has 1,500 acres of land, mostly open fields, with some wooded areas. The west branch of the Humber R. traverses the parkland and has been dammed at one point to create a large reservoir. The country is rolling and in many places exposed to wind, so skier should choose track according to weather.

Chedoke Winter Sports Park
Location: Hamilton on Aberdeen Ave. near Hwy. 403.

Cross-country skiing on 75 acres of land around a small, downhill ski resort. Snack bar.

Hamilton Cross-Country Ski Club
Location: South of Hamilton. From Binbrook on Hwy. 56, take Golf Club Rd.

A 20-mile creek runs throughout the 400-acre property. Wooded terrain with open spaces, gently rolling. Some wildlife may be observed, ducks, geese, foxes and deer. Open weekends, instruction may be arranged, rentals, pro shop, waxing area, food and liquor. Some grooming. Accommodation in Hamilton.

Mill Run-Toronto Ski Club
Location: From Uxbridge west 9.5 km (6 mi.) on Aurora Sideroad.
Length: Varied trails on 600 acres
Mill Run Golf Club is used as a weekend cross-country area by the Toronto Ski Club. Terrain is picturesque and ranges from open

fairways to woods with flat and rolling sections. Club house, snack bar, barbecues, ski instruction by appointment, trail fees. Information from ski club at 8 Colborne St., Toronto, N1S E1E.

Seneca College Ski Trails
Location: North of Toronto. From Hwy. 400 east 5 km (3 mi.) on King City Sideroad, through King City, then north 3 km (2 mi.) on Dufferin St. to college entrance.
Length: 11 km plus skiing on 40-acre lake.

The King Campus of Seneca College is located on 700 acres of wooded parkland and is a former estate of the Eaton family. Skiing through rolling woodland, some swamp and over frozen surface of lake. Skiers use sloping front lawn of the former mansion for learning downhill techniques. This campus specializes in recreation and outdoor education courses, including a number related to cross-country skiing and many Toronto and area residents have learned to ski there. Rentals, instruction, snack bar, waxing area and ski shop. Trail fee. Lessons days and evenings, ski touring and leadership. Trips to Haliburton for weekend skiing and winter camping trips. Winter survival and wilderness first aid. Pre-season and racing courses.

Cedar Springs Ski Club, Burlington
Location: Burlington. From Hwy. 5 north on Cedar Springs Rd. to club.
Length: 2 km.

Small, groomed trail around a downhill ski area which is mainly open weekends. Snack bar, instruction, fee.

Hilton Falls
Location: From Milton north on Hwy. 25 for 3 km (2 mi.), then west on County Rd. 9 for 5 km (3 mi.).
Length: 3 km.

This 534-acre site is managed by the Halton Region Conservation Authority and includes an attractive waterfall on the headwaters of a tributary of the Oakville Creek. There are several trail loops.

Christie Conservation Area
Location: West from Hamilton 32 km (20 mi.) on Hwy. 5.
Length: Main loop of 5.5 km with three small cut-offs. Time about 2 hr.

This is an 840-acre area with hilly, wooded and open areas. Trails marked and groomed. Warm-up area and food, skating, tobogganing, fire pit. Map at trail or from

View over part of the campus of Seneca College's King campus north of Toronto. This popular ski centre was a former estate of the Eaton family.

Hamilton Region Conservation Authority, Box 99, 838 Mineral Springs Rd., Ancaster, Ont. L9G 3L3.

Valens Conservation Area
Location: North from Hamilton on Hwy. 6 to Freelton, then west on Hwy. 97 about 5 km (3 mi.) to entrance on north side.
Length: 6 km of trails on 700 acres of land.
This is a rolling, partly wooded area with two trails. Wildlife includes deer, fox, raccoon and small animals. Trails marked with orange tape. Parking lot, warm-up hut with waxing area. Skating on large reservoir. Map from Hamilton Region Conservation Authority, Box 99, 838 Mineral Springs Rd., Ancaster, Ont. L9G 3L3.

Dundas Valley Trails
Location: Ancaster off Mineral Springs Rd. and Ancaster Rd.
Length: About 10 km. Can form a loop of about 3 hr.
Dundas Valley trails are on three tracts of conservation authority land at Ancaster with distinct trail systems. Area is wooded and hilly, considered intermediate terrain. Trails

groomed. Map available from Hamilton Region Conservation Authority, Box 99, 838 Mineral Springs Rd., Ancaster, Ont. L9G 3L3.

Fonthill Ski Centre
Location: Near Welland. From Hwy. 20 in Fonthill north. 8 km (5 mi.) on Lookout Point Rd.
Length: 3 km on 160 acres.
Located on golf course, groomed, rentals on weekend. Lodging in town and Niagara Falls region.

Nottawasaga Bay

Blue Mountain Ski Resort
Location: From Collingwood take Hwy. 26 8 km (5 mi.) west, then south 1.6 km (1 mi.) on Blue Mountain Winter Park Rd.
Length: 34 km of trails with travel time up to 5 hr.
Blue Mountain is one of the largest downhill ski resorts in Central Canada and in recent years has started a cross-country development. The downhill runs are spread

across 2 ½ miles of the Niagara Escarpment facing Georgian Bay and there is a large development of lodges, ski shops and chalets at the foot of the hills. The cross-country skiing includes trails at the foot and top of the 750-foot-high escarpment with both wooded and open country and the possibility of long downhill runs if the snow conditions are right and the cross-country skier capable of sustained turns. There is even a ski jump for the more daring.

Accommodation, food, bars, dancing, rentals instruction from the Ernie McCulloch ski school. Trails groomed. The area features several downhill races including the pro circuit. Accommodation information from Blue Mountain Lodging Assn., RR 3, Collingwood or Grey-Bruce Tourist Council, RR 4, Owen Sound.

Tyrolean Village Resort
Location: From Collingwood follow Hwy. 26 8 km (5 mi.) west, then south 1.6 km (1 mi.) to resort entrance.
Length: 10 km of trails.

Tyrolean Village is a development at the foot of the Niagara Escarpment and beside the major Blue Mountain Ski Resort, which has downhill and cross-country facilities. The cross-country trails at Tyrolean are in hilly country both wooded and open and provide good views of Georgian Bay. They are suitable for all levels of skier. Accommodation, food and such facilities as indoor tennis available at resort. Rentals and lessons nearby.

Georgian Peaks Ski Resort
Location: From Thornbury Hwy. 26 east 6.5 km (4 mi.).
Length: 5 km with up to 2 hr. travel.

Georgian Peaks, which has the highest downhill runs in Central Canada, also has cross-country trails running from the area along the Niagara Escarpment. The terrain is wooded and at places almost mountainous but suitable for all levels. Scenery is very good with excellent views of Georgian Bay, which is very close to resort. Instruction, rentals, restaurant, groomed trails, shelter, bar and dancing. Downhill races. Accommodation nearby and information from Grey-Bruce Tourist Council, RR 4, Owen Sound.

Cyril's Cross-Country Ski Centre
Location: From Collingwood west 9.6 km (6 mi.) on Hwy. 26, then south 1.6 km (1 mi.) on Arrowhead Rd.

Length: 2 trails, 3 and 5 km. Travel time 1 to 2 hr.

Located on wooded, mountainous terrain of the Niagara Escarpment. First level suited for beginners, top for advanced skiers. Spectacular view. Rentals, snack bar, instruction, shelter, downhill facilities nearby. For accommodation, contact Grey-Bruce Regional Tourist Council, RR 4, Owen Sound, Ont. or Blue Mountain Lodging Assn., RR 3, Collingwood, Ont.

Talisman Ski Resort
Location: In Beaver Valley. From Flesherton on Hwy. 10 east on Hwy. 4 for 3.2 km (2 mi.), north on County Rd. 13 through Eugenia and Kimberley. Resort 1.6 km (1 mi.) northeast of Kimberley.
Length: 10 km

Talisman Ski Resort was developed in mid-1960s as a major ski and year-round resort. Cross-country trails lead from resort through scenic Beaver Valley area. Excellent views from top of Niagara Escarpment on either side of valley. Valley bottom is mixed farmland and woods with Beaver R. passing through area. Lodge accommodation plus hotels and farmhouses in area. Restaurants, bar, rentals, ski shop, lessons from Lorne McFadgen Ski School. Tobogganing and extensive downhill skiing. Winter carnival. Talisman Ski Resort, Kimberley, Ont.

Beaver Valley Ski Club
Location: In Beaver Valley east of Markdale and northeast of Flesherton. Follow signs.
Length: About 15 km with access to Bruce Trail.

This is the original ski club located on the broad, eastern slopes of the beautiful Beaver Valley. Originally just a downhill area, it is operated as a club with some cross-country skiing. Trails in valley and atop slopes through woodlands and past farm fields. Excellent views of the valley area.

Kolapore Uplands Ski Trails
Location: Beaver Valley Region. From Thornbury south about 19.5 km (12 mi.) on County Rd. 2 to junction with County Rd. 19. From there south about 1.6 km (1 mi.) to start on west side of road just south of bridge.
Length: Series of trails totalling 35 km.

This network was developed in 1973 by the University of Toronto Outing Club with an Opportunities for Youth grant. Trails run mainly through hilly, forested country. Scenic. Some suitable for beginners but most for experienced skiers. Marked with triangular orange blazes. Club notes much land is privately owned and to preserve good relations with persons who allow its use, skiers are asked to stay on trails, carry out garbage and not build fires. Trails are marked with such colorful names as Wandering Rocks, Quiet Pastures, Labyrinth, Red Death Hill and Wild Mouse. Detailed map available from club: Kolapore Uplands Ski Trail, c/o University of Toronto Outing Club, Box 6647, Stn. A, Toronto, Ont. M5W 1X4.

Wasaga Beach Provincial Park
Location: From Wasaga Beach east on Hwy. 92 to River Road West, then south 400 m.
Length: Loop trails of 4.6, 6.2, 9 km. Travel time from 1 to 3 hr. Graded novice to advanced.

The trails are located in a provincially significant natural area. The combination of various sand dune features and rare plant life make this area unique in Ontario. Wildlife includes ruffed grouse, red fox, porcupine, deer and numerous species of birds. Trails are groomed. Two shelters with provisions for warming light lunches. Snowshoeing. Accommodation in Wasaga Beach. Contact Chamber of Commerce. Brochures available at beginning of trails. Nottawasaga Ski Club annual cross-country races second week of February.

Mountain View Ski Area, Midland
Location: 1.6 km (1 mi.) west of Midland. Follow ski area signs from Hwy. 27.
Length: Trails of 2.5 and 5 km and many touring areas using part of trails. Loop from clubhouse.

Trails wander through pine and hardwoods and open fields. Terrain is varied with flat lands and gentle, rolling hills. Open daily, rentals on weekends when no reservation needed, or by reservation during the week. Lunch counter and heated chalet. Trails marked and groomed. Downhill facilities. Accommodation nearby. Trail map posted outside clubhouse. Annual race about first weekend of January. For information contact Don Foster, RR 2, Midland, Ont.

Fern Resort
Location: From Orillia take Hwy. 12B South to Atherley, then northeast 3.2 km (2 mi.) on Rama Rd.

Length: Travel time 1 to 2 hr. and extensive travel possible on Lake Couchiching.

Resort estate has a mile of private lakeshore. Open terrain, wooded, good for beginners. Instruction, rentals. Trails groomed. Entertainment, licenced dining room and lounge, indoor pool, sauna, California hot tub, floodlit skating rink, curling, Shuffle Horseshoes, ping-pong, pool tables, snowmobiling. Resort situated in Huronia ski country. Babysitting can be arranged. Inn and cottage accommodation. For information write Robert and Mary Lou Downing, Fern Resort, RR 5, Orillia, Ont. L3V 6H5.

Horseshoe Valley Resort
Location: Northeast of Barrie. From Hwy. 93 east 5 km (3 mi.) on Horsehoe Valley Rd.
Length: 58 km in eight trails on 2,000 acres.

This is one of the best cross-country resorts in Ontario. It has been developed since the mid 1960s and is used by skiers from beginner to racing ability. Trails pass abandoned farmhouses. Terrain ranges from flat, previously farmed areas now reforested through gently rolling hardwood forests to challenging slopes for expert skiers. Scenic region.

Horseshoe Valley is both a well developed cross-country and downhill resort and in summer operates a golf course and other facilities. Large chalet with licensed lounge, snack bar, rentals, repairs, ski shop, instruction. Trails groomed and tracks set. Rest stations on long trails. Babysitting. Maps. Open 9 a.m. to 4:30 p.m. weekdays, 8:30 to 4 p.m. weekends and holidays. Lodging information from Barrie Chamber of Commerce, Fred Grant Sq., Barrie, Ont.; Huronia Tourist Assn., County Building, Midhurst; Orillia Chamber of Commerce, Sundial Dr., Orillia.

Snow Valley Resorts
Location: From Barrie north on Hwy. 27, then west on Snow Valley Rd.
Length: About 9 km.

Located on 300 acres of hilly land beside a downhill ski resort in a heavy snow belt area. Rentals, instruction, food. Trail fee.

Minnesing Swamp
Location: West of Barrie about 15 km (10 mi.).
Length: A swamp area of several thousand acres.

This is an area in Southern Ontario which acts as a wildlife refuge and water reservoir.

It is shot through with rivers and streams including the Nottawasaga, Pine, Willow and Mad. Bounded on north by Hwy. 26, south by Hwy. 90 and east by little-used Canadian National Railways line which some skiers use for access. No developed ski trails in this wild area and snow is often too deep and brush too heavy for snowmobiles. Anyone entering this area should be prepared and equipped for wilderness travel. For map use 1:50,000 Barrie West topographic series. Swamp area is in centre of map.

Molson's Park
Location: Just south of Barrie. From Hwy. 400 exit east on Essa Rd., then south on Fairview Service Rd. Park is located on farm just south of brewery.
Length: 16 km.

The cross-country ski centre is operated as a free public relations gesture by Molson's Breweries and includes free instruction. Trails range over 600 acres of farmland and bush. Some trails pass through a tree farm. Trails marked, groomed and graded beginner through advanced. Rentals available but skiers seeking them on weekdays should check with centre to see if equipment is available, as it is sometimes booked by groups. Skating pond, snack bar, tobogganing. Flea market on weekends offers local crafts and antiques.

Nottawasaga Inn
Location: East of Alliston. From Hwy. 400 west about 10 km (6 mi.) on Hwy. 89.
Length: 4 km.

Skiing on rolling countryside is free to guests of inn and there is a trail fee for day visitors. Lodging, food, rentals.

Ski Haven
Location: Take Hwy. 400 north to Hwy. 89. Exit east on Cookstown Rd. 9.5 km (6 mi.) toward Lake Simcoe.
Length: Loop trails of 16 km on 500 acres.

Interesting trails for all skiers. Beginners enjoy golf course trails with ease. More experienced skiers take off through wooded and hilly farm land. All trails clearly marked and groomed. Ski shop, rentals, barbecue areas with fireplace, shelter, picnic tables, large heated area for changing and waxing skis, special night skiing parties and for the bird watchers, bird feeders in clearings. Complete clubhouse facilities, licenced lounge, coffee shop and banquet room. For lodging information contact Ontario Tourist Assn., Hwy. 400, Barrie, Ont. Also accommodation in Nottawasaga Inn, Alliston, and 400 Motel at junction of Hwy. 400 and Hwy. 89. Trail maps available free of charge at clubhouse or write Roy Moe, Ski Haven, Gilford, Ont. Southern Ontario Ski Assn. race.

Mansfield Forest Club
Location: North of Mansfield 4 km (2.5 mi.) on Airport Rd. Downhill resort on west side and cross-country and snowmobile areas just to north on east side of Airport Rd.
Length: 33 km.

This resort has developed attractive land along the Pine R. into a winter sport centre with each activity slightly separated. The cross-country ski trails wander over flat land in the river valley and climb a scenic area known as Oak Ridges. There are good lookouts from several places. Area has full services including food, instruction, rentals and maps for marked and groomed trails. Trail fee.

Honeywood Ski Centre
Location: From Mansfield north 9.5 km (6 mi.) on Airport Rd., then west on Sideroad 25 for 9.5 km (6 mi.) and south on 1st Line West 500 m.

The 1,600 feet elevation of the farm provides attractive scenery and good snow conditions for the area. The only marked trail is a section of the Bruce Trail which passes through the farm. Otherwise are free to choose your own routes on 1,500 acres. Simple dormitory accommodation for 16 in old farmhouse, meals and, by arrangement, instruction. Limited rental equipment. For information contact Honeywood Ski Touring Centre, RR 3, Shelburne, Ont. L0N 1S0.

Algonquin – Haliburton – Muskoka

Algonquin Provincial Park
Location: Access to most developed trails from Hwy. 60 starting 44 km (27 mi.) east from Huntsville.
Length: More than 100 km by 1976.

Algonquin, one of the most evocative words to a canoeist, is now entering the skier's vocabulary as the park slowly starts moving to year-round operations. While the crowds on the portages have become almost oppressive in summer, a winter visitor will find the 2,910-square-mile park almost empty of humans. The Ministry of Natural Resources has marked but not groomed five trails off Hwy. 60 in 1975 and there are limitless possibilities for short or long winter tours through the massive wilderness of the park interior. Starting points of the five trails are given in miles from the west gate.

Western Uplands Hiking Trail—start from mile 2. A loop wandering for 35 km through the myriad of small lakes in the southwestern part of the park. This is rugged, wooded country for advanced skiers with stamina for a long, wilderness trip.

Cache Lake, Old Railway Line—start from mile 15.3. Skiing is possible on the route of an abandoned railway line which once wandered across Algonquin Park for about 70 km. The line crosses Hwy. 60 between Tanamakoon and Cache Lakes on the south and travels in a generally east-west direction. Skiing suitable for all levels of ability.

Highland Hiking Trail—start from mile 19.6. Two loops of 18 and 35 km. The main trail starts south from Hwy. 60, just west of Pewee L. and the shorter loop circles Provoking L. The longer loop strikes southwest to bluffs just inland from Head L. and skirts the portage trail of 1,200 yds. south to Harness L. It circles back to pick up the small loop south of Provoking L. As in the case of the Western Uplands Trail, skiers should be prepared and equipped for wilderness travel. While this is well-trodden ground in the summer, it is little used in the winter.

Pog Lake Trail—starts from mile 24. A 3 km loop south from Hwy. 60 at Pog L., just west of Lake of Two Rivers. Land ranges from flat to gently rolling and is suitable for all abilities. Uses the abandoned railway line for part of its length.

Sunday Lake Trail—start from mile 26.8. A 16 km trail along an old road north from Hwy. 60. The land is quite flat and trail could be used by novice skiers.

In addition to the organized trails, there are many other logging roads which crisscross the park and an immense system of waterways with 80 major canoe routes over 1600 km. There are also a number of other summer access roads around the perimeter of the park which could be skied. A word of caution about trying to adapt canoe routes: parks officials say some ice can be unsafe even in mid-winter and caution should always be used in ice travel. As well, there

can be problems in trying to follow portages which can be obvious as beaten paths in summer but not evident when snow covered. Some wind up and down very steep slopes. The skier should know the route or check with someone who does.

Winter camping is being practiced here by an increasing number of persons. For starters, the Mew Lake campground at mile 20.1 has a plowed parking lot, firewood and toilets. Campers who head for the interior should be prepared for deep snow and temperatures which can dip as low as minus 40 degrees Celsius. In addition to beautiful views of a frozen wilderness, they will find at least the tracks of such hardy wildlife as deer, moose, marten, fisher, fox and wolf. The ravens, Gray Jays and Boreal Chickadees haunt campsites for stray crumbs. The night silence will be pierced by the cracking of frozen trees and possibly the howling of wolves in the distance.

Algonquin is one of the most beautiful areas of Southern Ontario and despite heavy summer use and logging for a century, much of it is still wilderness — or about as close as one is going to get to it in such latitudes. It is Ontario's oldest provincial park (1893) and the second largest in Canada. The hundreds of lakes, rivers and streams, one 300 feet deep, are the result of glacial scouring as recently as 11,000 years ago. Area is on edge of pre-Cambrian Shield and straddles highlands with some spectacular cliffs and gorges. Five major rivers have their headwaters here.

The western two-thirds of the park is mainly in hardwoods of sugar maple, beech and yellow birch, with hemlock groves and scatterings of giant white pine left over from the major logging era. The drier, sandier eastern section sprouts white, red and jack pine. Spruce bogs occur in low-lying areas throughout the park. The area is sparsely inhabited in winter and there is no gasoline station open for the 70 km (45 mi.) between Oxtongue Lake on the west and Whitney on the east. Food and lodging in towns. Information from park personnel at east gate (near Whitney) weekdays (8 a.m. to 5 p.m.) and at Park Museum at mile 13. Canoe map gives an idea of waterways but is of limited use. Skiers should check with park officials for numbers of topographic maps. Write: District Forester, Algonquin Park District, Whitney, Ont. K0J 2M0.

Arrowhead Provincial Park
Location: On the east side of Hwy. 11, 8

Winter camping in the Haliburton Highlands. Heavy clothing and a good stove are assets when one intends to stay put in cold weather. Tenting out in the snow is becoming an increasingly popular sport.

km (5 mi.) north of Huntsville.
Length: 2 loop trails totalling 14.5 km. Travel time 2 ½ to 3 hr. Intermediate ability.

Algonquin type wood and water land. Area and trails ideal for families. Washrooms, shelters, winter camping, skating, tobogganing, ice fishing, snowshoeing, snowmobiling. Accommodation in Huntsville. Contact Chamber of Commerce, Huntsville, Ont. P0A 1K0. Free maps at park office or Chamber of Commerce, Huntsville.

Bear Trail Inn Resort
Location: At Algonquin Park's East Gate, on Hwy. 60, in Whitney, on Galeairy Lake Rd.
Length: Travel time from 1 to 8 hr. Some trails loop, others start 15-20 km inside Algonquin Provincial Park and end at Bear trail.

Most skiing is taking place in the Algonquin Provincial Park, wilderness of lakes, rivers and streams. In 1975 the first two ski trails were established by the Park's management as part of a larger winter sports program. Ski shop, free guided wilderness

tours for groups. Trails marked but not groomed. Snowmobiling, snowshoeing, skating, ice fishing. Licenced dining room. Topographic maps of the area for sale at the resort. For information write Gertrude and Fritz Sorensen, Box 158, Galeairy Lake Rd., Whitney, Ont. K0J 2M0.

Echo Ridge
Location: West of Algonquin Provincial Park. North of Huntsville. 1.6 km (1 mi.) east of Kearney, on Hwy. 518.
Length: A wide variety of trails allow trips of 1 hr. to 1 wk. on old logging roads, traplines and horseback riding trails leading to Algonquin Park.

Trails wander through wilderness bush, past beaver ponds and lakes, over hills with spectacular view over the Almaguin Highlands. Trails are suggested by ski instructors for all levels of ability. Ample wildlife, moose, deer, fox, wolf, owl, raven, etc. Downhill and cross-country skiing instruction available. Pro shop, rentals, survival lessons, packtrips and cookouts arranged. Washrooms, cafeteria, camper parking. Trails groomed. Snowshoeing instruction and guide service by reservation. Cross-country races and parties organized. Accommodation in many rustic lodges and cottages mostly with fireplaces. For information, contact Almaguin South Tourist Assn., c/o George Purdy, Lynx Lake, Kearney, Ont. P0A 1M0. Topographic map: Burks Falls S.E. For information on winter carnival, write c/o Kearney Fire Fighters Assn., Kearney, Ont. For more information on resort, write W. Schmidt, Echo Ridge, Box 137, Kearney, Ont. P0A 1M0.

Purdy's Lodge

Location: West of Algonquin Park. 40 km (25 mi.) north of Huntsville. 6.4 km (4 mi.) east of Kearney on the Clam Lake Rd.
Length: Travel time about 7 hr. to complete all main trails.

Wooded and rolling terrain. Wilderness trails easy to difficult. Very lightly used. Small lodge, can accommodate 6, home cooking. Open all winter. Trails broken but not groomed, guiding available. Travel unlimited on unused logging roads. Nearby downhill ski operation, Echo Ridge. Ski rentals there. Specializes in quiet accommodation and individual attention.

Timberline Lodge

Location: Kearney, west of Algonquin Park.

This lodge provides bring-your-own-sleeping-bag dormitory accommodation and hearty meals for skiers planning trips on an extensive trail system in the area. This is a land of rolling, tree-clad hills and frozen lakes and rivers. It is good terrain for skiers and snowshoers of all abilities. Many marked trails and unlimited opportunity for bushwhacking in the wilderness. To the east, Algonquin Park stretches in a vast expanse of frozen forests and waterways. The Kearney area is at the 1,400-foot elevation and receives about 400 cm (150 in.) of snow each winter and there is consistently good skiing until April most years .

Haliburton Forest Reserve

Location: Southwest of Algonquin Park. From West Guilford north 19.5 km (12 mi.) on Kennisis Lake Rd.
Length: 30 km of trails cleared, marked and mapped in 10,000-acre area.

The Haliburton Forest and Wild Life Reserve Ltd. is a privately owned 100 sq. mi. area catering mainly to snowmobilers but with a sizable section now reserved for cross-country skiers. This wooded, hilly area has a snow season that usually lasts from

late December to late April. Rugged country with almost unlimited possibilities for wilderness skiing.

This Kennisis L. region, about 150 mi. from Toronto, is forested mostly with beech, maple and other hardwoods. It is an area of rolling hills up to 450 feet high and with good views. The Gull, Black, Hollow, Madawaska and York rivers radiate from the high ground. Ski trails follow numerous logging roads. There is a hunting cabin for lunch stops and a remote cabin for overnight trips.

Map available and skier should obtain topographic map, Haliburton 31 E/2 in 1:50,000 series. Wild area with some markings not clear so should carry map and compass. Most accommodation at lodge booked by snowmobilers but some skiers bring trailers or find lodging in towns as much as 20 miles distant. Fees for trail use. For information write the reserve, RR 1, Haliburton, Ont. K0M 1S0.

Bracebridge Resource Trails

Location: 6.4 km (4 mi.) north of Bracebridge, on the east side of Hwy. 11.
Length: 3 loop trails of 4.8, 6.4, 8 km. Travel time from 30 min. to an hour.

Trails are graded easy to advanced. Wooded area and unplowed bush roads along the Muskoka River. The Bracebridge Resource Management Centre is an area of about 1,500 acres of Crown Land. Known history of the property dates back to 1868-1872, when it was first settled by 12 families under the authority of the "Free Grants and Homesteads Act of 1868." Farming and logging were carried on until 1954 when the land was bought for a sort of game preserve, especially for deer.

In 1966 the Crown purchased the "Patterson Property" for the purpose of demonstrating resource management techniques of the Ministry of Natural Resources. There the public has an opportunity to view techniques in the Ministry's field of timber, fish, wildlife and recreation. Trails groomed. Snowshoeing, hiking. Snowmobiling prohibited. Washroom facilities. Accommodation in Bracebridge. Contact Country Ski and Sports Centre, 72 Manitoba St., Bracebridge, Ont. Maps available at trail and from the Ministry of Natural Resources, Box 1138, Bracebridge.

Raymond Cross-Country Ski School

Location: Muskoka, 24 km (15 mi.) north of Bracebridge. From Raymond General Store

on Hwy. 141 (formerly 532) north 1.6 km (1 mi.) to entrance on west side of road.
Length: Four trails: 1 - 5 km in loops. More trails under development.

The school trails are for the use of students and organized groups which have made prior arrangements. Lessons by Ann Niederhauser, Level III Canadian Ski Assn. instructor. Terrain is gently rolling land just east of Lake Rosseau. Covered with mixed woods, rocky outcrops and streams. Trails marked and groomed for all levels, heated waxing area, ski shop. This is training base for Southern Ontario Division (CSA) cross-country ski team. For further information write Raymond Cross-country Ski School, RR 1, Utterson, Ont.

Tally-Ho Winter Park
Location: From Huntsville east on Hwy. 60 towards Algonquin Park.
Length: 10 km.

This year-round lodge north of the Lake of Bays is located on 50 acres of rolling, forested land of the Algonquin region. Groomed trails, lodging and food. Rentals and instruction.

Cedar Grove Lodge
Location: From Huntsville east 11 km (7 mi.) on Hwy. 60.

The lodge has skiing on 100 acres of wooded, hilly terrain. There is food and accommodation.

Britannia Hotel Ski Trails
Location: From Huntsville east on Hwy. 35 and 60 for 16 km (10 mi.), then south on South Portage Rd. 8 km (5 mi.), then left on Britannia Rd. to hotel.
Length: 4.5 km loop. Travel time 90 min.

Britannia Hotel, RR 2, Huntsville, is a 190-room resort on the Lake of Bays in Muskoka highlands. Area is wooded and hilly with wildlife, beaver dams, lookout. Instruction, rentals, skating, snowshoeing, curling rink, snowmobile rentals, downhill skiing, dining room, bar. Annual loppet.

Echo Hills Park
Location: From Huntsville east 16 km (10 mi.) on Hwy. 60.
Length: Loop trails of 4.6, 8.5 and 13 km. Travel time 30 to 90 min.

Very scenic area, slightly hilly, mostly heavily wooded, some open stretches. Some wildlife. Open daily. Rentals nearby. Trails groomed. Cookout area. Snowshoeing on unplowed road system on 200 acres.

Motels and cottages at Dwight, 2.4 km (1.5 mi.) east of parking area. Map available at entrance. For information write L. R. Cotterchio, Echo Hill Park, RR 2, Huntsville, Ont.

Hidden Valley Ski Club
Location: From Huntsville east 8 km (5 mi.) on Hwy. 60 and south on access road.
Length: 5 km.

Hidden Valley is one of the largest downhill ski resorts in the Huntsville region and has added cross-country trails on its 50 acres. Located on shores of Peninsula L., a scenic area. Instruction, rentals, skating, lodging, dining room.

Middle Gibson Area
Location: From Port Severn north about 19 km (12 mi.) on Hwy. 103, then east 6.5 km (4 mi.) on Muskoka Rd. 33 to small parking lot.
Length: 4 loops of 2.5 to 5 km with trips up to 16 km. Extensions started 1976 to double trail by pushing east to Southwood.

This is one of a series of wilderness trails cut by the Five Winds Touring Club on crown lands in the Muskoka area. The country, long popular with summer visitors, is rugged and scenic with a wide variety of plant and animal life. Trails can be skied by persons of intermediate ability in good physical condition but should be tackled only by groups familiar with wilderness travel and led by experienced skiers with ability in bushcraft, survival and navigation. Carry food, map, compass, spare clothing and emergency gear. Trails marked with orange or blue plastic tape and paint blazes. Detailed maps available from Ministry of Natural Resources office in Parry Sound or from Five Winds Club, 4 Belmont, Toronto, M5R 1P8.

Gibson-McCrae Area
Location: From Waubaushene north on Hwy. 103 for 16 km (10 mi.).
Length: 25 km.

Part of a series of wilderness trails cut by the Five Winds Touring Club on Muskoka area crown lands, this trail starts at Hwy. 103 and ends at same highway about 3 km north. Trail passes through rugged terrain with mixed hardwoods and softwoods and some open area with a scattering of oak and juniper. It passes below McCrae L., skirts the edge of a Georgian Bay inlet and ends below the Gibson R. There is one ice crossing at McCrae Narrows which must be used with caution. Some steep sections. Club advises most sections call for intermediate ability but skiers should be in good physical condition and led by someone experienced in bushcraft, survival and navigation. Carry food, map, compass, emergency gear. Trails marked with orange or blue tape and paint blazes. Detailed map available from Ministry of Natural Resources office, Parry Sound, or Five Winds Club, 4 Belmont, Toronto, M5R 1P8.

Coldgray Area
Location: North from Waubaushene on Hwy. 103, 22.5 km (14 mi.) to first entry point on west side at Go-Home Lake Rd. Two other entry points off Hwy. 103 below Muskoka R.
Length: Loop trails of 8 to 16 km.

Coldgray is the name given a series of connecting trails cut on wilderness crown land by the Five Winds Touring Club. They are located between a series of small lakes and streams between the Muskoka R. and Gray L. on the north and Coldwater L. on the south. Terrain is varied with some woods and open fields with juniper and oak. Some areas are rugged and as this is wilderness the club suggests that all parties should be led by someone experienced in such travel, survival and navigation. Should carry map and compass, spare food and emergency gear. Trails marked with orange or blue plastic tape and paint blazes. Detailed maps available from Ministry of Natural Resources office, Parry Sound, or Five Winds Club, 4 Belmont, Toronto, M5R 1P8.

Mount Madawaska Ski Area
Location: Barry's Bay
Length: About 15 km of interconnecting trails from base area.

The cross-country trails run from a downhill ski area base and pass through quite rugged terrain east of Algonquin Park with hills up to 400 ft. high. There are mixed woods, lakes, beaver ponds and many scenic lookouts.Lodge has ski rental and repairs, lessons, restaurant, licenced lounge, and four Adirondack type lean-to log shelters along trails.Trail maps and lodging information from ski area, Box 130, Barry's Bay, Ont. A cross-country ski weekend is held in March.
Madawaska Kanu Camp
Location: From Barry's Bay 14.5 km (9 mi.) southwest on Siberia Rd., then east on North Kamaniskeg Lake Rd.
Length: Variety of trails on old logging roads with trips from 30 minutes to full day.

The Madawaska Kanu Camp is better known as Canada's first white water school for kayaks and canoes. The operators, Hermann and Christa Kerckhoff, have expanded the operation into winter. Lodge is operated for three-day parties: Friday through Sunday. Area is 30 miles east of Algonquin Park on hilly, crown forest land, shot through with streams and rivers. Country is rugged wilderness but trails range from easy to expert. Snow depth as much as 3 metres (10 ft.). Hermann Kerckhoff provides instruction and guiding and is certified ski instructor. Christa cooks for skiers. Two-storey cedar chalet is on Kamaniskeg R., part of Madawaska River system. Instruction on equipment and waxing, ski movies, two fireplaces, dormitories, video tapes of students played at night for instruction. Trips are booked in advance through Kerckhoffs at 2 Tuna Crt., Don Mills, Ont. (416) 447-8845. Mini-bus from Toronto to camp and return included in package.

Muskoka Sands Inn
Location: From Gravenhurst north 5 km (3 mi.) on Muskoka Beach Rd.
Length: 10 km.

The inn is beside Lake Muskoka in one of the most scenic areas of Ontario and one of the most popular in summer. Skiing through woodlands and on lake.

Frost Centre Trails (Dorset)
Location: From Dorset south 11 km (7 mi.) on Hwy. 53.
Length: 25 km (to be expanded.).

The Leslie M. Frost Natural Resources Centre is the former Dorset Ranger or Forest Technical School, located on 55,000 acres in the Haliburton Highlands south of Algonquin Park. Cross-country facilities include a practice and warm-up area, marked trails and map. This is the centre where Ontario government conservation officers and forest technicians were trained by the former Dept. of Lands and Forests, now the Ministry of Natural Resources. There is now limited government training at the centre and much of it has been opened to the public for demonstration and educational projects in resources management, recreation and education. Programs are for day visitors and groups which have arranged to stay in the 83-room residences. Demonstrations include a sawmill, maple syrup operation, winter deer range management, fur bearing animal management, lake and stream management, geology and trail planning for activities including cross-country skiing. For more detailed information contact the centre at Dorset, Ont. P0A 1E0 or phone (705) 766-2451.

Nordic Inn
Location: From Dorset north 1.5 km (1 mi.) on Hwy. 35.
Length: Total of 16 km in 4 loops. Travel time about 5 hr. for all trails.

Trails are in rolling hardwood country. Yellow and Green trails are for beginners and intermediate skiers. Red trail is designed for experts and intermediate skiers, consisting of several steep declines and uphills, including sharp turns. Right in centre of trail system is one of the largest deer wintering areas and the animals are frequently seen by skiers. Warm-up and waxing hut. Night skiing on 2 km of lighted trail. Open year round, 7 days a week, fully licenced dining room. Accommodation for up to 40 people. Also two motels at Dwight, 18 km (11 mi.) to the north. Maps available at resort.

Sir Sam's Inn
Location: From Haliburton north 16 km (10 mi.) on Hwy. 519.
Length: 8 km.

The lodge, located on the shore of Eagle L., has groomed trails running through nearby woodlands. Accommodation, dining room and ski rentals.

Southeastern Ontario

Sibbald Point Provincial Park
Location: South shore of Lake Simcoe, 4.8 km (3 mi.) east of Sutton, 1.6 km (1 mi.) north of Hwy. 48.
Length: Total of 4.8 km in 3 loops.

Level terrain, partially wooded and open. Trails are marked and used for both snowshoeing and cross-country skiing. Skating rink, snowmobile trail. Open 7 days a week, entry fee. Camping in the park, electrical outlets, firewood. Motels on Highway 48 and in Jackson's Point. For brochure and information, write the Park Superintendent, RR 2, Sutton West, Ont. Cross-country ski races in conjunction with the Sutton Winter Carnival, organized by Chamber of Commerce, Sutton.

Mosport Park Ltd.
Location: From Bowmanville north 19 km (12 mi.) on Liberty St.

For much of the year this internationally known race track does not hear the whine of super-tuned engines and the scream of tires. It is actually situated on 700 acres of peaceful farming country suitable for such activities as cross-country skiing. Instruction, rentals, snack bar, trail fee. Open weekends.

Enniskillen Conservation Area
Location: In municipality of Newcastle, north of Durham County Rd. 7 on Rd. No. 10.
Length: skiing on 66 acre tract.

This area of open and wooded land is located on the Bowmanville Creek. Area has heated shelter and coffee shop, skating on farm pond, cross-country and downhill skiing, tobogganing and snowshoeing. Area operated by Central Lake Ontario Conservation Authority, 1650 Dundas St. E., Whitby, Ont. L1N2K8

Durham County Forest
Location: North 16 km (10 mi.) from Newcastle on Hwy. 115.
Length: About 20 km.

Two marked hiking trails, the red and blue, start from car park but there are other forest roads which can be used to add several more kilometres to any trip. Suitable for all levels of ability. Main trails lead past Lookout Hill which gives view of downhill Kirby Ski Area to south. No patrols, so skiers should be equipped with map, compass and some emergency supplies. It should be noted this is a popular area with snowmobilers. Topographic map of 1:50,000 scale is Scugog sheet. Primitive toilets at car park. Restaurants in Kirby area just to south.

Kendal Recreation Area
Location: North of Newcastle on County Rd. 9 between Kirby and Kendal.

The area has a snowmobile trail and a separated area for cross-country skiers, snowshoers and tobogganers. Parking, skating rink, washrooms. For skiers who make their way along nature hiking trail there are good views to north and south. Below trail wanders through cedar bush.

Ganaraska Forest
Location: From Oshawa east on Hwy. 401, north on Hwy. 115 and 35 to Kirby. 10 km (6 mi.) east on county road 9 to left turn. Follow signs.
Length: Loop trails of 4, 8, 13 km.

Hilly, wooded terrain with views of the Oak Ridges glacial moraine. Graded intermediate. Maps available on site or from Ganaraska Conservation Authority, 56 Queen St., Port Hope, Ont. For information about special events contact Great Pine Ridge Cross-country Ski Club in Oshawa.

Northumberland County Forest
Location: From Coburg, 13 km (8 mi.) north of Hwy. 401 on Hwy. 45, turn left at Beagle Club Rd.
Length: Loop trails of 3.2 and 4.8 km. Graded beginner to intermediate.

Trails wind through wooded, hilly terrain, pine plantations with views of Oak Ridges glacial moraine. Downhill ski club also in the county forest. Park at Beagle Club Rd. parking lot to avoid traffic of downhill skiers and snowmobilers. Maps available on site or from Ministry of Natural Resources, 322 Kent St. W., Lindsay, Ont.

Warsaw Caves
Location: From Peterborough northeast on County Rd. 4, north of town of Warsaw.
Length: 10 km.

This conservation area is based around an extensive collection of caves and kettles (potholes). Skiers use a system of trails also used for hiking during warmer months. Area of considerable geological interest. Caves were scoured from limestone bedrock by millions of gallons of water melting from Laurentide ice cap. Myriad of underground tunnels created by the Indian R., which is believed to have been 45 feet above its present level. Whirlpools filled with sand, pebbles and boulders believed to have scoured potholes. Area is mixture of mature forest, reforestation limestone plains, an area stripped to bedrock by fire and wind. For information and map contact Otonabee Region Conservation Authority, 727 Lansdowne St., Peterborough, Ont.

Cavendish Ski Area
Location: From Peterborough north 60 km (40 mi.) on Hwy. 507. Parking on west side, opposite Beaver Lake Rd. turnoff and at Red Lion Inn, 100 m. south.
Length: 6 km.

Ski area was developed in 1975 by four Toronto high school students working with an Opportunities for Youth grant and cooperation of landowners, the Coppys and Strongs. Traverses meadows, marshes, reforested areas, hardwood and mixed forest with stands of giant white pines. Generally rolling country with easy trails and advanced routes with some rugged sec-

tions. Three trails marked with colored arrows, paint and tape. Skiers are cautioned to expect the Coppy's horses on the trail and to give them the right of way. Also to keep gates closed and to treat the private property with respect. Red Lion Inn caters to skiers with rooms, meals, bar, washrooms, ski rentals and trail maps. Information and map from Glen Campbell, 55 Melrose Ave., Toronto, Ont. M5M 1Y6.

Connemara Camp and Centre
Location: Kawartha Lakes area. From Fenelon Falls north 27 km (17 mi.) on Hwy. 121 to Galway Rd., east 14 km (7.5 mi.) on Galway Rd. to Centre and sign.
Length: Loop trails ranging from 400 m to 8 km. For all levels of skiers.

Trails primarily wooded, some over open, hilly pasture, some over lake. Outstanding scenery and outdoor experience. Weekend program by reservation, instruction, lunch only, cookouts available. Group retreats, some overnight accommodation, natural marked trails. Weekday outdoor education sessions available for schools and youth groups. Snowbunny events for Juniors. For brochure and maps, write Connemara Camp and Centre, c/o Bruce and Patti Fleury, 52 Mid Pines Rd., Scarborough, Ont. or at the Centre RR 1, Kinmount, Ont.

Silent Lake Park
Location: North of Peterborough. From Apsley north 19.5 km (12 mi.) on Hwy. 28.
Length: 38 km in 3 loops for varying abilities: 2 to 6 hr. trips.

Silent Lake Provincial Park has a series of trails through a wooded, wilderness area around the lake. All water crossings are bridged. A 6 km trail suitable for novices or families has only gradual downhill runs. A 12 km route requires ability to sidestep up hills and snowplow down. The 20 km trail is for experienced touring skiers and winds around the lake with considerable variations in terrain and scenery. There are old roads and trails, open sections, flats and hills, beaver ponds, mature balsam and white birch stands along the way. The trail finishes with a good climb, then a downhill run to the finish in the parking lot. Grooming, map at start of trail. Lodging information from Apsley Tourist Assn., Apsley, Ont. K0L 1A0.

McKay Lake Trail
Location: Apsley.
Length: 5 km (about 1 hr.).

Trail in wooded terrain, starts from same

point as a snowmobile trail. Start is near motel and restaurant. This trail is less than 1 km from start of the annual Kawartha Tour, held each year in mid-February from Apsley to Buckhorn. Accommodation information from Apsley Tourist Assn., Box 383, Apsley, Ont.

Kawartha Ski Tour Trail
Location: Kawartha Lakes region north of Peterborough. Trail runs between Apsley and Buckhorn.
Length: 59 km in three major sections with small loops being added.

This is the scene, in the middle of each February, of the Kawartha Tour, a major event preceding the Canadian Ski Marathon. Tour runs from Apsley south and west to Buckhorn, 33 km (20 mi.) north of Peterborough. Trail is in three main sections: Apsley to Haultain (23 km, 4 hr.), Haultain to Deer Bay (20 km, 3 hr.) and Deer Bay to Buckhorn (16 km, 2 ½ hr.). This is a very scenic area, but aside from the time of the race is considered mostly wilderness and trail officials advise skiers to travel in parties with map, compass and proper touring equipment. Conditions are sometimes rugged and Haultain to Deer Bay section has considerable ice travel. Apsley to Haultain section has some difficult hills. In general a mostly wooded trail with some open areas. Good possibilities for spotting wildlife. Trail marked with orange signs. Maps from Kawartha Nordic Ski Club Inc., Box 1371, Peterborough, Ont. Information on the tour and lodging from Kawartha Tourist Assn., 393 Water St., Peterborough.

Buckhorn Wilderness Centre
Location: North of Peterborough. From Buckhorn east 6 km (4 mi.) on Hwy. 36.
Length: About 15 km.

For skiers who don't want to tackle the whole Kawartha Tour trail there is a sampling of the skiing at this centre. Located in hilly, wooded country just north of Lower Buckhorn lake in the Kawarthas. Shelters.

Ski Bethany
Location: West of Peterborough. From Bethany village north on Hwy. 7A. 3.2 km (2 mi.).
Length: 3 km loop.

Bethany Ski Club, founded in 1927, is one of the oldest in Ontario. It is mainly a downhill resort, with a 380-foot high ski hill but club members report there have always been some cross-country skiers. Trail

passes through cedar woods and is suitable for all abilities. Deer, small game and birds in area. Grooming, chalet, snack bar, cookout, waxing hut, instruction can be arranged. For information contact Bethany Ski Club Inc., Box 472, Peterborough, Ont.

Devil's Elbow
Location: West of Peterborough. From Bethany north 5 km (3 mi.) on road to Omemee.
Length: 7 km.

This is both a downhill and cross-country ski resort in cedar wooded country. Some grooming, instruction, rentals, snack bar.

Caribou
Location: West of Peterborough. From Bethany north 5 km (3 mi.) on road to Omemee.
Length: 7 km.

This is strictly a cross-country ski area in rolling, cedar-wooded hill country. Overlooks tributary of Pigeon R.

Kawartha Ski Tour Trail
Location: Kawartha Lakes region north of Peterborough. Trail runs between Apsley and Buckhorn.
Length: 59 km in three major sections with small loops being added.

This is the scene, in the middle of each February, of the Kawartha Tour, a major event preceding the Canadian Ski Marathon. Tour runs from Apsley south and west to Buckhorn, 33 km (20 mi.) north of Peterborough. Trail is in three main sections: Apsley to Haultain (23 km, 4 hr.), Haultain to Deer Bay (20 km, 3 hr.) and Deer Bay to Buckhorn (16 km, 2 ½ hr.). This is a very scenic area, but aside from the time of the race is considered mostly wilderness and trail officials advise skiers to travel in parties with map, compass and proper touring equipment. Conditions are sometimes rugged and Haultain to Deer Bay section has considerable ice travel. Apsley to Haultain section has some difficult hills. In general a mostly wooded trail with some open areas. Good possibilities for spotting wildlife. Trail marked with orange signs. Maps from Kawartha Nordic Ski Club Inc., Box 1371, Peterborough, Ont. Information on the tour and lodging from Kawartha Tourist Assn., 393 Water St., Peterborough.

Buckhorn Wilderness Centre
Location: North of Peterborough. From Buckhorn east 6 km (4 mi.) on Hwy. 36.

Length: About 15 km.

For skiers who don't want to tackle the whole Kawartha Tour trail there is a sampling of the skiing at this centre. Located in hilly, wooded country just north of Lower Buckhorn lake in the Kawarthas. Shelters.

Devil's Elbow
Location: West of Peterborough. From Bethany north 5 km (3 mi.) on road to Omemee.

Length: 7 km.

This is both a downhill and cross-country ski resort in cedar wooded country. Some grooming, instruction, rentals, snack bar.

Caribou
Location: West of Peterborough. From Bethany north 5 km (3 mi.) on road to Omemee.

Length: 7 km.

This is strictly a cross-country ski area in rolling, cedar-wooded hill country. Overlooks tributary of Pigeon R.

Kuglin Trail
Location: North of Belleville. Start at Kuglin Farm on Hwy. 14, 4.8 km (3 mi.) west of Foxboro.

Length: 13 km.

This trail runs as a loop through the Kuglin and neighboring Ketcheson farms. Marked with blue metal strips at eye level and white directional signs with skier symbol. Maps and more information about trails for winter and summer and about lodging from Quinte-Hastings Recreational Trail Assn., 14 Bridge St. W., Belleville, Ont. K8P 1H7.

Ganaraska Trail
Location: A partially completed 500 km trail through Southern Ontario from Port Hope to Glen Huron.

The Ganaraska was started in 1967 after the Bruce Trail was finished and first pushed north from Port Hope on Lake Ontario. In 1970 the trail association was formed to continue the new route until it joined the Bruce at Glen Huron, about 16 km south of Collingwood. By mid-1976, about 320 km of trail were complete, including sections from Port Hope north to Omemee, northeast of Lindsay in the Kawarthas, from Glen Huron to Coulsen and a branch trail from Weybridge to Coldwater in the Midland area. It was designed as a hiking trail but much of it is usable for cross-country skiing and snowshoeing.

The route is through pleasant rural land. In the Port Hope area there are pine forests, the Kawarthas have the scenic ruggedness of the Canadian Shield, west of Orillia there are sand hills, near Midland is the Wye Marsh Wildlife Centre and the Glen Huron area includes a section by the beautiful Mad River valley. A branch trail passes the historic Ste. Marie reconstructed Jesuit mission where priests were martyred during Indian wars four centuries ago. Trail marked with brown arrows on white, but maps necessary. Write: Ganaraska Trail Assn., Box 1136, Barrie, Ont. L4M 5E2.

Sidney Trail
Location: North of Belleville. Access points at: Pine Hill Crescent on Hwy. 62, 4.8 km (3 mi.) west of Foxboro; Gallivan Road at Hwy. 14, 8 km (5 mi.) northwest of Foxboro; southeast corner of Oak Hills Flying Club field, between Concessions VI and VIII; Concession VI and Fish and Game Club Road, 1.6 km (1 mi.) northeast of Frankford.

This is part of the original hiking trail suitable for cross-country skiing and is a linear trail, not a loop. It is marked with orange metal strips and orange symbols of a hiker. Maps and more information about trails for winter and summer and about lodging from Quinte-Hastings Recreational Trail Assn., 14 Bridge St. W., Belleville, Ont. K8P 1H7.

Camp Inn Trail
Location: From Hwy. 62, 800 m east on Concession XII of Huntingdon Twp. (Quin-Mo-Lac Rd.).

Length: 13 km.

This is a loop trail operated by Jamie Campkin's Camp Inn and the Quinte-Hastings Recreational Trail Assn. just south of Moira Lake. Snack bar and lounge. Maps and more information about trails for winter and summer and about lodging from Quinte-Hastings Recreational Trail Assn., 14 Bridge St. W., Belleville, Ont. K8P 1H7.

Loyalist Trail
Location: start at parking lot west of William R. Kirk School, West Bridge Street, Belleville.

Length: 8 km.

Trail runs as loop between school and Loyalist Community College and is marked with blue metal strips at eye level. Also white directional signs with skier symbol. Maps and more information about trails for winter and summer and about lodging from Quinte-Hastings Recreational Trail Assn., 14 Bridge St. W., Belleville, Ont. K8P 1H7.

Proctor Conservation Area

Location: Trenton area. Village of Brighton. From Hwy. 2 north on Kingsley St. for 400 m.

Length: 2.5 km. Loop trail starts at parking lot off Kingsley St.

The trail crosses a small stream, Butler Creek, into cedar bush and semi-open level area along the creek, then back into the cedar bush up to a steep hill close to a mature maple-beech woodlot. From there across an open field, down a steep hill and into the cedar bush, across the creek and up a short hill to the parking area. Scenic lookout, wildlife viewing, interpretive nature trails, snowshoeing and winter hiking. Accommodation in Brighton. For information on the Conservation Area and trail conditions, write Lower Trent Region Conservation Authority, Box 180, Frankford, Ont. K0K 2C0.

Macaulay Mountain Conservation Area

Location: From Hwy. 33 on eastern outskirts of Picton, southeast on County Rd. 8 (Union St.) to access road. Trail starts near Recreational Shelter.

Length: Loop trail of 8 km. Travel time 1 hr. Extensive touring possibilities on plateau.

Trails runs along and below an escarpment with a maximum drop of 100-150 feet. Slope varies, providing a gentle grade at the eastern edge. A mature forest exists along the escarpment. Open grassland predominates in lower areas, north of the escarpment proper, and the plateau to the south of the escarpment is predominantly flat terrain covered with red cedar. Generally, the trail is not too difficult, except for a small portion which is particularly steep. The escarpment portion of the trail is laid through a mature climax forest in which can be found some Carolinian species and an especially interesting stand of mature hemlock. The slope trail provides scenic views of Picton Bay and the surrounding area. For lodging information, write Quinte's Isle Tourist Assn., 116 Main St., Picton, Ont. Maps at Shelter, 9 A.M. to 5 P.M.

Gould Lake Conservation Area

Location: From Sydenham northeast 10.5 km (6.5 mi.). Follow signs. 35.5 km (22 mi.) northeast of Kingston.

Length: 5 km of trails within the Rideau Trail System.

The trails traverse glacial land forms, rather varied, mostly through woods. The area is used by skiers of all ability but is quite popular with the more advanced ones. This 1,500-acre conservation area is a wilderness land with tremendous scenic value. A large number of porcupines, beavers, raccoons and the occasional white tail deer inhabit the area as do numerous bird species. Accommodation in the Kingston area. Contact the Kingston Chamber of Commerce, 209 Ontario St. Trail guide available free of charge from the Cataraqui Region Conservation Authority Office, RR 1, Glenburnie, Ont. K0H 1S0.

Little Cataraqui Creek Conservation Area

Location: From Exit 102 on Hwy. 401 at Kingston, north 1.6 km (1 mi.) on County Road 10.

Length: Loop trails of about 9 km. Travel time 2 to 3 hr.

This trail system traverses rolling terrain in a 1,000-acre conservation area. Some trails go through the woods while others cross open fields. It services skiers of all ability. Open daily. Natural skating rink with a small changing shelter. Snowshoeing. Accommodation in the Kingston Area. Contact the Kingston Chamber of Commerce, 209 Ontario St. Trail map available free of charge from the Cataraqui Region Conservation Authority Office, RR 1, Glenburnie, K0H 1S0.

Lemoine Point Conservation Area

Location: From Kingston travel to the end of Front Rd. (follow Airport signs) to the area.

Length: 4 km loop trail. Maximum travel time 1 hr.

The trails are located on a 337-acre conservation area with over a mile of shoreline on Lake Ontario. It is a most picturesque location for skiing, snowshoeing or hiking. The trail goes across a flat open field, then enters a wooded area covering an elevated portion of the shoreline. Can be used by all levels of skiers. Accommodation in the Kingston area. Contact the Kingston Chamber of Commerce, 209 Ontario St. Trail guide available free of charge from the Cataraqui Region Conservation Authority Office, RR 1, Glenburnie, Ont. K0H 1S0.

Rideau Trail

Location: Kingston to Ottawa via Rideau Canal.

Length: 400 km hiking trail with 210 km suitable for cross-country skiing.

The Rideau is one of Ontario's four major hiking trails and parts of it with no steep sections are suitable for skiing though not groomed. Trail starts on L. Ontario shore in the marshes of the Little Cataraqui and winds north to the Chaudiere Falls near Parliament Hill. Terrain ranges from serene pastoral to rugged Eastern Ontario wilderness. There is abundant wildlife and many historic sites. Follows route of the Rideau Canal, built in 19th century.

From start, trail heads north to Sydenham, then plunges into the spectacular wild country of Frontenac Park, an area of rocks and beaver dams. It winds through the Rideau Lakes region, along the Tay R. and past Perth, Smith Falls and Merrickville. To north it enters Ottawa from southwest past Bells Corner and joins Ottawa R. near Britannia Bay. Camping and fires only with land owners' permission. Many access points from roads. Trail marked with orange triangles, side trails with blue. Like its sister trails, the Rideau was built by interested citizens, about 1971. Club holds ski seminars, clinics, outings. Must join club (about $5) to get maps. Write Rideau Trail Assn., Box 15, Kingston, Ont. K7L 4V6.

Lanark Ski Trails
Location: From Perth southwest 19 km (about 12 mi.) on County Rd. 1 and the Elm Grove Rd.
Length: 3 trails of 1.6, 3.2 and 3.2 km.

The trails pass through open fields and hardwood areas. Two are loop trails, one the "Rideau Trail" is on the Rideau Walking Trail and must be travelled both ways. For beginners mostly. Numerous motels and hotels within half hour drive. Map at parking lot or free from Ontario Ministry of Natural Resources, Box 239, Lanark, Ont.

Depot Lake Trails
Location: From Hwy. 38 at Verona, northwest on Snider Rd.

Second Depot Lake and Hinchinbrooke Conservation Areas have numerous wilderness unmarked trails. 2,372 acres of wooded rugged terrain and frozen lakes in the Canadian Shield. Abundant wildlife and beautiful scenery. Various motels on Hwy. 38. Also in Kingston and Napanee. Topographic map: Tichborne 31 C/10, 1:50,-000. Authority plans to mark trails.

Buells Creek Conservation Area
Location: From Hwy. 401 at north edge of Brockville follow Hwy. 29 north 5 km (3 mi.), then 2.5 km. (1.5 mi.) east on Centennial Rd. to entrance on north side.

The 1,315-acre tract is operated by the Cataraqui Conservation Authority, RR 1, Glenburnie, Ont., which publishes a brochure on the area. It is not specifically developed as a cross-country ski area but can be used as such. There is already a hiking trail from the northeast corner around the west side of the reservoir, which occupies half the area. The land is mostly flat and forms part of the Smiths Falls Limestone Plain. Soil is shallow and flat beds of underlying dolomite rock can be seen around south side of pond when snow cover is thin. Low ridges north and west of pond were formed after last ice age 10,000 years ago.

Wildlife includes white tailed deer, beaver, muskrat, porcupine and small mammals. Early and late in ski season waterfowl start to gather at pond including Mallard and Blue-winged Teal. Woods include tamarack, white cedar, red maple, ash, white pine, hemlock, balsam fir, sugar maple, basswood, gray birch, ironwood and butternut. Wetlands have willows, red-osier dogwood, cattails and bullrushes. Historically the reservoir was a mill pond later drained to extract peat. Now the Broome-Runciman Dam is used to control flooding.

Maitlands Trails
Location: From Hwy. 2 at town of Maitland. For main entrance to orange trail go north 400 m on County Rd. 15. Entrance on west side of road opposite Esso station. Parking. Other parts of trail start in town.
Length: 30 km. 3 loop trails plus crossovers. Longest (orange) trail is 10 km with average travel time of 1 - 1 ½ hr.

Wooded terrain with gentle slopes. Rated good for all levels of skiers. Wildlife: rabbit, grouse, raccoon and fox. Rentals in sports shop in Brockville, 6.2 km (4 mi.) west of Maitland. Ski school Saturday mornings, mid-January to mid-February. Maps available at White House Motel on Hwy. 2 and at Esso Station. Orienteering held here in fall and inter-school ski races during winter. Trails were started in 1973 by Maitland Trails, Box 89, Maitland, Ont. K0E 1P0, an active trail group. For accommodation information contact Brockville Chamber of Commerce.

Charleston Lake Provincial Park
Location: 14.5 km (9 mi.) north of Lansdowne, just off County Road 3, 22.5 km (14 mi.) northeast of Gananoque.
Length: Trails of 5, 6.5, 10 km, graded beginners to intermediate. Trip time 1 to 2 hr.

Charleston Lake is a 1,900-acre Natural Environment Park which preserves areas of natural, scenic and historical significance. It is situated on the edge of a narrow extension of the Canadian Shield, with fields, wooded valleys, open ridgetops, swamps, marshes and forest. Wildlife includes porcupine, ruffed grouse and red fox. Winter birdwatchers may find blue jays, white-breasted nuthatches, black-capped chickadees and woodpeckers. Trail grooming. Two warming cabins located along the trails with a stove and a supply of firewood. A toboggan, first aid kit and blankets are provided for emergency use. Two snowshoe trails. Trail brochure available free from park or Ministry of Natural Resources District Office in Brockville. 1:50,000 topographical maps of the Charleston Lake area are as follows: Westport 31 C/9, Brockville 31 B/12, Gananoque 31 C/8 and Mallorytown 31 B/5.

Ottawa Valley

Carillon Provincial Park
Location: 17 km (11 mi.) east of Hawkesbury on Hwy. 417.
Length: Loop trails of 8 km.

1,700 acres of wooded and open gently rolling terrain in a natural state along south shore of Ottawa River. There is a variety of wildlife and tree species. Lookout located at Carillon Dam. Ice travel on Ottawa River not recommended due to fluctuating water levels. This is a provincial park and maps are available at park office. Accommodation in Hawkesbury.

Larose County Forest
Location: East of Ottawa about 48 km (30 mi.) and 8 km (5mi.) north of Casselman. From Hwy. 417 take Limoges Exit.
Length: County forest of about 26,000 acres with 1,000 acres reserved for cross-country skiers. Much of the rest is available but used by snowmobilers, who have 160 km of trails. Snowshoeing. Hunting in season. Maps from Ministry of Natural Resources, Box 10, Bourget, Ont.

'Y' Ski and Outdoor Center
Location: From Ottawa west 16 km (10 mi.) on Queensway, north 6.4 km (4 mi.) on Hwy. 17, turn right, 90 m to Regional Rd. 8, turn right again towards Ottawa River, 6.4 km (4 mi.) to ski centre.
Length: Loop trails of 3.2 km.

144 acres of wooded area. 2.5 m wide trails on flat and hilly terrain. Trails groomed. Weekend operation with focus on instruction, novice to intermediate levels. Snowshoeing, skating, tobogganing, sleigh rides. Groups may rent facilities for parties. Dining hall and chalet. Bunk house accommodation, bring sleeping bag. For information, write Ottawa YM-YWCA, 180 Argyle Ave., Ottawa, Ont. Registration Office.

Ottawa Area
The National Capital Commission lists five distinct cross-country ski areas in Ottawa plus another in Hull. In addition there is a large cross-country and downhill ski resort at Camp Fortune, just north of Hull. Area residents can get a brochure with sketch maps of the areas by phoning the NCC (613) 992-4321. Skiing areas range from parkland in the middle of Ottawa to creeks and swamps on the outskirts. In addition there is skiing on the Rideau R. when ice conditions are safe, along some parts of the Ottawa R. shoreline and on parts of the bikeway. There are numerous possibilities in parks throughout the region.

Hogs Back and Vincent Massey Parks
Location: On east bank of Rideau R. north and south of Heron Ave.

Two modest trails form loops along the river bank and inland. From here a skier can travel further afield along the river bank using the bikeway system.

Stony Swamp Ski Trails
Location: Access at several points in Bells Corners, NepeanTwp., west of Ottawa. Major access from Cedarview Rd. near Bell High School.
Length: About 30 km of trails, mostly in loops, ranging up to 17 km. On 3,000 acres.

Stony Swamp is under the care of three organizations: the National Capital Commission owns the land, Ministry of Natural Resources manages the land and is planting trees and the Nepean Parks and Recreation Dept. has co-ordinated and extensively studied the development of ski trails since 1973. Parks officials feel it is a rare example of a major cross-country ski area so near a large urban area. Some waxing and ski instruction is offered. Maps at parking lot. Some races.

Trails wander from built-up area south and west into undeveloped land, skirting the occasional road. Terrain is mostly level and

Skiers setting out along a popular trail in Hiawatha Park.

there are fields, cedar bogs, pine barrens, coniferous and deciduous forests and beaver ponds. Area is a bird haven and animals include fox, squirrel, ground hog, skunk, beaver and porcupine. Geologically it is Nepean sandstone, sandy dolomite and limestone laid down during Cambrian and Ordovician periods, about 500 million years ago. Old Quarry Trail passes exposed rocks 450 million years old and fossil sea shells can be seen in the rocks. Other trails pass beaver cuttings and demonstration plots for forestry studies. Sketch map on NCC Winter Trails folder and information from Nepean Parks and Recreation Dept., 1701 Woodroffe Ave., Ottawa, Ont. K2G 1W2.

Pinhey Forest
Location: Nepean Twp. Starts at Sportsplex on Woodroffe Ave. just north of Slack Rd.
Length: 6 km.
Two trail loops have been developed north and south of Slack Rd. in area that is mainly forested but has some open fields. Surrounding area partially developed. Maps at Sportsplex and on National Capital Commission Winter Trails folder.

Green Creek-Mer Bleue Trails
Location: Centred around Blackburn Hamlet on eastern edge of Ottawa.
Length: About 30 km.
Just six miles from the Parliament Buildings, a long network of trails ranges through parkway belt land largely following the Green Creek inland from its mouth at the Ottawa R. near Lower Duck L. The trail passes west of Blackburn Village, then follows the creek as it swings eastward into the large swamp area known as Mer Bleue. The trail makes several loops along the way and brushes past the Magnetic Laboratory of the Dept. of Energy, Mines and Resources before heading further south across Borthwick Cr. There is access and parking at the toboggan slide at Orleans Rd. and at several other points including two places on the dead-end extension of Ridge Rd. east of County Rd. 42. Sketch map with fair detail on National Capital Commission Winter Trails folder.

Pine Grove
Location: Just south of Ottawa city limits, east and west of Hwy. 31 near Kempark and Canadian Forces Base Leitrim.

These are two loop trails in National Capital Commission greenbelt forest at the city's edge. The small loop of about 5 km starts at Capital Golf Gardens just north of Kempark. A much more extensive network of seven trails is located north of CFB Leitrim and touches several roads, including Davidson Rd., and Conroy Rd. Main access points off Davidson Rd. west of Hawthorne and Leitrim Rd. east of Hawthorne. Map on NCC Winter Trails folder.

Nangor Cross-Country Resort
Location: From Pembroke 8 km (5 mi.) east on Hwy. 17, then 29 km (18 mi.) northeast on County Roads 21 and 12. From Westmeath 8 km (5 mi.) to northeast.
Length: Four loops of 2, 2.2, 5 and 8.2 km. Links and connections give variety of 10 trails from 1 to 8.2 km. Unlimited off-trail skiing. All abilities.

The trails are in 400 acres of woodland with hills of 25 to 30 feet and one 55-foot hill of which 25 feet is man-made, possibly the only man-made cross-country ski hill in Canada. Some skiing on bay with ice normally safe from December to March. Abundant wildlife: birds, small animals and a few deer. Trails overlook Laurentian Hills. Lighted skating rink, moonlight skiing, lessons, snowshoeing, babysitting, snowmobiles prohibited. Dining room with lounge and fireplace. Accommodation at Nangor Lodge for 56 persons. Trail maps at lodge or write Nangor Lodge, Westmeath, Ont. K0J 2L0. Trails laid out and maintained by owner who has skied 45 years.

Petawawa Forest Station Trails
Location: From Chalk River south 6.5 km (4 mi.) on station access road.
Length: 50 km in a network of 7 trails plus connections.

Petawawa Forest Experiment Station of the Canadian Forestry Service has opened its large forest area to cross-country skiers. Many trails have been marked along fire control roads and others blazed by skiers including members of the forest station staff, with some official help by the station. This large network is used for some of the celebrations of the annual Silver Spoon Festival held on second weekend in February and based in nearby Deep River.

Trails are color coded and one is marked with signs explaining forest ecology and forestry operations at research station. No regular grooming. Station advises that terrain is not generally difficult but skiers should travel in groups and treat this as a wilderness outing. Varied species of trees and areas where trees undergoing special treatments. Hilly country with some ridges giving good views of surrounding countryside, small lakes. Various access points from road through station as plowed. Compass advisable. Maps available at station or write for maps and information to: C. E. Van Wagner, Canadian Forestry Service, Petawawa Forest Experiment Station, Chalk River, Ont. K0J 1J0.

Silver Spoon
Location: Eastern edge of Deep River, near Ottawa R. From Hwy. 17 east on Town Line Rd., then southeast on Pembroke-Mattawa Rd. about 500 m and park on south side of road.
Length: 14 km, about 2-3 hr. in five loops ranging from 1.5 to 5 km.

Site of Silver Spoon Grand Prix ski race, part of Silver Spoon Festival, traditionally held second weekend in February. Race draws several hundred competitors from recreational skiers to Olympic racers and is considered a preliminary for many who enter Canadian Ski Marathon at end of February. The trails run through woods and at places give good views of Ottawa R. and Laurentian Hills. Trails marked and maps posted at loop intersections. Loops run north and south of road, along Kennedy's Cr. and to edge of Ottawa R., crossing clearings, bridges and some open fields. For inexperienced to average ability. Maintained by club members. Lodging in Deep River.

3-M Ski Trail
Location: West end of Deep River, starting at the local Mount Martin Ski Hill.
Length: 5 km. Travel time 1 hr.

3-M ski trail (Mount Martin McAnulty) varies from wooded to open terrain and is very undulating but safe for skiers of all abilities. It has been designed as a race course for local program and is safe under even icy conditions. Fine views of the Ottawa River and the Laurentian Hills. Mount Martin Ski Club maintains a small chalet at top of ski hill. Downhill facilities. Accommodation in Deep River. Maps available in chalet. Local time trial races held most Saturday afternoons. Trail maintained by local ski enthusiasts.

Northern Ontario Trails

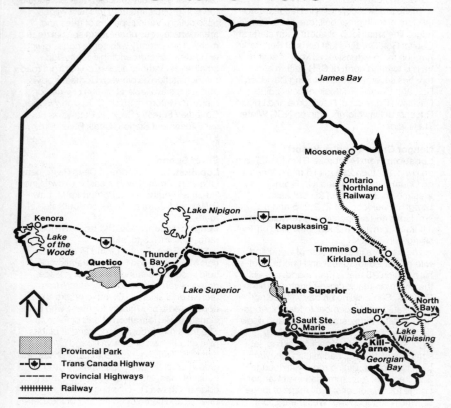

James Bay

Moosonee ○

Ontario
Northland
Railway

Kenora

*Lake
of the
Woods*

Quetico

Thunder
Bay

Lake Nipigon

Kapuskasing ○

Timmins ○
Kirkland Lake

Lake Superior

Lake Superior

Sudbury ○

North
Bay

*Lake
Nipissing*

Sault Ste.
Marie ○

**Kill-
arney**

*Georgian
Bay*

Provincial Park
Trans Canada Highway
Provincial Highways
Railway

Northeastern Ontario

Mattawa Wild River Area
Location: Along Mattawa R., east of North Bay from Trout L. to Samuel De Champlain Provincial Park.

The two parks along this beautiful, wild river, a major route of the voyageurs and explorers, comprise 14,000 acres of rugged Northern Ontario countryside. Skiing on trails, particularly portage trails used by canoeists in summer. Snowshoeing. Snowmobiling on park roads only. This is wild country, though it lies just north of Hwy. 17, and should be treated as such by anyone planning extensive travel.

Laurentian Ski Club
Location: In city of North Bay.

Length: About 5 km.

North Bay skiers have a combination cross-country and downhill ski area at their doorsteps. Part of loop trail system is on ski club property and part in adjacent forest. Climbs rolling, forested hills and provides excellent views over city and L. Nipissing. Lights for downhill night skiing illuminate some of the cross-country trails. Guided tours weekends. Ski school, rentals and food.

Larocque's Maple Sugar Shack
Location: Northern outskirts of North Bay, off Cedar Heights Rd. just east of Gormanville Rd.
Length: 6 km

This is a long, loop trail which can easily be broken into smaller loops by cutting over to the return track early. The Sugar Shack is located southeast of the intersection and the trail crosses Cedar Heights Rd. and runs parallel to Gormanville Rd.

North Bay Nordic Ski Club
Location: From North Bay east 16 km (10 mi.) on Hwy. 63, then south at Redbridge on the Songis Road for 14.5 km (9 mi.) to Camp Conewango.
Length: Four trails of 5, 7.5, 8.6 and 8.7 km.

Trails are in rolling, wooded country north of Mattawa R. and Lake Talon. Groomed by club with track setter. Rentals, cabins and some meals at Camp Conewango. Annual races and other activities of ski club. Map available from club or obtain 1:50,000 scale map North Bay 31 L/6 East.

Killarney Provincial Park
Location: South of Sudbury on north shore of Georgian Bay. From Hwy. 69 southwest on Hwy. 637.

Killarney is a uniquely beautiful area in Ontario. In addition to a generous sprinkling of lakes among its forests, it is traversed by the La Cloche Mountains, rising as much as 1,000 feet above the surrounding countryside. These low mountain ranges of white quartz are spectacularly beautiful as they rise precipitously from the shores of frozen lakes. The area has long been a favorite with artists, including members of the Group of Seven. One of its lakes is named OSA after the Ontario Society of Artists.

It is a beautiful land but also remote and wild, particularly in winter. Parties of cross-country skiers should be prepared for mountain-type skiing if they venture onto the high ground of steep cliffs and deep, snow-filled gullies. The area is very popular with canoeists in summer and it is possible to follow some canoe routes over lakes, rivers and portage trails when the waterways are well frozen. There is also a summer hiking trail, starting from the George Lake campground, but in many places it crosses steep ground and travel can be difficult on skis. Good map of 85,000-acre park available from sources including Parks Branch, Ministry of Natural Resources, Queen's Park, Ont.

Nordics Ski Club
Location: Starts at Dowling Community Hall, town of Dowling.
Length: Main trail is a 5 km loop with cut-off trails of 1, 2 and 3 km. Full trail takes 40 min. for average skier.

Dowling is 20 mi. northwest of Sudbury and trails are in area south and east of the town's community hall. The area is wooded with small conifers and hardwoods and the trails traverse some alder swamps. Arena near community centre has snackbar weekends and weekdays from 4-10 P.M. Skating in arena. Trails groomed and map available from Andy Ramta, President, Nordics Ski Club, Dowling, Ont. (send self-addressed, stamped envelope). Open race late December or early January. Winter carnival race mid-February. Accommodation in town and area.

Voyageur Trail
Location: A 400 km trail for hiking, cross-country skiing and snowshoeing from South Baymouth on Manitoulin I. to Gros Cap, west of Sault Ste. Marie. Runs along north shore of Lake Huron.

This ambitious trail project was started in 1973 by a group of northern residents with some help from Southern Ontario hikers, including members of the Bruce Trail Assn. The Voyageur route is seen as an extension of the Bruce, picking up across Georgian Bay from the tip of the Bruce Peninsula. It passes through such north shore communities as Little Current, Espanola, Spanish, Blind River, Thessalon and the Soo, then ends 40 km further west at a rock promontory in L. Superior. Long range plans call for it to push east to the Ottawa Valley and northwest across the top of L. Superior as a major link in what could become a transcontinental trail series starting with the Appalachian in Georgia and ending with the Pacific Crest in Baja California.

As of 1976, only some parts of the Voyageur have been completed and not all areas are suited for skiing as the country is very rugged. It wanders through hemlock forests, crosses many streams, skirts lakes and beaver ponds and climbs the glistening, white quartz hills of the La Cloche range just west of Killarney. For much of its length, the trail passes along a very rugged escarpment, twisting and turning to avoid major natural obstacles. In many areas blue blazes indicate side trails to points of interest and lookouts. Main trail is marked with white blazes, like the Bruce Trail. Every 500 m there are blue on yellow, diamond-shaped markers to indicate distance travelled. Numerous access points are marked with green and white signs.

Like the Bruce, this trail is being built by local clubs along its length and much of it crosses private land. Users are asked to respect this fact. Since this is dense wilderness in most places, skiers should be in parties experienced in and equipped for such travel. Map and compass necessary. For information and details on what parts of the trail are usable, contact Voyageur Trail Assn., Box 66, Sault Ste. Marie, Ont.

Fort Creek Conservation Area
Location: Geographic centre of Sault Ste. Marie. Runs north from Hwy. 550 (Second Line), 2.5 km (1.5 mi.) west of Hwy. 17.
Length: 4 km of trails on 180 acres.

The wooded ravine park in the heart of a major city is a unique feature and is within walking distance of many residents. It is used year-round for such activities as skiing, snowshoeing, hiking, canoeing and nature study. Ski trails groomed. There is a network of trails, including a Parcours Vita with exercise equipment at stations along one trail. Vegetation study stations have been established for students and other interested persons.

The natural forest covering the headwaters of the Fort Creek is located at about a 900-foot elevation at the foot of the Prince Landscape and runs three miles through watershed ravines to dam at margin of Algonquin Terrace. Flood control dam has created large reservoir. From there Korah Bench marks drop to Nipissing terrace and older parts of city. Part of woods are mixed Great Lakes-St. Lawrence, characteristic of Southern Ontario, while on cooler northern slopes there is Boreal forest of conifers. For winter, a warming hut can be used by contacting Sault Ste. Marie Conservation Authority, 99 Foster Dr., Civic Centre.

Hiawatha Park
and Crystal Creek Conservation Area
Location: From Sault Ste. Marie north 5 km (3 mi.) on Hwy. 17, then east 5 km (3 mi.) on fifth line road.
Length: A trail network from Sault Finnish Ski Club lodge. Trails of 2, 4, 5 and 10 km. Terrain varied with flat land and easy hills for short trails and more difficult terrain for longer runs. Area is wooded with hardwoods and some red pine reforestation. The Finnish club has built a large lodge of logs and, has snack bar, fireplace, steam baths and dance floor. Trails groomed and tracks set by machine. The area is popular with Soo skiers and is open all week. Club organizes a race in mid-winter and wilderness tours for members. Map posted in lodge. Accommo-

dation in Soo. Contact Chamber of Commerce, Sault Ste. Marie, Ont.

Lake Superior Provincial Park
Location: On east shore of Lake Superior between Sault Ste. Marie and Wawa.

This is a 500-square-mile park that is a favorite with wilderness touring skiers and snowshoers. Snowmobiles are prohibited. The country is mountainous and remote and skiers planning long trips should be well equipped. The Ministry of Natural Resources, Box 1160, Wawa, Ont. has topographic maps available and lists two trails. The Mijin-Old Woman Lake Trail starts from Hwy. 17 at Mijin Lake Access Rd., about 32 km (20 mi.) south of Wawa and the Gargantua Trail starts at Gargantua Rd., about 40 km (25 mi.) south of Wawa. These trails are maintained by the ministry but are under review. There are hundreds of miles of logging roads. The area is in the Algoma region, a rugged and high scenic part of Ontario favored by members of the Group of Seven Canadian painters. There are high cliffs and wild rivers and the spectacular Agawa Canyon, site of excursion train rides on Algoma Central Railway. Accommodation along Hwy. 17 and in Wawa.

Headwaters Program
Location: Temagami area.

Headwaters is an outfit which runs cross-country ski and snowshoeing trips through the frozen wilderness of Northern Ontario's Temagami region. The usual format is to bring groups in for one, two or three weeks and give people instruction not only in wilderness travel but in how to live in the Northern Ontario bush during winter. Some trips are specialized, that is for teachers or university students who are taking the program as an educational credit. The base camp is permanent but all groups spend at least two nights camping out. All equipment, including skis, winter clothing and sleeping bags, is provided. The travel is through heavy bush and across frozen lakes, with guides from the camp. For information write: Headwaters, Temagami, Ontario.

Temagami Area Trails
Location: A network of trails radiating from central area of eastern shore of Lake Temagami near town of Temagami.
Length: Range from less than 1 km to about 25 km, providing trips of one-half hour to one day.

The trails are maintained by Temtoa (Temagami Tourist Operators' Association) a group of eight camps, six of which are open in the winter. Write the association in Temagami, Ont. for brochure of members and they will provide details of the trails. The routes wander over lake and mainland logging roads and portage trails through pure Canadian Shield country: boreal forest of red and white pine, cedar, spruce, fir, poplar and birch. Trails are varied. Camps will pack a lunch or provide a hot meal if you return at noon. Ice fishing for lake trout, whitefish and pickerel. Loon Lake Lodge, Temagami, Ont., has ski and snowshoe rentals and will provide instruction if requested in advance.

Temagami has long been a favorite summer recreation area, particularly for canoeists and fishermen. It is starting to develop as a winter sports area. The wilderness around the region offers extensive possibilities for wilderness tours and winter camping.

Camp Wanapitei

Location: From Temagami 29 km (18 mi.) by ski plane or by Milne Lumber Co. forest road.

Length: Unlimited possibilities in wilderness with a number of regular trails on paths, portage trails, abandoned logging roads and frozen waterways.

Camp Wanapitei dates back to the early part of the century as a canoe camp, particularly for young people and is one of the better known ones in Ontario. Staff members always returned during the winter to cut and store ice for the summer season. At first they generally used snowshoes, but some acquired cross-country skis and from there came the idea of opening the camp for winter ski tours.

Temagami area is very scenic with numerous waterways, dense forests and rocky outcrops typical of Canadian Shield. Trails of 30 km and longer are used for long day trips and winter camping trips can be organized with staff as guides. Skiers must arrange accommodation in advance and can charter a small plane or drive to near camp and ski in last 1500 m. Lodging is in frame cabins heated by wood stoves and skiers bring own sleeping bags good for temperatures down to about 5 degrees Celsius in addition to ski and touring equipment.

Skiers usually head out for short or day trips with members of camp staff and pack a lunch. Trails range from novice to expert and cross areas from flat to hilly and heavy bush to lightly treed. There is an unlimited

opportunity for bushwhacking on skis or trying out snowshoes. At night skiers eat in dining cabin. Evenings tend to be convivial with singsongs, square dances and parties. Room for 35 visitors.

The camp is normally opened during the mid and late March to cover the period of school breaks as it is popular with families. If a group reserves ahead it can be opened other weekends. For information write: Tom Roach, Box 1093, Peterborough, Ont. or Bruce Hodgins, 7 Engleburn Pl., Peterborough.

Kettle Lakes Provincial Park

Location: From Timmins east 32 km (20 mi.) on Hwy. 101, then north 3.2 km (2 mi.) on Hwy. 67.

Length: 3 and 6 km loop trails. Maximum travel time 2 hr.

Wooded gentle to flat terrain, ideal for beginners. Open picnic shelter on 6 km loop. Privies. Accommodation in Timmins area. Marked trail system.

Porcupine Ski Runners

Location: Timmins area. 800 m east of Shumacher on Hwy. 101.

Length: 10 km of groomed trails.

Relatively flat wooded terrain. Trail is on private land owned by Pamour-Porcupine Mines Ltd. Trail fee or season membership. Very limited facilities, small waxing hut. Expansion planned. Accommodation in Timmins, contact Chamber of Commerce, Hwy. 101, Ont.

Raven Mountain Ski Resort

Location: From Kirkland Lake east 47.5 km (29 mi.) on Hwy. 66.

Length: Loop trails of .75, 2 and 4 km. One straight trail of 5 km.

All wooded trails with considerable slope. Some wildlife: moose, rabbits, birds. Downhill skiing. Accommodation available in Kirkland Lake. Contact Chamber of Commerce, Kirkland Lake or Bruce Morris, President, Raven Mountain Ski Club. Resort holds special events. Trails maintained.

Otto Lake Hiking and Ski Trails

Location: West of Kirkland Lake. Culver Park, Swastika.

Length: 4.8 km, several loops. Travel time 2 hr.

Trail wanders through rolling woodland. Wildlife in area, snowshoe hare, fox, squirrel, otter and moose. Scenic rapids can be seen from south side of trail. For lodging information, write Chamber of Commerce, Kirkland Lake. Maps available at Parks and Recreation Office, above Arena Kirkland Lake, Ont.

Kap-kig-iwan Provincial Park

Location: South of Kirkland Lake. From Englehart south 3 km (2 mi.) on park access road.

This attractive, 720-acre park on the Englehart R. is heavily forested with poplars and some hardwoods. Land is rolling with an attractive river valley and frequently steep banks. Park is known for very scenic High Falls and series of rapids upstream from the falls. Good photographic possibilities.

Hearst Cross Country Ski Club

Location: From Hearst north 4.8 km (3 mi.) on Hwy. 583.

Length: About 16 km of double set tracks.

All trails are about 3.5 m wide, double lane, identified with painted blazes on trees, distances well-marked, groomed. Flat to gently rolling terrain does not offer much challenge but various timber types and length of well-maintained trails provide good skiing potential. All water crossings bridged. Two shelters, coffee in main shelter (1 P.M. to 8 P.M.), 5 picnic areas with firewood, picnic tables, well-cleared hill area, rest of trails through forested area, 3 parking lots, outdoor privies. Monthly skiing night on Saturday nearest to full moon. For accommodation, write Hearst Board of Commerce, P.O. Box 1522, Hearst, Ont. Maps available on trails and panel board or main parking lot or through Board of Commerce.

Mattagami Ski Trail

Location: From Smooth Rock Falls, north on Hwy. 807.

Length: About 8 km. Extension planned to Legault's Lake.

Wooded, very hilly terrain, following the banks of the Mattagami River. Narrow scenic trail, one of the most challenging in area, natural and rustic. Open whenever snow permits. Trail marked. Warm-up cabin. Good ice fishing at Legault's L. Trapping in area. Accommodation in Smooth Rock Falls.

Chapleau Ski Club

Location: Starting point at the Chapleau Ski Hill on the north side of town.

Length: 11 km. Travel time 3 hr.

Easy trail, for beginners, located in heavily wooded area with some open spaces. Downhill facilities, snack bar. For accommodation, write Chamber of Commerce, Chapleau, Ont. Free map available from Chapleau Ski Club.

Northwestern Ontario

Nordic Ski Trail: Schreiber-Terrace Bay

Location: From Schreiber east 3.2 km (2 mi.) on Hwy. 17, then south on Schreiber dump road 500 m and east on road to gravel pit.

Length: About 4 km.

Trails of 3 loops up to total length of about 4 km and suited for novice to advanced ability. Land is wooded and ranges from rolling to hilly. It is close to the cliffs overlooking L. Superior. This trail has been established by the Ministry of Natural Resources, 435 James St. S., Box 5000, Thunder Bay, Ont. P7C 5G6 and the office should be contacted for map and information about condition of trails.

Sibley Park Trails

Location: Sibley Provincial Park. From Thunder Bay east on Hwy. 11 and 17 for 40 km (25 mi.) to Hwy. 587, then south to park entrance.

Length: About 50 km, 4 trails.

Sibley Park, located on a large peninsula jutting south into L. Superior, is a very scenic area. The high cliff at the south end has been dubbed the Sleeping Giant for the shape as seen from a distance. Cross-country and snowshoeing trails wander through this park, between lakes and streams, generally following summer park roads. They are groomed depending on use. One trail runs between two points on Hwy. 587, another forms a loop around L. Marie Louise and two others skirt the Sleeping Giant formation. As this trail is subject to review, users should first contact Ministry of Natural Resources, 435 James St. S., Box 5000, Thunder Bay, Ont. P7C 5G6. Map available.

Cascades Conservation Area

Location: In northeast section of Thunder Bay. From Hwy. 17, then Balsam St. N. to end.

Length: Two main ski trails totalling 3.7 km plus some small hiking trails on 353-acre park.

This park contains a variety of flora and fauna including large white pine and excellent views of the Current R. from rocky outcrops. It was named for a unique geological feature, a series of spectacular rapids which tumble down the river for 500 m. Trails are marked with colored triangular signs. Parking, picnic tables, snowshoeing. The park is part of a chain of ski trails reaching from Centennial and Trowbridge Falls parks in the city to Wishart Conservation area in the north. Maintained by Lakehead Region Conservation Authority.

Kamview Ski Area

Location: Southern outskirts of Thunder Bay. Southwest on Hwy. 61 10 km (6 mi.) then north 1.6 km (1 mi.) on 20th sideroad to parking on west side.

Length: Five loops totalling 15 km.

This cross-country ski area is in generally wooded area with terrain ranging from rolling to hilly. Some areas particularly, give good views of city of Thunder Bay, harbour and Kaministiquia River valley. Maps in box at plowed parking area. As this trail is subject to review, users should contact Ministry of Natural Resources, 435 James St. S., Box 5000, Thunder Bay, Ont. P7C 5G6.

Centennial Park

Location: Thunder Bay. From Hwy. 17-11 E. go south on Hodder Ave., then west on Arundel Street to Centennial Park Rd.

Length: Trail system includes 5 and 10 km racing trails and touring trails including one to Cascades Conservation Area, 10 km away.

Trails for all abilities including hilly and winding trails in forest area around park. Skiers cautioned to use trails since ice on Current River can be hazardous. All-night skiing at Trowbridge Falls Park to north along river. Parking. Some trail grooming by clubs, Ministry of Natural Resources. Sleigh rides, toboggan hill, some downhill skiing, skating on Boulevard Lake. Races organized by Thunder Bay Ski Club, Box 1085, Thunder Bay, Ont. and Reipas Sports Club, 879 John St., Thunder Bay. Lessons available to club members. Lodge, food. Maps on site and from City parks and recreation department, 141 South May St., Thunder Bay, P7E 5V3. Lodging information from Visitors and Convention Bureau, 193 Arthur St., Thunder Bay.

Wishart Conservation Area

Location: North of Thunder Bay on Hwy. 17, then north on Onion Lake Rd.

Length: 2 km on 525 acres.

This is part of a chain of parks leading from Thunder Bay and used for cross-country skiing. Tobogganing and snowmobiling. Maintained by Lakehead Region Conservation Authority.

Ignace Cross Country Ski Trail

Location: From Ignace southeast on Hwy. 17, then north 13 km (8 mi.) on Hwy. 599.

Length: Loop trails of 7 km in total.

Located in rugged northern Ontario wilderness, near the English River system. Wooded area. Trail skirts three small lakes. Trail groomed. Accommodation in Ignace. Map available free from Ministry of Natural Resources, P.O. Box 448, Ignace, Ont. P0T 1T0.

Kakabeka Falls Provincial Park

Location: From Thunder Bay west 29 km (18 mi.) on Hwy. 11.

Length: About 8 km.

Series of trails follow park summer roads to campgrounds through slightly hilly terrain on south side of area. Highly scenic region where Kaministiquia R. pours over 128-foot-high falls, called the Niagara of the North. History of the area tells that Green Mantle, daughter of an Ojibway chief, was captured by a raiding party of Sioux and was forced to guide the invaders to her tribe. Instead, she led them down the river to the mighty falls. Just before the attackers were swept over the cataract to their death on the rocks below, Green Mantle escaped and swam to shore. Legend says her spirit floats in the thick mists in the gorge below the falls and that the noise one hears is the rumbled anger of the Sioux.

Mink Lake Trail (Quetico Area)

Location: From Atikokan east 40 km (25 mi.) on Hwy. 11 to Dawson Trail Campgrounds, at east entrance of Quetico Provincial Park. Entrance on north side of highway.

Length: 3 loops ranging from 5 km (45 min.) to 15 km (2 hr.).

Trail was established by Ministry of Natural Resources on old logging roads just north of famous Quetico Provincial Park and trails are marked and groomed with a track setting machine after every snowfall. Snowmobiles prohibited. Area was formerly logged and trails are on rolling terrain with moderate hills. Suitable for all abilities and used by local schools. Free trail map from Ministry of Natural Resources, Atikokan, Ont. Area and contour maps available for a fee. Accommodation information from Atikokan Chamber of Commerce.

This trail lies just across the highway from Quetico, a favorite park with wilderness canoeists. It was the land of Ojibway trappers and route of the Voyageurs and the Dawson Trail, used by westbound settlers. Extensive wildlife including eagle, wolf, moose and small mammals and birds. Park is not marked for skiing but has obvious possibilities for the well equipped, touring skier. Canoeist's map available from Ministry of Natural Resources.

Sioux Lookout Trails
Location: In town of Sioux Lookout, central departure point at the curling arena on 3rd Ave.
Length: Network of 3 trails forming 2 loops of 4.8 km each or one of 8 km. Pelican L. is accessible directly from the trails.

The trails keep to gentle sloping valleys and are suitable for all levels of skiers. They pass through meadows and forests of spruce, pine, birch and poplars. Lodging information, write Sioux Lookout-Hudson Chamber of Commerce, Sioux Lookout, Ont. Topographical map: Sioux Lookout 52J, available at Ministry of Natural Resources, Sioux Lookout. Trails unmarked.

Dryden Ski Club
Location: From Dryden, north on Hwy. 601 for 11 km (7 mi.), then continue north on Reed Rd. for 9.5 km (6 mi.).
Length: Trails of 4.6, 6.8, 8, 9.6 km. Minimum travel time from 20 to 66 minutes. Graded intermediate.

Gently rolling terrain with a few small rock outcrops. All trails are interconnected and through treed area. Moose, deer, wolves can occasionally be found. Ski club open on weekends and holidays, lessons available. Downhill facilities. Food concession in ski chalet. Hills and trails patrolled by Canadian Ski Patrol. Accommodation available in Dryden. For further information contact Tourist Bureau, Dryden. Topographic maps available in the Ministry of Natural Resources office in Dryden. Annual club races for men, women and children around the first weekend in March. Skiers also use Wabigoon Lake and numerous snowmobile trails around the area.

Hopkin's Bay Cross-Country Ski Trails
Location: From Fort Frances east 16 km (10 mi.) on Hwy. 11, north on Reef Point and Hopkin's Bay Rds. Several access

points on east side of Hopkin's Bay Rd.
Length: Network of loop and open-end trails of about 12 km, tying in with Hydro Line (6.4 km), roads and Rainy Lake. Trails being expanded. Within the abilities of novice skiers.

Beautiful scenery along shore of Rainy L. and in forest of pine, birch, ash, cedar, and poplar. Hills up to 100 feet. Many summer cottages along the shoreline. Several resting spots with benches. Accommodation in Fort Frances. Maps available free of charge from Parks Supervisor, Ministry of Natural Resources, 922 Scott St., Fort Frances, Ont.

Mount Evergreen Ski Club
Location: From Kenora northeast 5 km (3 mi.) on Airport Rd.
Length: 4 loop trails from 4 to 13 km.

Beginner, intermediate and advanced trails. Canadian Shield offers wooded trails as well as gentle slopes (elevation up to 150 ft.). Open every weekend. Instruction available from certified instructors, rentals, chalet with change area and cafeteria, trails groomed and marked, cookout, downhill slopes. For accommodation information contact Tourist Reception Centre, Hwy. 17 W., Kenora, Ontario. Maps available. Club races for men and women in January, Kenora Carnival races in March.

Rushing River Provincial Park
Location: From Kenora east 26 km (16 mi.) on Hwy. 17, then south on Hwy. 71 to park.
Length: 3.2 km.

Trail follows unplowed summer road to campsites on the north side of Dogtooth Lake. Rushing River is a 395-acre Provincial Park bounded on three sides by Dogtooth L. and traversed by Rushing R. The attractive lake and landscape shelters a variety of animals—wolves, moose or deer. Winter visitors can see the tracks of red fox, ermine, mink, otter and beaver. There are many birds in the park. The ruffed grouse lives in the park all year round. The dominant forest tree is the jack pine, seeded naturally after a forest fire burned over this area in the early 1900s.

About 7,500 years ago, this region was covered by Lake Agassiz, the last glacial lake. The rounded bolders in the park were deposited by the last glacier. The park bedrock belongs to the Pre-Cambrian Shield. For more information, contact The District Manager, Ministry of Natural Resources, Provincial Building, Kenora, Ont.

Québec

A lunch break for a party of skiers touring through the wilderness of Québec's Parc des Laurentides.

At 594,860 square miles and with a population of more than six million, Québec is the country's largest province and its second most populous. It is also one of the best places to go for big cross-country ski trails – trail networks of more than 100 km. Nature made this possible with rolling, sometimes mountainous, forested countryside and on that structure skiers have cut and marked thousands of kilometres of trails.

Among the trail blazers of Québec and of Canada one man stands out as the person responsible for not only creating many of the routes but for inspiring others to continue and expand the work. That man is Herman Smith-Johannsen better known across the country as Jack Rabbit. He is known not only as an explorer of ski routes but as an inspiration to people to pursue the sport as he has done for a century.

One symbol of his work was the famous Maple Leaf Trail, a 130 km route running from near his home to Labelle, north of Mont-Tremblant. In the tradition of the European trails he laid the route between hotels so he and the skiers who followed would always find a place to sleep. Now much of that landmark of early Canadian skiing has been covered by the Laurentian Autoroute, but it inspired hundreds of more trails which now lead to and from inns and villages in this ski region just north of the metropolis of Montréal.

Since the days of the Maple Leaf Trail, cross-country skiing has blossomed across Québec. Some of the best trails systems are, of course, in the Laurentians, but the ski region of the Eastern Townships is developing an impressive collection. Like the upper Laurentians this area is semi-mountainous, thanks to the hills of the Appalachians. More centres of skiing lie along the south shore of the St. Lawrence and further east in the Gaspé. To the north are ski regions around the twin towns of Rouyn and Noranda, Québec City and along the north shore. Skiing is enthusiastically pursued far to the north at iron ore mining towns along the Labrador border.

The climate ranges from cold and stable in the north and northwest to temperate but changeable in the south. Ski seasons vary both with latitude and altitude so mountainous southern regions may hold snow into May. In the north weather can be severe through February and ski outfits often consist more of insulated clothing than knickers during the dead of winter. However, the ski season lasts on into spring.

Geographically Québec is divided into three regions. The northern four-fifths is a massive sweep of Precambrian Shield: boreal forests, granite peaks and cliffs, plateaus, rivers, lakes, swamps and muskeg. This is an area of vast resources such as wood, iron ore and hydro-electric power. The Appalachians, south of Québec City and in the Gaspé, are a continuation of the mountain range commonly associated with New England. The highest peaks in the province are in the 3,000 to 4,000 foot range. Most of the population has followed the earliest traditions of the French settlers and stayed in the third region, the rich agricultural area of the St. Lawrence and Ottawa River valleys.

The outstanding feature of Québec is the fact it is a Francophone province with a language and culture different from those in the rest of the Americas. For the tourist there is much to see, ranging from such historic and architectural features as the lower town and Plains of Abraham in Québec City to the Montréal showplaces of the Expo 67 site and the Olympic installations. There is a great variety of potables, ranging from a quart of beer to be swigged at a small grocery store or a bottle of French wine on the table to such traditional items as pea soup, maple syrup and Brome Lake duckling.

As a province with thousands of skiers and thousands of kilometres of ski trails, Québec was bound to develop its share of cross-country events. It is the scene of one of the world's major ski races, the Canadian Ski Marathon. Though it was only

		Mean Temperature In Celsius (Fahrenheit)		Snowfall In Mean Centimetres (Inches)
		Min	Max	
Montreal	Dec	-10.4 (13.3)	- 2.9 (26.8)	57.4 (22.6)
	Jan	-14.3 (6.2)	- 5.4 (22.2)	54.9 (21.6)
	Feb	-13.4 (7.8)	- 4.2 (24.5)	58.2 (22.9)
	Mar	- 6.4 (20.4)	1.8 (35.3)	35.1 (13.8)
Québec	Dec	-11.3 (11.6)	- 4.3 (24.2)	70.9 (27.9)
	Jan	-14.7 (5.6)	- 6.6 (20.1)	72.9 (28.7)
	Feb	-13.2 (8.3)	- 4.9 (23.1)	66.3 (26.1)
	Mar	- 7.1 (19.3)	.7 (33.3)	42.7 (16.8)
Magog	Dec	-10.7 (12.7)	- 2.4 (27.7)	81.8 (32.2)
	Jan	-14.9 (5.1)	- 4.4 (24.0)	77.0 (30.3)
	Feb	-14.1 (6.7)	- 2.9 (26.7)	75.4 (29.7)
	Mar	- 7.9· (17.7)	1.6 (34.9)	44.2 (17.4)
Gaspé	Dec	-10.7 (12.7)	- 3.0 (26.6)	58.4 (23.0)
	Jan	-15.1 (4.8)	- 6.1 (21.1)	80.0 (31.5)
	Feb	-15.1 (4.8)	- 5.3 (22.5)	74.9 (29.5)
	Mar	- 9.9 (14.2)	- 0.7 (30.8)	59.9 (23.6)
Trois Riviéres	Dec	-13.3 (8.1)	- 4.1 (24.6)	64.0 (25.2)
	Jan	-17.4 (0.6)	- 6.6 (20.2)	55.6 (21.9)
	Feb	-16.6 (2.1)	- 4.8 (23.4)	54.6 (21.5)
	Mar	- 9.3 (15.2)	1.6 (34.8)	40.1 (15.8)
Chicoutimi	Dec	-14.4 (6.1)	- 6.3 (20.6)	57.7 (22.7)
	Jan	-19.8 (- 3.6)	- 9.6 (14.8)	51.3 (20.2)
	Feb	-18.3 (- 1.0)	- 7.2 (19.1)	46.5 (18.3)
	Mar	-10.7 (12.8)	- 0.1 (31.8)	34.3 (13.5)

started in 1967, as a Centennial project, the mighty Marathon now draws thousands of skiers from across the continent and from Europe. In 1976 organizers set a limit of 3,000 skiers and had to turn away 300 late entries. The Marathon is a 160 km wilderness ski race through southwestern Québec from Lachute, just north of Montréal, to a point just north of Hull. Though racers may try to complete the course in two days to win gold medals, many citizens, ranging from as young as five years to skiers in their seventies and older, will ski one or more of the ten sections as their abilities dictate. Shuttle buses move people around and hot food and drink is handed out at checkpoints.

Traditionally the event is held in the last weekend of February, literally rain or shine and skiers contemplating a run at it are advised to have a medical checkup. Those entering the Coureur de Bois event must have a medical to ensure they are capable of trying to ski 80 km a day, some of them with a pack containing their food and sleeping gear for an overnight stay on the trail. Despite these teeth-gritting aspects rule number one of the event is: "All skiers must be cheerful and have a good time." The fact that thousands show up each year is an indication they do

Following is a list of some commonly used words both general and for the sport:

s'il vous plaît— please		raquette— snowshoe	
merci— thank you		piste— trail	
gaz— gasoline (in Québec)		relais— shelter	
fait le plein— fill it up		chauffé— heated	
ou est— where is		casse-croûte— snack	
je suis— I am		location— rental	
nombre— number		salle de fartage— waxing room	
longeur— length		réparation— repair	
boisé— wooded		chambre— hotel room	
colline— hill		hébergement— lodging	
pente— slope		garderie— babysitting	
facile— easy		parc— park	
débutant— beginner		stationment— parking lot	
intermédiaire— intermediate		voiture— car	
difficile— difficult		sortie— exit	
dangereux— dangerous		Nord— North	
attention— danger		Sud— South	
eau— water		Est— East	
neige— snow		Ouest— West	
glace— ice		ski de fond— cross-country skiing	
balisées— marked		ski de randonnée— ski touring	

just that. For information write: Canadian Ski Marathon, Box 315, Stn. A, Ottawa, Ont. K1N 8V3.

Second only to the Marathon in difficulty is Le Grand Fond, an event only for the experienced competitor or wilderness tourer. It was started in 1971 and is run through wilderness from Camp Mercier in Parc des Laurentides north of Québec. In 1976 there were ninety-four skiers who made it over a 70 km course with no exits. The first runner, who had to break trail through fresh snow at some points, completed the trip in just under six hours. Only 100 experienced skiers, usually those holding competitor's cards, are allowed to enter. For information write: SkiQuébec, 1415 est, rue Jarry, Montréal, Que., H2E 2Z7, or contact the Canadian Ski Assn., 333 River Rd., Tower A., Ottawa, Ont. K1L 8B9.

Anyone in Québec during early February will want to participate in the famous Winter Carnival. The pre-Lenten festival is similar to those in New Orleans and Rio de Janeiro and Europe. It is a let-your-hair-down celebration that draws thousands of people to Québec City from all over eastern North America for a week or more of merrymaking, culminating with a mammoth parade and the famous boat races across the icy St. Lawrence. For details on the exact time, events and lodging contact Québec Winter Carnival, 290 Joly St., Box 8, Que.

The Québec government publishes a wealth of details on winter activities in the province and many regions have their own publicity and lodging organizations. The province even maintains an information office in Toronto. For general information on skiing and tourism in Québec write: Ministry of Tourism, Fish and Game, 150 est, boul. Saint-Cyrille, Que., G1R 4Y3. There are specific booklets on cross-country skiing and snowshoeing, downhill skiing, lodging, winter events and the parks of Québec.

In addition you may find it useful to contact SkiQuébec; the Laurentian Ski Zone, 306A, Carré Youville, Montréal, H2Y 2B6; Office du tourisme de l'Outaouais, 768, boul. Saint-Joseph, C.P. 666, Hul, J8X 3Y8; or Hospitalité Québec Inc., 17 rue St-Louis, C.P. 9, Haute Ville, G1R 4M8.

Quebeckers are hospitable but contrary to popular belief in some parts of the country they do not all speak English. While virtually all the people a tourist would normally deal with are bilingual, it is useful to know a few words of French so you can read signs and brochures and ask for gas or directions in less touristic parts of the province. It is also a nice gesture to at least be able to say "Bonjour" (hello and goodbye in Québec) and "merci" to fellow skiers.

One of the many pleasures of cross-country skiing: relaxing around a roaring fire. This group has just returned from an outing at Lac Simon in the Outaouais region.

Hudson Bay

James Bay

Schefferville

Fermont

Sept-Îles

Laurentian Mountains

St. Lawrence River

Forillon
Gaspé

Lac St-Jean

Saguenay River

Gaspésie

Chicoutimi

Laurentides

Amos
Noranda
Rouyn

La Mauricie

Mont-Tremblant

Labelle

Trois-Rivières

Québec

Mont-Tremblant

Hull

Ottawa River

Montréal

Provincial Park
Trans Canada Highway
Provincial Highways

Québec Trails

Montreal-Laurentians

The Laurentians

This region can be called the cradle of skiing in Canada for it is here that cross-country and later downhill trails were blazed during the 1930s. There had been skiing in various parts of the country for as long as a century thanks to Scandinavian immigrants who brought their skis, but it was a rather individual effort. In the Laurentians skiing—cross-country skiing—became an organized sport.

With about 20 major ski communities, each having a cluster of ski centres, the Laurentian area north of Montréal is one of the major ski regions of the continent. The peaceful, rural valleys are dotted with such picturesque villages as St-Sauveur, Ste-Agathe, Ste-Adèle, Val-David and, of course Mont-Tremblant, in the shadow of the 3,000 ft. peaks which are mecca for so many skiers. There is rugged terrain too, such as the Johannsen route to the Tremblant peak named for Herman (Jack Rabbit) Smith-Johannsen, and there are more trails like this for the touring skier or mountaineer.

Dotted along the trails like beads are dozens of hotels, restaurants, ski shops and boutiques in and around the villages. Here one can find anything from a fresh tube of wax or suntan cream to the latest in ski fashions. Or, for a change of pace, you may want to browse through some of the handicraft shops. Here, too, along this trail system one can enjoy ski touring in the European manner. With a packsack on your back, containing some essential ski supplies and a change of clothing, you can tour from the Shawbridge area north 60 km to the Mont-Tremblant area, sampling restaurants and staying in hotels along the way.

Many ski resorts are realizing the popularity of cross-country skiing and offer ski weekends or ski weeks for guests who would like to make day tours from a central point. Often the hotels are located in regional ski trail networks of more than 100 km, allowing a good week of touring without skiing the same trail again. Lodging can range from the simple but comfortable to the luxurious resort hotel with features such as indoor swimming pool, curling rink, posh restaurant and dance band.

Parc Du Mont-Tremblant

This 990-square-mile provincial park 144 km (90 mi.) north of Montréal has some of the most rugged and spectacular terrain in Québec. For cross-country skiers it forms the northern extremity of a huge series of trails reaching from Shawbridge 60 km (35 mi.) to the south. Inside the park there are two separate cross-country areas maintained by the government. The Lac Monroe region is in the south end of the park not far from the north slope of the downhill Mont-Tremblant ski resort. The St-Donat area is to the east with access from that village.

The park is located in the northern Laurentians, just south of the Shield in a geological area known as Grenville. Heavy glaciation left exposed rock layers in deep gorges and extensive valley systems. Depressions scoured in the ground formed the basis for seven rivers, many streams and 965 lakes. Forest cover ranges from deciduous and evergreens in the valleys to hardwoods on the mountain peaks which reach into the 3,000 foot range. These peaks provide the highest downhill ski runs in eastern Canada.

While the interior of the park is in a mostly natural state and skiers must bring all the food and equipment they need, outside the park there is a wide range of resorts, ranging from simple and comfortable to posh. Equipment may be bought or rented in surrounding villages.

Mont-Tremblant - Secteur Lac Monroe

Location: In south end of Parc du Mont-Tremblant. From Route 117 exit north at St-Faustin and continue through Lac-Carré and Lac-Supérieur then past the cutoff to the north slopes of the downhill resort. Parking at Lac Monroe centre.

Length: Twelve trails totalling 48 km.

This trail network branches out along two valleys for easy runs and starts climbing passes to higher altitudes to challenge intermediate and expert skiers. Trails pass several small lakes but skiers are warned to beware of ice, particularly on Lac Monroe where currents keep it thin even during cold weather. Two heated shelters along trails, waxing room, toilets. Skiers are advised to check in and out at the reception centre. Normal season from mid-December to late March.

Mont-Tremblant - Secteur St-Donat
Location: From St-Donat northwest on Route 125 to reception centre just inside eastern park boundary.
Length: Three trails totalling 18 km.

This ski centre is located on the west shore of Lac Provost and has skiing around the rugged Mont-Cascade. There are two easy trails totalling 8 km and one difficult route which climbs the back side of the mountain to provide a viewpoint over the countryside. Skiers advised to register at the reception centre as the terrain is wild and mountainous. Trails marked, mapped and patrolled. Waxing room, heated shelter on trail, toilets.

Camp Mère Clarac
Location: St-Donat in the Laurentians. In park beside Lac Ouareau at southern end of village.
Length: 13 km, travel time 4 hr.

This is a private trail network used mainly by school classes in the region. For information contact Camp Mère Clarac, St-Donat, Que.

Mont-Garceau
Location: North side of village of St-Donat in Laurentians.
Length: Two trails of 3 and 8 km one way.

The 3 km trail winds its way for 1,500 ft. up the nearby mountain, also used for downhill skiing, to provide an excellent view over the St-Donat area and Lac Ouareau to the side. Trail marked and groomed, shelter, food and lodging at the village. The 8 km trail, for intermediate to expert skiers, crosses hilly, wooded terrain to a peninsula on Lac Ouareau.

Club de Golf St-Donat
Location: Access from Route 18 just south of village of St-Donat.

The golf club has a small network of trails in a hilly area with open and wooded areas. Elevation change of up to 500 ft. Good area for relaxed skiing with some routes for more experienced skiers. Food and lodging in area.

Mt-Legault
Location: About 8 km (5 mi.) south of village of St-Donat. Exit from Route 329 to Chemin Guay.

Length: 25 km. Travel time about 8 hr.

This beautiful trail through the Laurentian hillside rises 1,200 ft. to Mt. Legault for an excellent view of the area. Shelter on trail. Route used by snowmobiles. Food and lodging at St-Donat.

Auberge la Perdrière
Location: In Laurentians at southern edge of Parc Tremblant. From Laurentian Autoroute continue through village of St-Donat for 2.8 km (1.7 mi.) to the hotel.
Length: Three loop trails from hotel totalling 26 km.

Hotel is located on the shore of Baie de Tire and trails fan out through the wooded, mountainous countryside, across the frozen surface of the bay or along the shore of the Rivière Pimbina. There is a 16 km route allowing trips of one half day for intermediates and experts and 5 km trail each for experts and novices. Trails well marked and patrolled on weekends. Since much of the land is private, skiers are asked not to litter or make fires. Ski and snowshoe rentals, maps, lodging and food at the hotel. Downhill skiing nearby at Mt-Garceau.

St-Jovite — Mont-Tremblant
Location: Northern Laurentians along southeast edge of Parc Mont-Tremblant. Series of trails from village of St-Jovite north of Mont-Tremblant village and ski hills.
Length: Twenty-six trails totalling about 100 km.

This represents the northwestern sector of the Laurentian ski trail system and connects hotels in the area. Such a route is maintained by the two municipalities and the various hotels along the way. It provides skiers with European style touring in which one can ski from hotel to hotel. You can stop for a drink, a meal or an overnight stay on the trip.

There is a central trail of about 20 km leading between the two villages. Skiing ranges from very easy outings for beginners through intermediate and expert trails to semi-mountaineering. Hardy skiers can follow the tracks of skiers like Jack Rabbit Johannsen and climb more than 2,000 vertical feet to a peak named after him. The region is mountainous and has the highest downhill peaks in the Laurentians. Tree cover ranges from pines and spruce to birch and maple.

Night ski trips organized by the Club de Ski de Fond, Mont-Tremblant - St-Jovite, the co-ordinator of this trail network. The club also organizes obstacle course races and other special events. Services include rentals, sales, repairs, instruction, guide service, babysitting by hotels for children of guests, downhill skiing and snowshoeing. Excellent choice of hotels and restaurants, many with entertainment. For map and information write: Bureau Touristique St-Jovite - Mont-Tremblant, St-Jovite, Que.

Base le P'tit Bonheur
Location: On Lac Quenouille south of Parc Tremblant. East of Lac-Carré.
Length: Five trails totalling 50 km.

This year-round sport centre on a Laurentian lakeshore is still expanding its trail network into the nearby wooded, mountainous country. Both cross-country and downhill skiing at the resort. Lodge with restaurant. Trails range from about 2 km to 16 km loops and a 20 km trip one way with a shelter at the end for overnight trips. Ski equipment provided free for guests of lodge. Ski events include Traversée Des Laurentides. For information write Auberge P'tit Bonheur, CP 30, Lac-Carré, Que. J0T 1J0

Otter Lake Haus
Locations: At Huberdeau in western Laurentians.
Length: 21 km.

Two trails, a beginner and intermediate known as the Lac a La Loutre (Otter Lake) and an expert trail, the Grand Rouge, start from the front door of this lodge. Good scenery. Snowshoeing. Guide service, baby sitting, rentals. Downhill skiing in area. The family lodge is trilingual with German added to the two official languages and the cooking features both German and Canadian food. Huberdeau Winter Carnival. For information write Otter Lake Haus, Huberdeau, Que. J0T 1G0.

Ste-Adèle Region Trails
Location: Series of ski centres around the Laurentian ski town of Ste-Adèle.
Length: Six trail centres totalling 150 km.

Located north and west of the Mont-Rolland trails, the Ste-Adèle trails include the Johannsen, connecting the southern region. Ski centres comprising the Ste-Adèle system include Auberge Yvan Coutu, Far Hills Inn, Alpine Inn, Centre de Ski Mont-Alouette, Hôtel Chantecler, Centre de Ski Le Chantecler and Hôtel Sun Valley.

Ste-Adèle is in a central point in the massive Laurentian cross-country ski trail system and connects with Mont-Rolland and Shawbridge in the southeast, Morin Heights in the west and Ste-Agathe to the north, leading to Mont-Tremblant. The Ste-Adèle region is known for its good hotels and food and has services including ski shops, rentals, instruction and downhill skiing.

Ski Mont-Alouette
Location: Ste-Adèle in the Laurentians.
Length: 6 km.

The downhill ski resort maintains this trail from its slopes to Hotel des Monts at nearby Mont-Rolland via L'Os-Qui-Fume restaurant at Ste-Adèle. Ski rentals at the downhill area, cafeteria, snowshoeing.

Centre de Ski Le Chantecler
Location: At downhill ski hills by Chantecler Hotel in Ste-Adèle in the Laurentians.
Length: Three trails totalling 13 km.

A series of trails for beginners, intermediates and experts winds above, below and around the downhill ski facilities at this hilly resort town. The area is mostly wooded with some open areas, such as the golf course. Extensive ski area includes chalets, restaurants, bars, indoor swimming, sauna, ski shops, rentals and instruction. Trails marked and maintained. These routes also connect with much larger ski trails passing through the area. Ski map free from Service de la Publicité, Le Chantecler, Ste-Adèle, Que.

Alpine Cross-Country Ski Centre
Location: On road from Ste-Adèle to Ste-Marguerite Station in the Laurentians.
Length: 9 km.

This large and luxurious inn has three loop trails for novices and intermediates. Terrain is wooded and rolling and some trails give nice downhill runs. Trails groomed and marked. Trail fee, waxing hut, instruction, accommodation, lodging and bar. Indoor pool, curling and skating rinks.

Hotel L'esterel
Location: In Laurentians 80 km (50 mi.) north of Montréal. Just east of Ste-Marguerite.
Length: 33 km.

This large and modern resort hotel on a 5,000-acre estate has both daily skiing and cross-country ski weeks for those who want to use the trail system. There are routes ranging from about 1 km and 45 min. travel time to 10 km trails which require about a day of travel and there is access to the Maple Leaf trail which passes through the area. The region is wooded and hilly and some trails cross Lac Dupuis and Lac Castor. Trails used for Quebec Cup and zone championships.

This ski centre, which also features downhill skiing, snowshoeing and snowmobiling, has very extensive facilities, including instruction, rentals, sales, guides, skating, night skiing, repairs, picnic areas and shelters. The lodge offers such niceties as indoor swimming pool, sauna, whirlpool, playroom and badminton.

Mont-Rolland Trails
Location: Village of Mont-Rolland, just east of Ste-Adèle in the Laurentians.
Length: Thirteen trails totalling about 100 km.

This trail network, reaching north, south and east from the village forms the eastern edge of the massive cross-country ski trail system in the southern end of the Laurentian resorts area. The Mont-Rolland trails, including routes like the Whizzard and Johannsen, fan out through forested and open countryside with a variety of terrain, ranging from flat to mountains and valleys. Trails pass downhill ski resorts and run close to or climb to panoramic viewpoints. In many cases they cross small lakes which dot the Laurentian countryside.

There are numerous departure points, including the Hôtel des Monts, Centre Equestre, Cie de Papier Rolland, Hôtel Chaton-Rose, Domaine Mont du Rocher and Lac Bellevue. Area has services including hotels, restaurants, bars, picnic areas with fireplaces, snowshoeing, rentals and sales. The village is a centre for such arts and handicrafts as painting, weaving and sculpture.

The trails are marked and maintained by Club des Monts, founded by Jean-Paul Fortier. For information on lodging write Bureau Touristique, Ste-Adèle, Que. Map of trail system prepared by Mont-Rolland Council and *chambre de commerce.* Available from Eddy Fortier, Hôtel des Monts, Mont-Rolland, Que., J0R 1G0.

Mont-Gabriel
Location: Trails start near Auberge Mont-Gabriel at the top of Mont Gabriel in the Laurentians.
Length: 3 trails with travel time ranging from 30 min. to about 2 hr.

The trails lead down wooded hillsides near a downhill ski area and are suitable for experienced skiers. Trails end near downhill ski resort so cross-country skiers have access to bar, restaurant, motel, skating

and babysitting. Lodging in area including Auberge Mont-Gabriel. Map available at hotel.

Piedmont Ski Club
Location: St-Sauveur region of the Laurentians.

This summer golf and winter ski club is located just north of Piedmont. The club is a starting point for access to a 100 km trail network which passes through this region. Club has ski rentals, instruction, bar, restaurant, lodging and there are torchlight ski tours on club grounds Saturday nights. For information write Club de Golf et de Ski de Fond, Piedmont, Que.

Morin Heights Trails
Location: Laurentians, north of Montréal. Trails centred around the village of Morin Heights west of St-Sauveur.
Length: About 250 km of trails with network under expansion.

This impressive trail network, comprising the southwestern sector of the massive Laurentian trail system, is itself a combination of two interlocking trail nets. The northern trails emanate from the Scan Sport Nordic Ski Centre on the eastern edge of Morin Heights while southeast of the village another series is based at the Viking Ski Club. The trails form an elaborate system of interlocking loops over about 150 square miles of Laurentian countryside about 65 km (40 mi.) north of Montréal.

The trails circle the village and range through hardwood and evergreen forests, across open fields, along streams, around many small lakes, across roads and over hilly and flat areas. From this region they reach out like arms to Ste-Agathe in the north, Ste-Adèle and Mont-Gabriel in the east and to the Shawbridge area to the southeast. Trails are marked and groomed. Night skiing section. The Morin Heights area has a full range of services for skiers including hotels, restaurants, bars, babysitting, equipment rentals, sales, exchange and repairs and instruction. For map and information contact Nordic Ski Centre, C.P. 151, Morin Heights, Que.

Camp Edphy
Location: Val-Morin in the Laurentians. Access from 14ième ave.
Length: Trails totalling 32 km.

This is best known as a summer camp for children but has wooded mountain skiing for all levels of skier and trails are open to all in the winter. It is located in a beautiful part of the Laurentians along the Rivière du Nord. Ski rentals and accommodation. For information write: Centre d'Education Physique et de Plein Air Edphy, 14ième ave., Val Morin, Que. J0T 2R0.

Mont de Lanaudière
Location: Northeast from Montréal, on Routes 40 and 347 to St-Gabriel-de-Brandon.
Length: Four loop trails totalling 32 km. Trails of 3, 8, 9.5 and 11 km with routes for all level of ability. Shorter trail for novice, longer trails for experts. Mostly on wooded, mountainous terrain. Rentals. Waxing room. Tobogganing. Bar, restaurant, snack bar. Downhill facilities. On-site accommodation. For information write Club de Ski Lanaudière, 1851 Chemin du Mont de Lanaudière, St-Gabriel-de-Brandon, Que.

La Mauricie National Park
Location: From Trois-Rivières north 56 km (35 mi.) on Route 55 and enter the park by the road through St-Jean-des-Piles. After 5 km (3 mi.) you will reach the parking area and start of trails.
Length: More than 40 km.
The park offers one 4.9 km loop trail for intermediate skiers, one 12.4 km loop trail for experts and a trail of 14.9 km one way running along Lakes Isaïe and A la Pêche. Novices can ski part of this trail but a complete round trip is beyond the abilities of a beginner. Two shelters on this trail. One shelter at halfway point on 12.4 km loop. All trails are marked and groomed and have been laid out through dense forests and along the shores of frozen lakes. Skiers must register at entrance. For maps and information write Information Services, Parks Canada, 1141 Route de l'Eglise, Box 10275, Ste-Foy, Que. G1V 4H5.

Vallée-Pruneau Ski Trails
Location: Grandes-Piles, 8 km (5 mi.) north of Grand-Mère on Hwy. 155.
Length: 24 km in total.
Vallée-Pruneau has four trails ranging from 1.6 to 8 km in length, suitable for beginner, intermediate and expert skiers. One trail is lighted for night skiing. Terrain is wooded and about half is mountainous. Downhill facilities. Ski school, ski shop. Bar, dining room. Babysitting available. Snowshoeing. Accommodation in Grand-Mère, contact Chamber of Commerce. For information write Gilles Verrette, Manager,

Bd. Ducharme, Grandes-Piles, Laviolette County.

Vallée du Parc
Location: Just north of Grand-Mère on Boulevard Vallée du Parc to Mauricie Park in the north.
Length: 3 trails totalling 15 km.
Starting from the ski chalet, also used for a downhill area, a network of trails for beginner, intermediate and advanced skiers fans out through open, wooded and mountainous country. One trail is sometimes lighted for night skiing. Instruction, rentals, skating, snowshoeing, guides, restaurant, bar, dining room, lodging in area. Map at chalet. Lockers.

Parc du Mont Saint-Bruno
Location: From Montréal, east 24 km (15 mi.) on Route 20, exit Saint-Bruno, then secondary road 30 to Saint-Bruno.
Length: 25 km.
Marked and groomed trails ranging from 3 to 9 km. One trail is classified as easy, two as intermediate and one as difficult. Wooded terrain with oaks and maple trees. Open 7 days a week. Reception centre. Snack bar weekends only. Two heated relay stations. Snowshoeing. Downhill facilities. Skating. Trail expansion planned. Accommodation in Saint-Bruno, Saint-Basile, Sainte Julie. For information write Parc du Mont Saint-Bruno, 1635 rue Montarville, Saint-Bruno, Que., or Direction des Parcs, Ministère du Tourisme, de la Chasse et de la Pêche, 5075 rue Fullum, Montréal, Que.

Centre de Ski Ayers
Location: From Lachute, north 16 km (10 mi.) on Route 327, just past Pine Hill.
Length: More than 100 km.
This trail system, based on some routes in the area of Lac Notre Dame, was greatly expanded by a 1973 Opportunities for Youth project, which pushed the network southwest about 15 km. Trails are located in wooded, mountainous area, sometimes follow rivers and cross lakes. Focal point for trails is a downhill ski resort. Wide trails, marked and groomed. Rentals, waxing room, shelters and restaurant. Trail fee, maps for sale. Lodging in Lachute. Closed Tuesdays.

Centre Recreatif Mont-Laval
Location: From Montréal 9.5 km (6 mi.) on Autoroute des Laurentides, exit 6 west, to Laval.

Length: Three trails totalling 9.6 km.

Trails are located in the centre of the city of Laval. They loop from one another so beginners may travel for 4.8 km, intermediate skiers for 8 km while experts can ski the full 9.6 km trail. Mostly through wooded terrain. Trails are marked and groomed. Patrol. Tobogganing, snowmobiling, snowshoeing. Downhill facilities. Instruction and rentals available. Cafeteria, dining room, disco bar. Ski shop. Map included in trail fee. Usually three special events are organized each year. For information write Centre Récréatif Mont-Laval, 675, Boul. St-Martin, Ste-Dorothée, Laval, Que.

Parc Paul-Sauvé
Location: West of Montréal at mouth of Ottawa R. Just east of town of Oka.
Length: About 35 km.

The closest of the provincial parks to the metropolis of Montréal, this small park is highly developed for winter recreation. There are five trails ranging from 3 to 13 km with more planned and there is a good distribution of types with easy, intermediate and one difficult route. The park is open from 8 A.M. to 4 P.M. and is patrolled. Skiers have maps, nature interpretation signs along the routes, warming huts and picnic areas. Trails are groomed twice daily. The park is located on a former seigniory and is forested with hickory, maples, linden, ash, walnut, oak and elm. The forest and hillsides are inhabited by hares, squirrels, fox, lynx, coyote and many birds, including grouse.

Outaouis-Northwest

Camp Fortune-Gatineau Park
Location: Trails begin along Gatineau Parkway near Mountain St. at western edge of Hull, but greatest concentration is at Camp Fortune. Access to camp via Route 5 north to Kingsmere Exit then left through Old Chelsea. About 25 km (15 mi.) from Ottawa.
Length: Total of about 150 km with 115 in the Camp Fortune section.

This is the major trail system in the Ottawa-Hull region and runs from the doorstep of the urban centre. The Gatineau trails run on and beside the parkway with offshoots to nearby areas. At Kingsmere they link up with the intensely developed Camp Fortune area. This is both a downhill and cross-country ski centre and as such has extensive facilities for day visitors. The trails are cut through the Gatineau countryside and are mostly on hilly, forested countryside. More than half are rated as easy but some of the rest are challenging for experts. Skiers can also use unplowed roads running through the area.

Camp Fortune, home of the 3,000-member Ottawa Ski Club, maintains, grooms and marks the trails for the National Capital Commission. Four huts, spaced about 2.5 km apart, have wood stoves maintained on the weekends and wood in them for fires during the week. Three have phones. Ski routes are patrolled by Trail Rider Ski Patrol on weekends. Four cafeterias on weekends, ski school, sales and rentals, waxing hut, babysitting and ski buses from Ottawa. Lodging at Wakefield or in Ottawa-Hull area. Maps and information from National Capital Commission, 48 Rideau St., Ottawa, Ont. K1N 8K5.

Club Rivière Rouge
Location: West of Montreal, on Route 20, exit at Côteau-du-Lac, then take Route 201 north for 5 km (3 mi.) to Club de Golf Rivière Rouge.
Length: 16 km. Travel time 3 hr.

Secondary trails ranging from 800 m to 3.2 km, branch off a main trail of 5 km. The network allows skiers to travel from 5 up to 16 km, depending on their ability and time. Routes are on flat terrain and suitable mostly for beginner and intermediate skiers. Trails pass through forests of coniferous and mixed trees. Chalet, restaurant, bar. Trail system is marked and groomed. Accommodation in Côteau-du-Lac and Valleyfield. For information write Club de Ski de Fond Rivière Rouge, 169, route 201, Côteau-du-Lac, Cté Soulanges, Que.

Centre La Petite-Rouge
Location: From Montebello north on Route 323 to St-Emile-de-Suffolk.
Length: Nine trails totalling 32 km.

Trails located in both open and forested country on western edge of Laurentian region. Suitable for beginners and intermediates. Cross-country clinics. Rentals, repairs, shelter and ski shop. Lodge with cafeteria, group activities. Snowshoeing, tobogganing and skating.

Chateau Montebello
Location: At Montebello, on Route 148, east 60 km (40 mi.) from Hull and west 130 km (80 mi.) from Montréal.
Length: Four trails totalling 64 km.

Marked and groomed trails in open fields

Herman (Jack Rabbit) Smith-Johannsen, puts in an appearance at the famous Canadian Ski Marathon, held each year in southwestern Québec.

for beginners and through hilly, forested areas for more experienced skiers. Shelter on trail, rentals, waxing room, repairs, guided tours on request. The 200-room hotel has luxurious accommodation on site and a good restaurant.

Mont Cascades
Location: North of Hull. From Cantley on Hwy. 307, on Chemin Mont Cascades.
Length: 20 km total. Travel time about 2 hr. per trail.

Scenic Gatineau Trail of 10 km passes along Pike Lake lookouts, joins Edelweiss ski lifts to the north, and loops around to the south, following the Gatineau River before joining other trails. Cascades Trail and Clifford Trail form loops on mountainous terrain and traverse some bush and field areas. Downhill facilities. Ski school. Restaurant, shelter with picnic area and firepit. Babysitting. Accommodation at Tulip Valley Motel in Cascades and in Wakefield. Free maps available at ski chalet. Ski tour on the Gatineau Trail, from Edelweiss to Mont Cascades, in February, organized by Mont Cascades Ski Club.

Mont Chilly Ski Trails
Location: Near Ft. Coulonge about 115 km (70 mi.) up the Ottawa R. from Hull. From town travel north about 5 km (3 mi.), then turn right on access road.
Length: 3 main loops of 1 to 3 hr. travel time plus logging roads.

The Mont Chilly ski patrol maintains a system of trails through wooded, hilly country near a small downhill resort. There is a 1-hr. trip for novices and longer trails for more expert skiers. All routes marked in red. In addition, skiers can wander unmarked logging roads and cross three small lakes in the region after freeze-up. Chalet at ski hill serves lunches from 10 A.M. until dark. Some skiers take the T-bar as a shortcut to trails atop the small mountain. Map at hill. Lodging in Ft. Coulonge.

Mont Ste-Marie
Location: 88 km (55 mi.) north of Hull. Take Hwys. 5 and 105 north, then turn east, just before Kazabazua, to reach town of Lac Ste-Marie. Turn right after Lac Ste-Marie for another 5 km (3 mi.).
Length: 5.5 km. Travel time 1 to 1 ½ hr.

Very scenic trails suitable mostly for intermediate skiers. They pass through tall pine forest, across a couple of open brooks and along the edge of high fields with beautiful views on the lakes and the mountains. There are 4,500 acres of land and skiers can roam all over the property. Trails are designated for expansion and to connect with the "Gatineau Trail." Mont Ste-Marie is a major downhill resort. Sales, rental and instruction available. Warming hut. Snowshoeing. Cafeterias, coffee shop, dining room, disco bar and piano bar, nursery, conference centre. Accommodation at the resort, in a hotel, motel or lodges. Also in Lac Ste-Marie. For information write Mont Ste-Marie, C.P. 92, Lac Ste-Marie, Que. J0X 1Z0.

Association Nor-Fond
Location: From Rouyn-Noranda, east 40 km (25 mi.) on Route 117, to Cadillac. Start of trails nearby at Lac Normand.
Length: Five trails totalling 24 km.
Groomed trails include three routes for beginners and two for intermediate skiers. Wooded, hilly terrain. Wildlife includes rabbit and moose. Shelters. Reception centre, snack bar. Babysitting Sunday afternoons. Trail fee. Map available. For information write Association Nor-Fond, 3220, Latulipe, Rouyn, Que.

Centre Récréatif Evain
Location: About 8 km (5 mi.) west of Noranda, on Route 117. Off rang 8,9.
Length: 24 km.
Four groomed, easy trails, on wooded terrain. Shelters at Lac Lebrun and Lac Flavrian. Reception centre, snack bar. Open weekends. Trail fee. Map available. For information write Centre Récréatif Evain Inc., 57 de L'Eglise, Evain, Que.

Sentiers Amos-Piste du Camp Scout
Location: Western Québec west of Lac Abitibi. From town of Amos east 6 km (4 mi.) on Route 395 to chalet.
Length: Three trails totalling 35 km.
Trails are located in mostly wooded area with gentle slopes, so routes are not particularly difficult. Enjoyable for outings. Forest with moose, hare and grouse. There are trails of 5, 11 and 19 km. Marked and maintained by town of Amos.

Mont Kanasuta
Location: From Rouyn-Noranda west 35 km (22 mi.) on Route 117.

Length: 20 km. Travel time up to 2 ½ hr.
System of trails ranging from 2.5 to 5 km. Most are loop trails located on wooded terrain. Three are classified as easy and two others on mountainous sections, as intermediate and difficult. All trails are groomed and start at Chalet Kanasuta. Patrol, instruction available, restaurant. Downhill facilities. Accommodation in Rouyn-Noranda. Bus service on weekends. For information write Chamber of Commerce, Rouyn-Noranda, Que.

Sentiers Amos - Piste du College
Location: Start from Collège d'Amos, 800, liere rue est, Amos, in western Québec, west of Lac Abitibi.
Length: Four trails totalling 43 km.
Trails start from behind college in hilly, wooded country and the expert loop is in mountainous terrain. At the high point there is an observatory where one can look out over town and the Rivière Harricana. Wildlife includes moose, hare and grouse. Shelter in middle of trail system. Marked trails. Groomed by town of Amos.

Base de Plein Air Lac Mourrier
Location: From Malartic in western Québec, south 20 km (13 mi.) on Chemin Colonie Fournière.
Length: 48 km.
Loop trails ranging from 3 to 14.5 km. Travel time 30 min. to 2 hr. Also, 20 km trail going to town of Malartic, travel time 2 ½ to 3 hr. On wooded, slightly mountainous terrain. Suitable for beginner and intermediate skiers. Marked and groomed trails. Shelters, reception centre, snack bar. Rentals and instruction available. Waxing room, ski repairs. Snowshoeing, skating on the lake, ice fishing. Babysitting. Accommodation on site and in town of Malartic. Maps can be obtained at base lodge or from Association Régionale de Ski de Randonnée de l'Abitibi-Temiscamingue, 426 Central No. 2, Val d'Or, Que. Site of Québec Regional Games.

Eastern Townships

Bromont
Location: In the town of Bromont, in the Eastern Townships, on Autoroute 10.
Length: 17 km.
Beginners trail is on golf course and covers 5 km. Intermediate and expert trails of 4 and 8 km are located on wooded terrain, easily accessible. The equestrian events in

A scenic route in the Outaouais region of Québec.

1976 summer Olympics were held on this site. Instruction and rentals available at ski shop. Downhill facilities. Ski chalet with cafeteria and bar. Equestrian club may be used as a shelter by skiers. Accommodation in Bromont. Contact Association Touristique de Bromont, C.P. 29, Bromont, Que. J0E 1L0. Sketch map available.

Association Plein Air Coaticook
Location: Eastern Townships, near Vermont Border. In Coaticook on Hwy. 147.
Length: 2.5 km. Expansion planned between Coaticook and Compton.

One trail starting north of Coaticook. Many access points in town. On wooded terrain, follows a brook and goes down steep slopes with sharp turns at bottom. Suitable mostly for intermediate skiers. Trail is part of a project to develop Coaticook Gorges area. They are 245 feet deep, and offer beautiful scenery and wildlife only 800 m from centre of town. Accommodation in Coaticook. For information write Club A.P.A.C., Mr. Alain Roy, 424 rue St-Joachim, Coaticook, Que. J1A 2L7.

Mont Scotch Hill
Location: Eastern Townships area, near Asbestos. From Danville south on Route 116 for 3 km (2 mi.)
Length: 12 km.

The base Plein Air at Mont Scotch Hill has a very attractive location in partially wooded, rolling countryside. The view is excellent and you can see as far as the Appalachian Mountains in the United States. The centre is in the process of adding 30 km of trails to the present system which has routes for all levels of skier. Trails marked and groomed, ski patrol and instructors. Races, ski clinics, torchlight tours and an after ski life including dancing to an orchestra at the lodge. Food and bar. For information write Mont Scotch Hill, Danville, Que. J0A 1A0.

Ski Wilvaken
Location: Eastern Townships. From Magog south on Route 141 and road to Fitch Bay, then follow signs on private road to lodge.
Length: 50 km.

There is a wide network of ski trails at this summer childrens' camp which becomes a ski centre for all ages in the winter. There are straight and loop trails ranging from 1 to 12 km with a great variety of interconnections possible. Routes are generally in secluded, wooded areas with some travel on fields, hillsides and on one small lake. Night skiing on fields and lake. Trails marked, maps available. Shelters, some areas for fires. Rentals, instruction can be arranged. Simple accommodation for skiers who bring their own sleeping bags may be had at lodge and guests are expected to help clean up after meals. Lodging in Magog as well. Trail fee.

Sutton en Haut
Location: Eastern Townships. South of Lac Brome. From town of Sutton east on road to Mont Sutton ski resort.
Length: Five trails totalling 30 km.

There is a good trails system on both sides of the access road to Mont Sutton downhill ski area, a few hundred metres to the east. The Sutton en Haut cross-country trails are in forested mountain country and many run along a stream through the property. Average travel time for each trail is 2 hr. Routes for all levels of skiers. Trails marked, groomed, patrolled by the Ambulance St-Jean and at closing each afternoon by ski patrollers on snowmobiles. Rentals, instruction may be arranged, maps. Trail fee. The trails pass three hotels where skiers can stay. Shelters on trails. Carnaval celebrations third weekend of February.

Parc du Mont-Orford
Location: Eastern Townships. From Magog northwest 10 km (6 mi.).
Length: Seven trails totalling 22 km.

Trail network in wooded, mountainous terrain in the beautiful, 15-square mile provincial park noted first for a good downhill ski centre. Routes evenly divided between flat, uphill and downhill. Most trails are along the Etang de la Rivière aux Cerises but skiers are warned to stay off the ice because of frequently unsafe conditions. Four heated shelters, centre for registration. Operates daily from 9 A.M. to 4 P.M. Groups of 15 or more persons are asked to give at least two weeks notice before arrival. Ski instruction on weekends. Waxing room. Skiers must register for all trips.

The Monteregian hills are located in the climax region of the northern Laurentian hardwood forests and on the edge of the Appalachian region. Tree cover includes maples, linden, beech, ash, eastern hem-

lock and many other species. Forests are inhabited by deer, porcupines, hare, raccoon, beaver and several species of birds. For information write Parc du Mont-Orford, C.P. 146, Magog, Que. For lodging information write Station de Ski Mont-Orford, bureau des réservations, C.P. 248, Magog, Que.

Baldwin Recreation Centre
Location: Eastern Townships. At Baldwin Mills near Lac Lyster, close to Vermont border. Southeast of Coaticook.
Length: Ten trails totalling 37 km.

Located on the hilly shores of Lac Lyster this ski centre has a series of trails mostly in wooded countryside. Trails start from Restaurant Cabana and there are four heated shelters along the way. Marked and groomed. Trail fee includes map. Lodging in Coaticook or Ayer's Cliff.

Owl's Head
Location: Mansonville in Eastern Townships.
Length: Two loop trails totalling 19 km.

Trails start at a major downhill ski resort in this popular ski region. They pass through hilly, wooded and open country. Marked routes, shelter, waxing room. One trail for beginners, the other for intermediates. Cafeteria. Instruction and rentals. Accommodation at Owl's Head Lodge at base of the mountain. Trails open 9 A.M. to 4 P.M.

Bolton Glen
Location: At Knowlton in Eastern Townships south of Lac Brome.
Length: 8 km loop. Travel time about 4 hr.

This trail, starting from a youth hostel lodge, passes through wooded, mountainous country and is suitable for intermediate or expert skiers. Snack bar, rentals, skating, snowshoeing, downhill skiing nearby. Accommodation at lodge. Topographic map, 1:50,000 scale, 31 H/W Menphramagog. Operated by Canadian Youth Hostels.

Mont Bon Plaisir
Location: At Eastman in the Eastern Townships.
Length: Five trails totalling 55 km. Travel time between 1 and 6 hr.

Two trails for beginners and intermediates and three for experts run through wooded and hilly country in this Sherbrooke area resort. Woods of spruce, pine and maple. Trails marked, groomed weekends, maps available. Ski shop, rentals, restaurant, bar-salon around fireplace. Snowshoeing on 15 km of trails. Sleigh rides. Downhill skiing nearby. Lodging at four motels close to ski trails. This is the site of a winter carnival in late January and early February. Information from the resort at C.P. 54, Eastman, Que., J0E 1P0.

Base de Plein Air Mont Bellevue

Location: In Sherbrooke, rue Jogues.

Length: Eleven trails totalling 16.5 km.

Trails are marked and groomed and classified as 3 easy, 5 intermediate and 3 difficult. Trails are wide enough so two skiers can glide side by side. About two-thirds of the routes are on wooded terrain, the rest on open sections. Mountainous region. Chalet, snack bar. Rentals, instruction available. Snowshoeing. Downhill facilities. Accommodation in Sherbrooke. For information contact l'Office Municipal du Tourisme de la Ville de Sherbrooke, 48 rue Dépôt. Map available from Service des Loisirs de la Ville de Sherbrooke, 229-8e avenue nord, Sherbrooke, Que. For topographic maps, write Services Techniques de la Ville de Sherbrooke, 1300, rue Galt ouest, Sherbrooke, Que.

Copains des Neiges Ski Trail

Location: From Windsor, Route 5-22 towards Sherbrooke. Turn onto Rang 12, in front of Auberge des Cantons.

Length: 16 km in two loop trails. Travel time about 1 ½ hr.

Trails pass through wooded terrain with some mountainous and some flat sections. Beautiful countryside. Three heated relay stations with snack bar in one of them. Snowshoeing. Accommodation in Windsor. In 1975, race organized on this site for the ''Jeux de Québec.'' For information write Club de Ski Copains des Neiges, Roger Godbout, 30, rue Principale, Windsor, Que.

Club Saint-Romain

Location: From Sherbrooke northeast on Route 108 to St-Romain.

Length: Five trails totalling 20.5 km. Travel time about 8 hr. to complete the system.

You can start on the trails right in the centre of town, in front of the Town Hall, or at the Pont Dostie, 1.6 km (1 mi.) from the village on a road called ''Route chez Dostie.'' Network of marked and groomed trails, ranging from 1.3 to 9 km, suitable for beginner and intermediate skiers. One difficult section on trail 1. Trails pass through beautiful forests of maple and coniferous trees,

and along the banks of Rivière Felton and Rivière Sauvage, in a very scenic countryside. Abundant wildlife includes hare, grouse and porcupine. In spring, skiers may spot beavers, otters and mink. Sugar cabin in maple forest. Three relay stations. Accommodation in St-Romain. Maps available. For information write Club de Ski de Fond de St-Romain Inc., St-Romain, Que.

Base de Plein Air Jouvence

Location: West of Sherbrooke. At Bonsecours on Route 220.

Length: Four trails totalling 18.5 km. Travel time from 30 min. to 2 ½ hr.

Beginners have a choice of three trails of 1.5, 2 and 6 km. One trail of 9 km for intermediate skiers. All pass through wooded terrain. Lodge with access to trail system. Accommodation by reservations. For information write Base de Plein Air Jouvence, RR 1, Bonsecours, Cté Shefford, Que.

Loisirs St-Adolphe

Location: At St-Adolphe de Dudswell, 40 km (25 mi.) northeast of Sherbrooke.

Length: 11 km.

Trails are located on mostly wooded, mountainous terrain in a very picturesque countryside. Suitable for all levels of ability. Trails subject to revision.

Centre Ski-Raq

Location: From Montréal, east 72 km (45 mi.) to Granby. Then north 8 km (5 mi.) to Roxton Pond.

Length: 20 km.

Series of loop trails on mostly easy routes with a few difficult sections. Trails go through forests for the most part, passing on bridges across small rivers. Skiers must register at entrance. Two shelters. Rentals. Restaurant nearby. Snowshoeing. Accommodation in Granby. Maps available at control booth.

Parc des Voltigeurs

Location: Trans-Canada Highway Route 20, exit 111, Drummondville. Park is 3 km (2 mi.) from town.

Length: 7 km. Travel time about 2 hr.

Trails loop on each side of Trans-Canada Highway. Some of the routes follow the St-Francois River, mostly through woods of coniferous and deciduous trees. Suitable for beginner and intermediate skiers. Open 7 days a week. Marked and groomed trails. Reception centre, dining, rental, waxing room, patrol. Two heated relay stations with toilets. Night skiing, snowshoeing, skating. Map available at the park. Accommodation in Drummondville. For information write Parc des Voltigeurs, Box 878, Drummondville, Que. J2B 6X1.

Quebec - North Shore

Parc Mont-Ste-Anne
Location: North shore of St. Lawrence River. From Québec east 40 km (25 mi.) on Route 360.
Length: More than 60 km of trails.

First developed in the past decade as one of the major downhill ski centres in eastern North America, Mont-Ste-Anne is now being groomed as an important cross-country trail network. It will receive international prominence in 1979 when it will be the site of the world nordic championships, a year before the Olympic competitions in Lake Placid, N.Y. As a result, the trail system and facilities such as the chalet are undergoing expansion. Centrepiece of the area is the 2,600 ft. mountain, towering over the St. Lawrence R. and providing views along the valley and over the South Shore, across the water.

Trails are marked and groomed but pass through rugged, heavily forested terrain so most are rated for intermediate or better skiers and registration is required. At several points the routes cross the Rivière Jean Larose and at times climb the steep hillside in a series of switchbacks.

Park has rentals, sales, shelters, snowshoeing, restaurants, bars, boutiques, nursery, first aid post and ski school. Skiing starts in late November or early December and lasts into April on the north slopes. For map and information write Parc de Mont-Ste-Anne, C.P. 400, Beaupré, Que. G0A 1E0.

Centre de Ski St-Raymond
Location: At St-Raymond de Portneuf, west of Québec.
Length: About 77 km.

Trail system offers a choice of 3 beginner trails of 3.6, 4.6 and 6.2 km, 2 intermediate trails of 4 and 5 km, and 3 expert trails of 12.3, 15.8 and 25 km. Located mostly on wooded, mountainous terrain, these trails lead past panoramic viewpoints and give skiers a chance to spot wildlife in its natural habitat. Marked and groomed. Chalet, snack bar, waxing room, rental and sale of

equipment, two heated shelters along trails. Maps available. Trail fee. Downhill facilities. Annual tour end of February. Accommodation in St-Raymond. For information write Parc Naturel St-Raymond Inc., C.P. 1176, St-Raymond, Que.

Club le Refuge
Location: St. Adolphe, about 30 min. drive north of Québec City.
Length: 85 km.

This is a cross-country ski club with season membership located in the hill and river country north of Québec City. Trails follow Rivière des Hurons at one point and long trails circle local hills. Site of two loppets: Aventure Castor in February and Marche ou Crève in March. Rentals, snack bar, picnic areas with fireplaces, shelter, night skiing, babysitting. Trails marked and groomed. Lodging at Hotel Normande, Lac Beauport, or in Québec.

La Tuque Rouge
Location: West of Laurentides Park at town of La Tuque on Route 155 beside Rivière St-Maurice.
Length: About 40 km of trails.

The Club de Ski de Fond La Tuque Rouge has developed an extensive trail network between the edge of town and the river. Most trails are for beginners and intermediates and pass through fields and wooded areas, mounting three terraces with views over the area. The non-profit club charges a modest membership fee to maintain such facilities as two heated shelters with washrooms and to produce free maps available in town or at the trails. Parking at trails, grooming. Trails are marked and signed with small sketches. Lodging in town. Races and other events held at the ski trails. For map and information write the club at C.P. 1, La Tuque, Que. G9X 3P1.

Camp Mercier
Location: In Parc des Laurentides, 58 km (36 mi.) from Quebec, on Route 175.
Length: About 48 km in total.

There are 15 trails, ranging from 500 m to over 8 km. Five trails are classified as easy, nine as intermediate and one as difficult. They pass through mainly coniferous forests. Reception centre: dining, rental and repairs of equipment, waxing room, patrol, guided tours. Five heated relay stations with toilets. Detailed map distributed on site. Snowshoeing.

The park covers 3,696 square miles of

After checking out the trail map, skiers prepare for a trip in Parc du Mont-Orford in the Eastern Townships, southeast of Montréal.

heavy coniferous forests surrounded by stands of white birch, mountain tops reaching between 3,000 and 4,000 feet in the eastern section, rivers flowing towards the four cardinal points. During the past few years, the Department has been attempting to reintroduce the caribou to the park and the animals are now roaming free. Other wildlife include moose, wolf and lynx. Skiers might be interested in viewing experimental forests at the nearby Montmorency Research Station. For lodging, a few cottages are available, reservations required. Also lodging in Stoneham, 11 km (7 mi.) from the camp. For information write the Ministère du Tourisme, de la Chasse et de la Pêche, Parc des Laurentides or 150 est, Bd. St-Cyrille, Québec, Que.

Club de Ski de Fond d'Alma
Location: Lac Saint-Jean area. From Alma east on boulevard Auger and follow signs for about 10 km (6 mi.)
Length: 10 trails totalling more than 70 km.
This trail network is one of the finest available and was highly praised by a Canadian technical expert on ski areas. The trails run through wooded northern Quebec countryside and many of the hilly routes offer exceptional views of the Saugenay River area. There is a choice ranging from a beginners trail of 1.5 km to a competition trail of 5 km with intermediate trails of 3 to 15 km in length. All routes are laid out in loop pattern so there is great variety in travel possible. Trails are groomed. Competitions held including cup race for junior skiers in March. Lodging in Alma.

Tobo-Ski Club
Location: Lac Saint-Jean area. From St-Félicien southwest 10 km (6 mi.) on rural road.
Length: Loop trails of 24 km in total.
Double track trails of 2, 5, 7 and 10 km. Groomed and marked. Located on wooded, mountainous terrain. Longer trails cross elevation of as much as 250 feet. 2 km trail is easier. Shelter in middle of 10 km trail. Wildlife includes hare, grouse, small animals. Downhill facilities. Restaurant, dining room,

A party of skiers turns into a line of silhouettes in the soft light of a winter afternoon.

waxing room, ski patrol, ski school, rentals. Snowshoeing in area. Accommodation at St-Félicien or in private homes in the area. Map posted at chalet. Local and regional competitions. For information write Tobo-Ski, RR 6, St-Félicien, Que.

Peribonka Ski Club
Location: North of Lac Saint-Jean. From Péribonka on Route 169 north 13 km (8 mi.).
Length: Loop trail of about 10 km. Travel time approximately 45 min.

Mostly wooded hilly terrain with some difficult slopes. Suitable for intermediate skiers. Beautiful countryside, abundant wildlife.

Open weekends. Groomed trails. Rentals, repairs. One relay station. Night skiing, picnic in the forest once a month. Accommodation in Péribonka. Map is posted at the chalet. Special event in the area includes 50 km crossing of Lac Saint-Jean, organized by the Club de Roberval, in mid-march. For information write Club de Péribonka, Péribonka, Que.

Centre Plein Air C.E.R.F.
Location: North of Lac Saint-Jean. Near Saint-Monique on Route 169.
Length: Loop trails of 6 km in total. Travel time about 2 hr.

One short trail of 1.5 km and a longer one

of 4.5 km. Both trails make one loop and are located on mostly wooded, flat terrain with one sharp downhill slope and 500 m on open land. Beautiful countryside. Suitable for beginners. Trails are groomed. Snowshoeing. Patrol service. Service station, restaurant. Centre plans expansion of its food and lodging facilities. For information write Centre Plein-Air, Base C.E.R.F. (Centre écologique de récréation en forêt), Ste-Monique, Lac Saint-Jean, Que. G0W 2T0.

Club Passe-Partout
Location: South of Lac Saint-Jean. From Roberval west 5 km (3.5 mi.) on Rang 2.
Length: Loop trails of 27 km in total.

Trails range from 1 to 10 km. They are mostly on wooded terrain. Some slopes up to 100 m. Open everyday from noon, weekends from 9 A.M. Groomed and marked trails. Rentals. Snack bar. Snowshoeing. Skating. Accommodation in Roberval. Special event "Le Lac Saint-Jean 50 km." Crossing of the lake from Péribonka to Roberval, organized by the club for the first or second Saturday of March. For information write Club Passe-Partout, 769 Simard, Roberval, Que.

Club Les Sakis
Location: Outskirts of Tadoussac.
Length: 13 km in two loops of 6.5 km each. Travel time about 2 hr.

Trails through mountainous wooded and open country at mouth of spectacular Saguenay R. Marked and groomed. Wildlife frequently seen on trails. Site of annual rally followed by celebrations. Restaurant and three hotels with 2 km of trails. For maps write: Club Les Sakis, CP 202, Tadoussac, Saguenay, P.Q. G0T 2A0.

Le Grand Walker
Location: From Port-Cartier on Route 138. Turn north on road to Lac Walker Provincial Park, for about 10 km (6 mi.)
Length: Eleven loop trails totalling 66 km.

There are 5 trails for beginners ranging from 1.5 to 2.5 km, 3 for intermediate skiers ranging from 4.1 to 9.5 km, and 3 expert trails of 10 to 13 km. Most of the trails are on mountainous terrain with a beautiful view of Port-Cartier from the top. Groomed trails, one relay station, patrol. Reception centre. Instruction, night skiing. Accommodation in Port-Cartier. You can phone the Service de l'Aide aux Migrants (418) 766-3094. Free maps available from Claude d'Auteuil, C.P.

1314, Port-Cartier or from Harold Tremblay, C.P. 1866, Port-Cartier, Que.

The club is very active and organizes many special events during the year. This club draws its name from the title once given to the superintendents of lumberjack gangs. These hardy men, wearing cross-country skis or snowshoes have travelled, it is said, the entire forest region of Québec seeking new areas for their men to cut.

Club "Rapido"
Location: From Sept-Iles, north 8 km (5 mi.) on Hwy. 138, then on Lac Rapide Rd. to parking lot.
Length: 32 km.

"Rapido" Cross-Country Ski Club was founded in 1974 and has developed a series of trails around the Lac des Rapides area. Trails are marked and groomed. Mostly in forests with some open lands. Five warming huts. Accommodation in Sept-Iles, on the North shore of the St. Lawrence River, the largest among 70 north shore ports between the mouth of the Saguenay River and the Strait of Belle-Isle. For lodging contact the Centre d'information Touristique, 546 Dequen Ave., Sept-Iles, Que.

Centre de Plein Air Lasallien
Location: North of Québec, on road to Lac Beauport.
Length: 11 km total.

The Centre has developed four trails of 1, 2, 3 and 5 km. The last one is suitable for experts only because of a steep downhill slope on the return trip. Terrain is mostly wooded and mountainous. Trails pass through very beautiful countryside. Open seven days a week. Rentals of cross-country and snowshoeing equipment. Instruction and guide services can be arranged. Accommodation for groups by reservation. Topographic map available. For information write Centre de Plein Air Lasallien, 78 Chemin du Brûlé, Lac Beauport, Que. G0A 2C0.

Centre Sportif Bean Lake
Location: Near Schefferville on Labrador border. From town follow mine road for 6 km. (4 mi.).
Length: Four loops totalling about 20 km.

This ski centre, including downhill runs, is located just outside the remote mining town of Schefferville, in the rugged, forested mountain country of eastern Quebec. Three of the trails are rated for advanced skiers while the fourth, of 4.5 km, is considered suitable for more relaxed outings. There are unlimited touring possibilities for skiers equipped for the cold and for navigation in the vast wilderness.

The four trails are marked and lead to excellent viewpoints over the town and endless forest of black spruce. Skiers may spot the occasional hare, squirrel, fox or grouse. Chalet used by downhill and cross-country skiers has rentals, instruction, food, bar, waxing area and snowshoes. Race of 6 km organized by sports club at Easter. Topographic map at 1:50,000 scale is Knob Lake.

Club Norfond

Location: Baie Comeau on North Shore. From town follow Route Forestière QNS for about 1.5 km almost to Base Plein-Air Mont-TiBasse.

Length: 15 trails totalling 72 km.

This large trail network has been developed by a highly active club of about 2,000 members. Trails have been cut and marked for all levels of skiers. About 70 per cent of the trails pass through forested areas with almost half of that mountainous. The rest of the trails are along lake shores. The nearby sport centre TiBasse has instruction, rentals, food and shelter. There is night skiing and snowshoeing. Downhill skiing at TiBasse. Extensive ski activities including night ski trips and festivities at Christmas and in spring and the Québec games during the winter.

Clairval - Club de Fond Saguenay

Location: From Chicoutimi south 8 km (5 mi.) on Route 175, then follow Boulevard Talbot to Clairval.

Length: 35 km in 5 trails.

This Saguenay area ski resort has mostly intermediate and expert trails through hilly coniferous forests, with one easy trail in the open. Trails of 5 to 10 km long. Site of four regional races each year. Map at area. Hotel at ski centre or lodging in area.

Centre de Ski Stoneham

Location: Stoneham, Rang du Hibou, on Hwy. 175, 40 km (25 mi.) northwest of Québec.

Length: 7 km.

First trail goes east for 4 km towards the Mont Hibou and can be continued to Lac Delage and St. Adolphe. Second trail makes a loop of 3 km. Both trails are suitable for intermediate skiers and traverse mostly wooded and mountainous terrain. Downhill

facilities. Restaurants, bar, rentals, baby-sitting. Accommodation in Stoneham. For information write Yves Bussière, Manager, 825 Ave. du Hibou, Stoneham, Que.

Centre de Ski de Fond de Duchesnay

Location: At Duchesnay Forestry Station on western shores of Lac St-Joseph, 42 km (25 mi.) northwest of Québec.

Length: 12 trails totalling 121 km.

This forest research and public nature intepretation centre is located in the hardwood-forested foothills of the Laurentides. It is close to the major population centre of Québec and provides parking for 1,500 cars, cafeteria for large numbers of skiers and a major marked and groomed trail system. Skiers will find most facilities including rentals, repairs, picnic areas, waxing huts, heated shelters, maps, guides and snowshoeing on a 7 km trail. Ski season normally runs from Christmas to early April. Lodging in small hotels and motels in Ste-Catherine and St-Raymond nearby or in Québec. Snow conditions by phone (418) 875-2711. For information write: Station forestière Duchesnay, Duchesnay (Portneuf), Que.

South Shore - Gaspé

Levis-Lauzon Ski Club

Location: In Levis, on Hwy. 173, off Autoroute 20.

Length: 20 km in total.

First trail is a loop starting Rue des Buissons in Levis. It is an easy trail mostly on wooded terrain. Second trail "La Martinière" begins Centre Monseigneur Guay in Lauzon. Suitable for intermediate skiers, it follows the St. Lawrence river, on wooded terrain. Magnificent views of the river at certain points of the route. Loops back to Lauzon. Accommodation in town of Levis. Club organizes also excursions outside Levis.

Centre de Plein Air Montmagny

Location: Notre-Dame-du-Rosaire, 14.5 km (9 mi.) east of Montmagny.

Length: 55 km.

The Sentier de Ski de Fond L'Inconnu of Centre de Plein Air de Montmagny Inc. is a network of 11 trails ranging from 2 to 8.5 km. It takes an average of 3 hr. to make a circuit of the perimeter trails. Trails start from chalet near 400-car parking lot and head past Lac Merisier or toward R. des Perdrix. Trails marked, groomed and patrolled by

Cross-country skiers and snowshoers meet at the starting point of separate trails in the Parc des Laurentides north of Québec city.

Ski-Secours. Wooded area of streams and rivers, few steep descents. Three heated warming huts along perimeter trails. Skiers bring own food and drink to chalet. Though centre closes about 4:30 P.M., some remain for night skiing. Restaurants and lodging in Montmagny. This the most extensive trail network in the area. For more information write: Ministry of Lands and Forests, Information Office, 200, Chemin Ste-Foy, Québec G1A 1P4.

Base Mont Orignal
Location: In Appalachian area south of Québec City. From town of Lac Etchemin north 5 km (3 mi.) on Route 277, then southwest on Route du Mont Orignal.
Length: Eight trails totalling about 90 km.

This is both a downhill and cross-country ski centre with a very extensive trail network. Starting point is at base lodge at the foot of the mountains and trails traverse the valley area and mount the hills through small passes. Trails for all levels of skier range in length from 3 to 28 km. Marked and groomed. Excellent views from the hill, overlooking Etchemin R. and the town. Base lodge has food, bar, waxing room, recreation room, instruction, rentals, sales, ski patrol office. Registration is required and patrol may inspect ski equipment to ensure it is suitable for the trip planned. Extensive lodging in area. Maps at area.

Frampton Trails
Location: South of Québec City in village of Frampton.
Length: Almost 200 km.

This huge network of 17 trails is located in and around the village and in the surrounding countryside. There are three departure centres for the ski trails: Club Chasse et Pêche Ste-Marie, Club de Golf Dorchester and Station Multiair Inc. About half the trails are maintained. Most of the skiing is in forested and hilly country in the Appalachian area east of the Chaudière R. There are woods of maple, yellow birch, elm, spruce and pine. From Mont Frampton and Mont O'Neil (2,050 ft.) skiers have magnificent perspectives over the region.

There are many activities at the area including races and tours and such relaxed trips as tours across the melting spring snows to sample sugar from the maple bushes or pull taffy. Numerous services including rentals, instruction, night skiing, snowshoeing, toboggan slides, sleigh rides, skating. There are lodging, food, bars, babysitting, picnic areas, shelters and guides.

The major centre is Station Multiair, a year-round resort which provides food and accommodation, particularly for groups, such as students. It features ecology study trails, visits to rock grottoes formed by erosion and an area of massive boulders. For maps and information contact Chambre de Commerce de Frampton, Frampton, Cté. Beauce Nord, Que. or Station Multiair Inc. Frampton, Beauce Nord, Que.

Sentier du Grand Portage
Location: From Rivière-du-Loup, follow route 185 to St-Modeste. From Cabano, follow Route 232 to Fort Ingall.
Length: About 60 km.

The Portage du Temiscouata is a major hiking and ski trail in the south shore region of Québec. A ski tour of the entire trail may be done in about two days or you can break the trip where the trail crosses a road. There are six log cabins, one every 10 km along the route with stove, toilets and room for six to eight skiers with sleeping bags. The trail passes through wooded terrain, open fields, some mountainous areas and across lakes. Maps can be obtained from: Le Sentier du Grand Portage, 4, Avenue de Gaspé, Riviére-du-Loup, Que.

The portage was first an Indian trail, then became a military and postal road for the French. Later it was the scene of British army operations. Halfway down the trail you will find the downhill ski resort of Mont Citadelle, with a cafeteria and ski shop. For information about lodging, write La Corporation du Tourisme de Rivière-du-Loup, 116, St-André, Rivière-du-Loup, Que.

Mont Saint-Mathieu
Location: Take Route 132 from Trois-Pistoles. Centre is 19 km (12 mi.) east of Trois-Pistoles.
Length: Three trails totalling 22 km.

Trails of about 5, 8 and 9 km. Average difficulty. They go through wooded, mountainous terrain, following a lake, in a very beautiful countryside. Marked and groomed trails, rentals. Snowshoeing, downhill facilities. Accommodation in Trois-Pistoles. Annual race for Regional Games. For information write Centre de Ski Mont Saint-Mathieu, Jean Claude Pelletier, Trois-Pistoles, Que.

Le Castor Trail - Forillon
Location: In Forillon National Park. From Gaspé east 42 km (26 mi.) on Route 132.
Length: Loop trail of 7 km. Travel time about 2 hr.

This is an easy trail, suitable for family outings. It allows easy exploration of the wooded lower levels of the park in the Cap-des-Rosiers area. An old sugar cabin serves as a shelter. There are good opportunities to see Virginia Whitetail deer. Trail marked and groomed. Map at park. Topographic map for area is Gaspé Comté de Gaspé-Est, 22 A/16. Lodging in hotels in nearby Cap-des-Rosiers or Cap-aux-Os.

Les Lacs Trail - Forillon
Location: In Parc National Forillon. From Gaspé east 29 km (18 mi.) on Route 132.
Length: 23 km loop with average travel time of 5 hr.

This is an expert trail leading to some of the highest mountains in this rugged park. Skiers will climb 1,500 ft., passing four small lakes along the way, and from the highlands have excellent views over the Baie de Gaspé. Trail marked and groomed. Two shelters. Self registration system. Map available free or skiers may want to obtain topographic map: Gaspé Comté de Gaspé-Est, 22 A/16. Lodging nearby in Cap-aux-Os or Cap-des-Rosiers.

Val d' Irène
Location: At edge of the village of Ste-Irène in the Matapedia region of the Gaspé.
Length: Three trails totalling 16 km.

The ski region claims ''the best snow conditions in Québec'' and boasts of opening in October and continuing until mid-May with snow still on the ground. Hilly area along the river valleys with excellent views over the forest regions. Near a downhill ski resort there is a small but well laid out network of cross-country trails around rivers and lakes with one trail to the top of the ski hill. Map at chalet. Lodging in hotels, motels or nearby farms. For information write: Val D'Irène, Ste-Irène, Cté. Matapedia, Que.

Centre de Plein Air St-Edgar
Location: From New Richmond north 15 km (9 mi.) on Chemin St-Edgar.
Length: 15 km. Travel time approximately 5 hr.

Four trails ranging from 2.4 to 5.2 km, suitable for all levels of ability. Mostly wooded and mountainous terrain. Groomed trails. Waxing hut. Heated shelters. Instruction and rentals available. Ski patrol. Chalet with cafeteria. Snowshoeing. Downhill facilities. Tobogganing. Parking for campers and trailers. Accommodation in New Richmond. Map available. For information write Centre de Plein Air St-Edgar, B.P. 218, New Richmond, Bonaventure, Que.

New Brunswick

An old-fashioned sleigh ride is one of the diversions a skier can find at New Brunswick's Mactaquac Provincial Park, near Fredericton.

Lying in the shadow of Québec's Gaspé region New Brunswickers share not only the two languages but an enthusiasm for skiing with the neighboring province. Though much of the activity has been centred around Fredericton, the capital, cross-country clubs are springing up around New Brunswick.

While new trails are being cut, some of them near downhill ski areas and others in forest and open lands across the province, many skiers have used existing paths to ski. For example there is 90 km of abandoned rail line running down the St. John R. from Fredericton to St. John and there is a 50 km hiking route, The Dobson Trail, from Moncton to Fundy National Park. Part of this trail is skiable.

There are numerous ski trails now in use in the national and provincial parks and the parks are often open to such related activities as winter camping. In Mactaquac Provincial Park, just west of Fredericton, skiers can also try skating, sleigh rides and Saturday night potluck suppers. Those who can't wait for dinner will find stacked firewood in the kitchen shelters. In St. John there is skiing in and around the city while at Moncton an old reservoir promises to be the site of 8 km of ski trails when developed.

This 28,345 square mile province has many attributes for cross-country skiing. The northern part lies on the plateau of the Acadian Highlands, an area of low, rounded hills (the highest is 2,690 ft.) and rolling uplands. In the south and east the land dips to the sea level and in Fundy National Park the coast is rugged and beautiful. Within the park there are many lakes and rivers that have cut deep channels through the forested terrain as they flow to the sea. As in most of the Maritime provinces the population (675,000) tends to gather near the water, either along the coasts or in the fertile St. John valley. Upstream in this valley is some of the finest potato growing land in the country.

Due to the influence of the Atlantic the southern part of New Brunswick tends to get milder weather with frequent fog and rain but south of Fredericton a snowbelt begins. The capital tends to hold its snow well and often has temperatures well below freezing. Further north the climate is continental, with extreme heat in summer and cold in winter and temperatures of minus 40 are not uncommon in midwinter. This kind of climate makes for snow accumulations in the 320 cm (125 in.) range and a ski season of December through March and into April in many years. Combined with a forested interior region this makes for excellent wilderness touring.

The most active booster of skiing in the province is probably the Wostawea Cross-country Ski Club, based in Fredericton. It has gone to considerable lengths to publicize the sport and has encouraged the training of instructors to continue the proselytism in other population centres. According to Toby Graham, a University of New Brunswick history professor whose avocation is the development of cross-country skiing in the province, there is tremendous potential in the many new clubs that have sprung up over the past three years.

Wostawea, a Micmac Indian word meaning snowy or snow-covered, has been central in the recent founding of the Maritime Marathon, a two-day, 80 km event held in mid-February. By 1976 the marathon was drawing skiers from the three adjacent Maritime provinces and from states across the border. The trip starts at the Crabbe Mountain downhill resort west of Fredericton and wends its way toward the city over a weekend. This is billed not as a race but as a long tour and skiers can tackle as many of the 8 to 15 km stages as they can master. Many skiers treat it as a warmup for the Canadian Ski Marathon a week later. At each section there are hot refreshments and the chance of a ride back to a central point for those who are ready to call it a day. Entrants have often participated in a Skiathon as part of the trip to raise money for the development of skiing in the province. They obtain pledges of so much money for every mile skied. For information write: Angus

Hamilton, RR 4, Fredericton, N.B.

There are several contacts for information about the development of skiing in the province. A major one is Toby Graham, 9 Spruce Terrace, Fredericton. Another is Brian Ferguson, 341 Canada St., Fredericton, a senior member of the provincial ski association.

In the northern part of the province you will find Rudi Richter, RR 1, Plaster Rock, E0J 1W0 one of the province's major ski trail designers. Worthy of note is a place called the Moncton Trail Shop Co-operative, 343A St. George St. This is a place to pick up first hand information and secondhand equipment for skiing in winter and backpacking or canoeing in the summer.

The provincial government has information about skiing in the parks and publishes a booklet on accommodation. Included in the booklet is information about Dial-A-Nite, a toll-free phone reservation service in the province. Contact: Tourism New Brunswick, Box 12345, Fredericton, E3B 2B4.

		Mean Temperature In Celsius (Fahrenheit)		Snowfall In Mean Centimetres (Inches)
		Min	Max	
Fredericton	Dec	-10.8 (12.5)	- 1.5 (29.3)	67.6 (26.6)
	Jan	-14.0 (6.8)	- 3.7 (25.3)	63.0 (24.8)
	Feb	-13.8 (7.1)	- 2.3 (17.9)	67.8 (26.7)
	Mar	- 7.4 (18.6)	2.5 (36.5)	43.9 (17.3)
Moncton	Dec	-10.2 (13.7)	- 0.6 (31.0)	53.1 (20.9)
	Jan	-13.6 (7.6)	- 2.6 (27.3)	62.0 (24.4)
	Feb	-13.6 (7.5)	- 1.9 (28.6)	58.2 (22.9)
	Mar	- 8.1 (17.5)	2.5 (36.5)	48.0 (18.9)
Saint John	Dec	- 7.3 (18.9)	0.7 (33.2)	40.4 (15.9)
	Jan	-11.0 (12.2)	- 2.1 (28.2)	60.2 (23.7)
	Feb	-10.3 (13.4)	- 1.1 (30.1)	53.3 (21.0)
	Mar	- 5.1 (22.3)	2.9 (37.3)	39.1 (15.4)
Campbellton	Dec	-11.4 (11.5)	- 3.7 (25.4)	67.6 (26.6)
	Jan	-15.6 (3.9)	- 6.1 (21.0)	82.3 (32.4)
	Feb	-15.4 (4.2)	- 4.8 (23.3)	78.7 (31.0)
	Mar	- 9.2 (15.4)	0.7 (33.3)	68.8 (27.1)

New Brunswick Trails

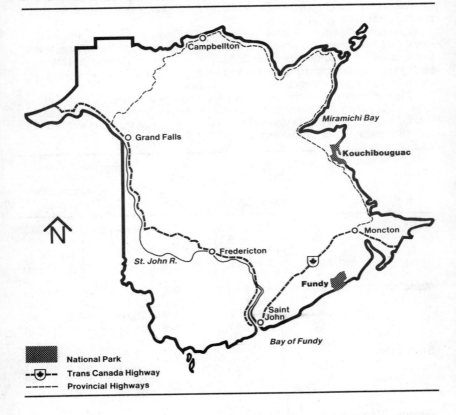

National Park
Trans Canada Highway
Provincial Highways

Fredericton Trails

The Fredericton area is a hotbed of cross-country skiing and is home for some of the more active promoters of skiing in New Brunswick. Skiers have about 10 km of trails at 350-acre Odell Park in the centre of the city. These are basically summer hiking and riding trails along the side of a hill and offer some challenging downhill runs at points. The area is about half wooded.

This park is used extensively not only by citizens trying out their equipment but by school groups taking up the sport. The University of New Brunswick (UNB) has provided equipment for skiers in the area. The main wildlife in the park is a pen of deer in a stream area in the park. Skiers use the bottom of a lodge for shelter, waxing and classes. Trail map at area. Skating. There is

also skiing on the rather flat UNB woodlot at the south end of the city and at the Woolastock nature park about 30 km (18 mi.) north of the city. The most extensive skiing area is at the Wostawea trails in Silverwood Park to the west. For more information on skiing in the area contact: Prof. Toby Graham, 9 Spruce Terrace, Fredericton, N.B.

Silverwood

Location: In Silverwood suburb of Fredericton. Access from Trans-Canada Highway (Hwy. 2) and Hanwell Rd.
Length: More than 40 km.

A large network of trails is located in the woods and fields along tributaries of the St. John R. Seven trails range in length from 500 m to 11 km in a series of connections fanning out from parking lots and the Silverwood Winter Park in a suburb of the same name. Trails range from easy skiing to hilly, scenic but very difficult loop near downhill resort. Trail near farm passes through heavy woods. Routes marked with colored tape. Country is traversed by Springhill Brook and Garden Creek and at times skiers pass by or over beaver ponds.

Mactaquac Provincial Park
Location: From Fredericton west 25 km (15 mi.) on Hwy. 105.
Length: Total of 45 km of trails including run to Crabbe Mountain.

This park on the north shore of the St. John R. is shared by skiers, snowshoers and snowmobilers. There are three loop ski trails ranging from 2.5 to 7.5 km on the property, with a 30 km trail leading to Crabbe Mountain near Millville to the northwest. This trail has been used for part of the Maritime Marathon. Skiing in the park is on flat and rolling country including a golf course and trails pass through mixed forests of spruce, balsam fir, poplar and maple. One trail leads to the Mactaquac Headpond where skiers can try their luck at ice fishing.

The ski area was the site of the 1973 Canadian Junior cross-country championships. Facilities include a comfortable lodge with bar, dining room, shower and changing rooms, waxing and maintenance area. Campground has shelters which can be used for winter camping. Electrical outlets, dry toilets, well water and kitchen shelters with stoves and firewood. Tobogganing and sleigh rides at park.

The Railway Line
Location: Old railway route from Saint John up the south side of the Saint John R. to Fredericton.
Length: About 100 km plus of skiing.

This abandoned rail line allows epic ski trips along the Saint John Valley between the two major cities of New Brunswick. It also links up with ski areas in the Fredericton area and the route can run another 30 km up to Crabbe Mountain. Much of the railway route is used by snowmobilers but it allows relatively easy skiing for considerable distances. The route passes from the Saint John area, which has relatively low snow accumulations, to the inland area where a snow belt begins.

Crabbe Mountain Area
Location: Western New Brunswick. Near Millville on Hwy. 104 and 610.

This is hilly country with a downhill resort featuring a 750 ft. vertical rise, one of the highest in the province. Skiing here is mainly on old logging roads. A 30 km trail runs southeast to connect with the cross-country ski resorts of the Fredericton area. At Crabbe, skiers share a clubhouse and cafeteria with downhill skiers.

Fundy National Park
Location: On south shore where Chignecto Bay meets Bay of Fundy. About 40 km (25 mi.) south of Moncton.
Length: Seven trails totalling more than 35 km.

Hiking trails in this rugged park have become favorite ski trails for residents of the east coast, especially those from nearby Moncton.

This 80-square-mile park along the shoreline has an extensive network of hiking trails and the less rugged ones are used by skiers. Trips range from as little as 1 km to jaunts of 10 km one way.
Trips include:
– *Tracy Lake Trail* from Bennett Lake Parking lot to the lake. An easy 4 km trip through spruce and fir forest.
– *Matthews Head Trail* from behind Dept. of Agriculture Research Station for just over a kilometre to an abandoned farm atop a cliff overlooking the bay. Excellent views.
– *East branch Trail* from Hwy 114 north of park headquarters for about 2.5 km to the East Branch River. This follows an old logging road and has one steep pitch near the end where it drops to an old log-driving dam.
– *Coppermine Trail*. The only loop trail for skiers is about 5 km long. It starts at the Point Wolfe parking lot and reaches the abandoned site of a copper mine. Good views of the Bay of Fundy.
– *Bennett Brook Trail* starts north of park headquarters on Hwy 114 and reaches 4 km to the meeting point of Bennett Brook and Point Wolfe R. Originally a logging road. Leads through second growth forest, across a hardwood ridge and down an old growth of spruce and fir.
– *Goose River Trail* follows the Marven Lake Trail for a few hundred metres before heading toward Goose R. About a 9 km trip each way, with two steep river valleys to cross. Along the way you pass the remains of a small settlement and sawmill.
– *Marven Lake Trail* starts from a fire end of main road at Point Wolfe Campground and follows a fire road for 11 km to several inte-

rior lakes. Trail has several steep pitches.

The park is in one of the first settled areas of the province, and just across the Alma R. from the village of Alma. The area was farmed and logged in the past but settlement of what is now the park was abandoned when farming the rough glacial deposit proved fruitless and the timber ran out.

Eight miles of coastline is fronted by cliffs of 30 to 200 ft., divided at intervals by streams flowing through deep valleys from the interior. The interior plateau, a remnant of an ancient mountain range, averages 1,000 ft. above sea level but is deeply cut by rock-walled valleys, exposing lava and ancient sediments. The rolling plateau is covered with a mixture of broad-leaved and evergreen trees with birch, red spruce and balsam fir along the cool coastline and maple, beech, birch, spruce and ash in the interior. Skiers may spot the white-tailed deer, snowshoe hare, racoons, porcupines, squirrels or even a bobcat if they are lucky. For information write: Superintendent, Fundy National Park, Alma, N.B.

The Dobson Trail
Location: From Riverview, just south of Moncton south to Fundy National Park.
Length: Skiing on about 30 km of hiking trail.

Many parts of this hiking trail are now used by Moncton area skiers. Travel over open fields and marshes, through hardwoods of the Acadian Forest region and across some rugged land approaching the coastline of Bay of Fundy. The trail crosses roads at eight points, allowing trips of from about 3 to 15 km between roads and skiers either make the return trip or organize transportation at the end of each leg. The 50 km hiking route, part of which is too rugged for skiing, was originally called The Fundy Hiking Trail but was renamed for Dr. J. Arthur Dobson and his father, who worked extensively on development of the route.

Riley Brook
Location: East of Grand Falls area. From Plaster Rock north on Hwy. 385 and past village store at Riley Brook 1.6 km (1 mi.) to sign "R. P. Richter."
Length: 5 km loop.

Rudi Richter, one of the major cross-country ski trail designers in New Brunswick, has laid out this circuit on rolling, wooded terrain behind his own home. The large house serves as dining room, waxing room and lodge for skiers who make reservations. Trail used by most skiers in the area including school groups from Plaster Rock. Rentals available. For information write Rudi Richter, RR 1, Plaster Rock, N.B. E0J 1W0.

Rockwood Park
Location: Sandy Point Rd. north of Saint John.

Cross-country skiers range through summer walking trails in this suburban city park of about 500 acres. Trails lead through mostly level, forested area with considerable evergreen tree cover. Park includes small Lily L. Skiers share chalet with downhill area at 150 ft. hill.

Sugarloaf Provincial Park
Location: Just west of Campbellton on Hwy. 11 in northern New Brunswick.
Length: Two loops totalling 10 km.

This popular downhill resort, with its 500 ft. hill, has seen cross-country skiing mushroom in popularity in recent years. Rudi Richter, a ski trail designer, laid out two interlocking 5 km loops on a forested plateau on the top of the mountain. A novice-intermediate trail ranges along the top of the slopes while an intermediate trail pushes in to circle Pritchard L. Trails have been cut and cleared to about 15 foot width. Ski shelter at parking lot where trails start. At bottom of mountain all skiers share chalet with cafeteria and film projection room. Rentals, some sales, lessons. Lighted skating rink.

Kouchibouguac National Park
Location: On east coast along Hwy. 11 between Moncton and Chatham. Access via Frigot Rd. to park office.
Length: 6 km loop.

This 93-square-mile park lies along Kouchibouguac Bay and includes beaches, dunes, lagoons and marshes along the shore and forests including 30 species of trees inland. The cross-country trail, which reaches to the St-Louis R., flowing into the bay, is marked with green ribbons and sign posts. It crosses generally level terrain. Snowshoeing and snowmobiling on separate trails. Park naturalists are available weekends for guided walks and organized groups can arrange special programs by calling 876-3973.

Nova Scotia

Winter lies deep and heavy in the sheltered interior regions of Nova Scotia. Cross-country skiers are just beginning to explore the snowy travel possibilities.

Skiing is rapidly developing in this Atlantic province as enthusiasts start organizing into clubs and begin the process of transforming frequently used cross-country routes into marked and groomed trails. Two of the focal points of trail development so far have been in the national parks. Cape Breton Highlands park, which includes areas reaching from the sea to the 1,700 foot level, has a large number of trails which are used for hiking in summer and skiing in winter. In addition there is downhill skiing at the park. Here the country is rugged and forested with small rivers and lakes in the interior.

The second is Kejimkujik National Park in the central part of the southern peninsula. There are several trails plus extensive wilderness skiing in this area of rolling, dome-shaped hills, lakes, rivers and innumerable streams.

In addition there is considerable skiing on the many logging roads that lace the interior of the province. Sometimes these are organized with the help of timber companies but the changing needs of these businesses often force revision of the trail systems to keep them away from cut-over areas and heavy traffic of lumbering machinery. One of the most active organizers in the province has been the Metro Cross-country Ski Club in Halifax. Information about trail development is being collected by Janet M. Eaton, 6269 Edinburgh St., Halifax. Another active group is the Canadian Youth Hostels Assn., Maritime Region, 5516 Spring Garden Rd., Box 3010 South, Halifax, N.S. B3J 3G6. The same address is shared by Sport Nova Scotia.

The province that is known for the Bluenose and fishing is 21,425 square miles of land almost totally surrounded by water. Most of the population of more than 800,000 live in harbor towns and cities along the often rugged coastline or in valleys such as the beautiful apple producing region of Annapolis.

In fact there is a series of valleys between the five detached pieces of uniform upland plateaus that make up this province. The countryside is dotted with many lakes and rivers and streams abound. Weather can be unstable according to the whims of Atlantic storms. These may dump many centimetres of snow on the province at one time or there may be rain and fog.

For general tourist information on Nova Scotia write: Department of Tourism, Box 130, Halifax, N.S.

		Mean Temperature In Celsius (Fahrenheit)		Snowfall In Mean Centimetres (Inches)
		Min	Max	
Halifax	Dec	- 3.9 (24.9)	2.8 (37.1)	40.4 (15.9)
	Jan	- 6.8 (19.7)	.5 (32.9)	53.1 (20.9)
	Feb	- 7.2 (19.1)	.6 (33.0)	56.6 (22.3)
	Mar	- 3.6 (25.6)	3.8 (38.8)	39.1 (15.4)
Sydney	Dec	- 4.8 (23.4)	1.8 (35.2)	57.7 (22.7)
	Jan	- 8.2 (17.2)	- 0.7 (30.8)	66.8 (26.3)
	Feb	- 9.7 (14.6)	- 1.3 (29.6)	62.7 (24.7)
	Mar	- 6.1 (21.1)	1.2 (34.2)	60.2 (23.7)
Truro	Dec	- 7.8 (18.0)	1.2 (34.2)	57.9 (22.8)
	Jan	-10.7 (12.8)	- 1.3 (29.7)	57.7 (22.7)
	Feb	-11.3 (11.7)	- 1.4 (29.4)	52.6 (20.7)
	Mar	- 7.0 (19.4)	2.3 (36.1)	42.2 (16.6)

Nova Scotia Trails

Mainland

Metro Halifax Trails
Locations: Point Pleasant, Dingle and Shubie Parks in Halifax and Dartmouth.
Length: Total of about 12 km of skiable trails in the three parks.

Dingle and Point Pleasant parks along the Northwest Arm in Halifax and Shubie in the Port Wallace region of Dartmouth are not reserved as skiing parks but give residents a chance to try out their equipment and get a bit of exercise when snow conditions are good. The best time to ski of course is when the snow is fresh and not tracked into a hard, uneven surface by pedestrians. Point

Pleasant Park has about 8 km of trails, the largest selection of the three. There are level runs along the water's edge and some hilly sections just a bit inland. Good views of the waterfront. Lights from nearby docks for container ships give some illumination allowing a bit of night skiing.

Up the Northwest Arm, across the water from the RCMP barracks, lies Dingle Park, in the suburb of Armdale. There are just under 2 km of trails along the shore and inland to Frog L. Suitable for beginners. In Dartmouth the Shubie Park, just off Waverley Rd., has about 3 km of trails, two of them running along the canal. In addition smaller trails across the park interior provide options, including climbs up a steep slope to the southeast. Dartmouth recreation department has talked of creating a more formal trail system. (Metro Halifax information courtesy of Janet M. Eaton, Trail Co-ordinator, Cross-country committee, 6269 Edinburgh St., Halifax, N.S., and editor of *Cross-country Ski Trails of the Halifax Area* by the Metro Cross-country Ski Club.)

Twin Oaks Ski Area

Location: 2.4 km (1.5 mi.) from Middleton on the North Mountain.

This is a downhill ski resort but cross-country skiers are discovering the mountain trails in the area and are making use of the facilities. Modern ski chalet with canteen, lounge, change area and rentals. Accommodation in motels and tourist homes available in Middleton.

Old Orchard Inn Trails

Location: Exit 11 on Hwy. 101, between Wolfville and Kentville.
Length: About 12 km of trails.

The Old Orchard Inn has four marked trails ranging from 1.6 km to 4 km. Terrain varies from flat to gentle hills, with some steep up and down sections on trail 4. Very scenic views at top of trails 2 and 3. Ski shop. Accommodation at the inn. Motel, chalets, lounge, dining room, dancing, swimming pool, sauna. Skating and snowmobiling. For information write Old Orchard Inn, Box 1090, Wolfville, N.S.

Wentworth Youth Hostel

Location: Turn left onto Valley Road 1.6 km (1 mi.) north of the downhill ski hill, off the Trans-Canada Highway, Route 104. Turn left again at the first intersection, about 1.6 km (1 mi.). The hostel is approximately 800 m (one-half mi.) further on the right.
Length: Total of 60 km of trails.

Trails pass through primarily wooded areas of coniferous and deciduous trees with some open meadows and fields. Many routes follow old logging roads. Generally the trails make a steep climb to the top of the hills above the hostel, then become mostly level with some undulations about 1.5 km from the start. However there are also several kilometres of relatively flat terrain.

Marked and groomed trails range in length from 6.5 km to 40 km. In addition, skiers will find many kilometres of unmarked trails. Deer, moose, rabbit, porcupine, as well as a variety of birds have been seen in the area.

Ski instruction. Downhill facilities nearby. Snowshoeing, tobogganing. Accommodation in Wentworth youth hostel.

The hostel was built over 100 years ago by John Livingstone, a merchant and member of the Nova Scotia Legislature. He opened a dry goods store in the section of the house now being used as a ski centre. Hand-hewn beams secured by wooden pegs and square iron nails support the walls and roof. The hostel has a kitchen, dining room, large common room, 5 dormitory bedrooms and 2 double bathrooms with showers. The large room at the back has a wood stove in the centre. Lodging and food by reservations. Motel and private guest houses also available nearby. Ski sales and rentals at the Wentworth Valley Outpost, at the hostel. This is a branch operation of the Trail Shop, 6260 Quinpool Rd., Halifax. Sketch maps available at the hostel. Topographic map of 1:50,000 scale, 11 E/2. Site of Nova Scotia Marathon Ski Tour each February and of a number of other cross-country ski races. Hostel plans to expand its trail system to 160 km over the next five years. For information and reservations write Canadian Youth Hostel Association, Chebucto Branch Office, 6260 Quinpool Road, Halifax, N.S. B3L 1A3. Telephone (902) 423-8736.

Kejimkujik National Park

Location: Southern Nova Scotia. At Maitland Bridge on Hwy. 8 it is 50 km (30 mi.) southeast of Annapolis Royal and 70 km (45 mi.), west of Bridgewater.
Length: 32 km.

Park is open year round and has marked seven trails ranging from just under 2 km to 13 km, mostly along park roads. The 145-square-mile park of rolling hills, lakes, rivers and innumerable streams has several much longer hiking trails and possibilities for extensive wilderness skiing. Park reviewing winter policy and trail system may be changed. Ice travel generally unsafe as ice is thin and especially treacherous in areas of springs. Presently marked routes suitable for beginners and intermediates. Winter camping in an open field and wooded area near Jacques Landing about 8 km inside park. Water and heated washrooms. Warden on duty daily on weekends. Overnight campers must obtain permit from warden, park office or self-registration stations in park.

Kejimkujik, a Micmac Indian word meaning "place that swells" is taken from the vocabulary of the original inhabitants of the

This area is popular with cross-country and downhill skiers and with families who come just to slide on the snow in the simplest manner.

area. Park has one large lake and several small ones, and a diversity of gently rolling, dome-shaped hills. Tree cover is extensive and includes oak, maple, beech and birch on hills and well-drained areas with spruce, larch and hemlock in wet regions and along shorelines. Large, treeless bogs border some lakes. There is considerable wildlife including deer, porcupine, raccoon, bobcat, varying hare, flying squirrel, otter and beaver. Topographic map: 21 A/6 Kejim-kujik Lake. Information on park from Super-intendent, Kejimkujik National Park, Box 36, Maitland Bridge, Annapolis County, N.S. B0T 1N0.

Dalhousie Mountain Trails
Location: Pictou County, northern main-land Nova Scotia. From Salt Springs west 10 km (6 mi.) on Route 4 then north on Glen Rd.
Length: Eight trails totalling 10 km.
Series of loop trails from the area of a small lake along Glen Rd. At times road may not be plowed and you will have to ski in to

main trail area. Trails along logging roads through hardwood stands and across farm fields. Trails developed by Scott Paper Co. and New Glasgow Recreation Commission. Maps from Scott or from the recreation commission, Box 7, New Glasgow, N.S. Topographic sheets at 1:50,000 scale are 11 E/10W and 11 E 11/E.

Bowater Mersey Trails
Location: On company lands near St. Mar-garet's Bay, Hwy. 103, between Halifax and Bridgwater.
The Bowater Mersey Paper Company Limited of Liverpool opened 2,000 acres of its forest area for cross-country skiing in 1976, and provided extensive skiing on log-ging roads during weekends when no heavy equipment was moving. It was established on The Old Annapolis Road, just northeast of Big Indian Lake, around logging camp 18. The Old Annapolis Road was con-structed, after the War of 1812, as a route for discharged soldiers to settle inland Nova Scotia. It was planned to connect Halifax

with the Annapolis Valley but was never completed. Note that as a result of logging operation the cross-country ski trails may be relocated from time to time. Contact the company for specific trail location, at Box 1150, Liverpool, N.S. B0T 1K0.

Cape Breton

Cape Breton Highlands National Park

Cape Breton Highlands National Park is located near the north end of Cape Breton Island. It covers more than 300 square miles of mountains, forests, barren lands, rivers and waterfalls and rises from the rocky sea coast to a peak of 1,747 feet in its mountainous interior. The Cabot Trail connects Chéticamp at the southwestern corner of the park to Pleasant Bay at the northwestern corner, traverses to Neil's Harbour on the east coast and circles down to Ingonish and Ingonish Beach on the southeastern corner of the park.

There are many entrances to the park at warden stations along the Cabot Trail. The administration building is located at Ingonish Beach. There is a government owned lodge, the Keltic Lodge and Motel, in Ingonish, Victoria County. There are extensive cross-country skiing possibilities in the park and officials have already begun to map out and mark routes for winter visitors.

No permit is required to use the ski trails but skiers are urged to notify the park wardens of their travel plans. The wardens can give information on wildlife, weather and snow conditions, as well as provide assistance in an emergency. In Chéticamp you can usually find a warden at the Fire Equipment Building near the compound entrance.

Skiers may also contact the park interpreter on weekdays for information on various features of the area by phoning the administration office in Ingonish Beach, (902) 285-2270 or in Chéticamp at 224-3403. Ski rentals are available at the Cape Breton Ski Centre.

This is also the site of the major downhill runs in the Maritimes. The ski centre, at the seashore along Route 105 near Ingonish, has a vertical drop of 1,000 feet, which puts it in the Québec category of challenging hills. The view from the top of this hill looks out over the sea, dotted with white ice pans and range after range of mountains stretching toward the interior. Skiing starts in early December and often lasts until the end of April. For more information about all skiing in the park, write Superintendent, Cape Breton Highlands National Park, Ingonish Beach, N.S. B0C 1L0.

Branch Pond Lake

Location: Cape Breton Highlands National Park. Trail starts on the Cabot Trail at the Warren Brook Warden Station, 1.6 km (1 mi.) north of village of Ingonish.
Length: About 12 km one way. Travel time approximately 5 hr return.

The trail proceeds on the Mary Ann Falls Road (the old Cabot Trail) for 5.5 km, then turns sharply west a further distance of 6.5 km to Branch Pond. The trail gradually climbs from sea level to about 1,100 feet at Branch Pond. It passes through stands of spruce, balsam fir and mixed hardwoods and crosses over some sections of open barren. Trail can be handled by novice skiers. A warden's cabin on the north side of the trail near Branch Pond is open to skiers. Excellent lookout aboout 3 km after turning west off the old Cabot Trail, over the village of Ingonish and Cape Smokey.

The trail is frequented by moose, deer, lynx, fox, snowshoe hare, spruce grouse and ruffed grouse and many other species of birds. Note that the weather can change markedly between the Cabot Trail and Branch Pond. The first section on the Old Cabot Trail is also a designated snowmobile trail. Trail used for snowshoeing. Accommodation 5 km (3 mi.) from beginning of trail: Deervale Cottages in Ingonish, Victoria County and Keltic Lodge Motel, Ingonish Beach, Victoria County. Map available at the park administration building or from park wardens.

Warren Lake Trail

Location: Cape Breton Highlands National Park. Trail starts on the Cabot Trail at the Warren Brook Warden Station, 1.6 km (1 mi.) north of village of Ingonish.
Length: About 6.5 km.

For about 1.5 km the trail follows the road to Warren Lake where it joins the summer hiking trail. It then circles Warren Lake for a distance of about 5 km and returns to the Warren Lake road at the picnic area. Along the lakeshore the trail follows a sandy beach, goes through a coniferous forest on the south side, through some stands of old hardwood at the west end of the lake and comes back on the north side through a mixed forest of hardwood and softwood. After a slight increase in elevation from the Cabot Trail to the lake, the trail is for the most part level. Warren Lake is the largest lake in the park.

Various species of wildlife may be observed along the trail such as moose, white tail deer, lynx, fox, beaver, snowshoe hare, ruffed grouse and spruce grouse and many other kinds of birds. Trail can be handled by novice skiers. Used for snowshoeing. Accommodation 5 km (3 mi.) south from beginning of trail: Deervale Cottages, Ingonish, Victoria County and Keltic Lodge Motel, Ingonish Beach, Victoria County. Map available at the park administration office or from park wardens.

Clyburn Valley
Location: Cape Breton Highlands National Park. Trail starts on the north side of the Clyburn Bridge, where the Clyburn Valley Road joins the Cabot Trail. 1.6 km (1 mi.) north of the village of Ingonish Beach.
Length: About 3 km. Travel time 1 hr.

The trail runs parallel to Clyburn Brook from about 1.5 km, then crosses the brook at the suspension bridge. It comes back along the south side of the brook and returns to the highway at the Clyburn Brook picnic area. The trail is generally on level terrain, through mostly open country on the north side of the brook and wooded terrain on the south side. Suitable for all levels of skiers. The trail provides excellent scenery as the Clyburn Valley is one of the most picturesque areas in the park. Beautiful coniferous and deciduous forests can be seen along the way. It is possible to observe such wildlife as moose, white tail deer, snowshoe hare, lynx, red fox, beaver, ruffed grouse and spruce grouse and many other species of birds. Trail used for snowshoeing. Accommodation 1.6 km (1 mi.) south of beginning of trail: Deervale Cottages, Ingonish, Victoria County, and Keltic Lodge Motel, Ingonish Beach, Victoria County. Map available at the park administration office or from park wardens.

Salmon Pool Trail
Location: Cape Breton Highlands National Park. Trail starts near the information bureau at the Chéticamp entrance, 3 km (2 mi.) north of Chéticamp.
Length: About 6.5 km. Travel time approximately 2 hr.

The trail actually begins at the east end of Chéticamp campground and follows the north side of the Chéticamp River. There is a warden's cabin about 3.5 km from the start of the trail. The skiers must return by the

Solitary skier pauses to enjoy the view.

same route. The trail is quite level with rugged mountain terrain on both sides and passes through beautiful stands of spruce, fir and mixed hardwoods. Trail is wide, in good condition and fairly easy, with very few steep sections.

Wildlife such as moose, white tail deer, lynx, red fox, snowshoe hare, red squirrel, spruce grouse and ruffed grouse and many other species of birds may be observed. Excellent area for snowshoeing. Accommodation in Chéticamp, Inverness County, Acadian Motel and Lauries Motel. Map available at the park administration office or from park wardens. For information write Cape Breton Highlands National Park, Ingonish Beach, N.S. B0C 1L0.

Green Cove to Old Cabot Trail
Location: Cape Breton Highlands National Park. Trail starts near the entrance to Green Cove Picnic Area on Cabot Trail, north of village of Ingonish.
Length: About 6.5 km.

Trail begins on Cabot Trail and goes to the Mary Ann Falls Road (the Old Cabot Trail). It starts practically at sea level alongside the coast and climbs up 400 feet before joining the Old Cabot Trail. Abundant wildlife in the area. Accommodation at Deervale Cottages, Ingonish, Victoria County and at Keltic Lodge Motel, Ingonish Beach, Victoria County. Use hiking map, available at the park administration office or from park wardens. For information write Cape Breton Highlands National Park, Ingonish Beach, N.S. B0C 1L0.

Lake of Islands Road and Trail

Location: Cape Breton Highlands National Park. Trail starts from the Mary Ann Falls Road (the Old Cabot Trail), 5.5 km (3.5 mi.) of Warren Brook Warden Station. Follow signs.

Length: About 13 km one way.

The first part of the trail follows the Lake of Islands road for about 8 km. At the end of the road you can take an offshoot trail to Branch Pond, less than 1 km away. An alternative is to pick up the main trail of about 5 km to Lake of Islands. The trail begins through thick conifers and emerges on dry barrens, 1,200 to 1,400 feet above sea level. Considerable wildlife in the area. Accommodation at Deervale Cottages, Ingonish, Victoria County, N.S. and at Keltic Lodge Motel, Ingonish Beach, Victoria County, N.S. Use hiking map, available at the park administration office or from park wardens. For information write Cape Breton Highlands National Park, Ingonish Beach, N.S. B0C 1L0.

Paquette Lake Road and Trail to Lobster Lake

Location: Cape Breton Highlands National Park. Route starts on the Cabot Trail at the top of South Mountain, 9 km (5.6 mi.) west of Neil's Harbour.

Length: 14 km including offshoot trails, one way.

The first part of the trail follows the Paquette Lake road to Paquette Lake for about 2.5 km. From the parking lot at Paquette Lake you pick up the main trail of about 9 km to Lobster Lake. Short trails branch off Lobster Lake Trail, going to Mica Hill Lake (1.2 km), Glasgow Lake (350 m), John Dee Lake (700 m) and Round Pound (500 m). Trail passes through dense forests of conifers and emerges on dry barrens. Abundant wildlife. Accommodation in Neil's Harbour. Use hiking map, available at the park administration office or from park wardens. For information write Cape Breton Highlands National Park, Ingonish Beach, N.S. B0C 1L0.

Middle Head Trail

Location: Cape Breton Highlands National Park. Trail starts at the eastern end of Keltic Lodge parking lot, Ingonish Beach.

Length: About 2 km one way.

The trail follows mainly the southern part of the peninsula. At 800 m from the start, it is possible to return to Keltic Lodge on a trail of 1.2 km along the north side of the peninsula. Or, you can continue to the tip of Middle Head. The trail passes through a series of four rounded, forested hills or knobs, and three grassy, mostly treeless valleys and slopes. It is a typical headland of the Cape Breton variety. Accommodation in Keltic Lodge, owned by the government of Nova Scotia, and nearby cottages and motels. Use hiking map, available at the park administration office or from park wardens. For information write Cape Breton Highlands National Park, Ingonish Beach, N.S. B0C 1L0.

Beulach Ban Falls Road and Trail

Locations: Cape Breton Highlands National Park. Route starts near the Big Intervale Warden Station, on the northern edge of the park, east of Pleasant Bay.

Length: 6 km, one way.

The first part of the trail follows the road to the Beulach Ban Falls for 2.4 km. It then continues into the valley for another 2.4 km through a nice hardwood forest. At this point the road becomes a footpath going up the side of the mountain for 1.2 km. For the most part, the trail goes along the North Aspy river. Highly scenic route with views of the falls and the river. Abundant wildlife. Accommodation at Pleasant Bay. Use hiking map, available at the park administration office or from park wardens. For information write Cape Breton Highlands National Park, Ingonish Beach, N.S. B0C 1L0.

Cape Breton Ski Club

Location: At Ben Eoin, overlooking the Bras d'Or Lakes, 27 km (17 mi.) from Sydney on Route 4.

This is a downhill ski resort but there are also many kilometres of maintained trails available for cross-country skiers. Chalet with canteen, sundeck and lounge. Ski shop. Ski bus service provided daily throughout the industrial Cape Breton area.

Prince Edward Island

In recent years cross-country skiing has developed into a popular winter pastime in Prince Edward Island. There is skiing across the province.

Some enthusiastic island skiers and the provincial government helped get cross-country skiing established in Canada's smallest province during the early 1970s. The government put cross-country rental equipment into the small downhill operation at Brookvale resort not far from Charlottetown. Residents were convinced this was an ideal sport and started buying equipment. Actually the rolling farm and forest lands of P.E.I. are far more suited to cross-country than downhill. The highest elevation is the 600-foot hill at Brookvale and cross-country skiers boast of navigating its slopes when conditions are not too icy for their lignostone-edged skis. The provincial government now has three areas for cross-country skiing—one at each end and one in the middle of the island, while the national park has skiing in the woods and dune land along the north shore.

In addition to the developed trails skiers make use of the many hiking trails, unplowed country roads and logging roads. Many of these are best found by contacting local skiers. Generally the 2,184 square mile island is low and rolling and many parts of it have good tree cover to shelter skiers from the wind. Actually the whole island is sheltered from the severe Atlantic storms by Nova Scotia and Newfoundland so the weather in P.E.I. tends to be more moderate than to the east. Temperatures hover around or below the freezing point during January and February and lift over that point in March. There are usually a few cold snaps. Snow can be a bit of a problem if a warming trend moves in, but generally the season is from Christmas until mid-March, and it may last until May. In the winter of 1974-75 there was 250 cm (about 8 ft.) of snow in the bush and skis sold briskly. Enough of the 119,000 residents had taken up the sport by 1976 that the first island ski marathon was held and it drew 138 skiers.

For information about skiing on the island and ski clinics which are held in various centres contact: Dave Mills, Recreation co-ordinator, Department of Tourism, Parks and Conservation, Box 2000, Charlottetown, P.E.I., C1A 7N8.

		Mean Temperature In Celsius (Fahrenheit)		Snowfall In Mean Centimetres (Inches)
		Min	Max	
Charlottetown	Dec	- 7.0 (19.4)	- 0.1 (31.8)	65.3 (25.7)
	Jan	-10.6 (12.9)	- 2.8 (27.0)	75.9 (29.9)
	Feb	-11.3 (11.6)	- 3.2 (26.3)	65.5 (25.8)
	Mar	- 6.7 (19.9)	0.4 (32.7)	51.8 (20.4)
Summerside	Dec	- 7.2 (19.0)	- 0.3 (31.4)	55.1 (21.7)
	Jan	-10.9 (12.4)	- 3.1 (26.5)	61.5 (24.2)
	Feb	-11.1 (12.0)	- 2.9 (26.8)	57.9 (22.8)
	Mar	- 6.6 (20.2)	0.7 (33.3)	49.3 (19.4)

Prince Edward Island Trails

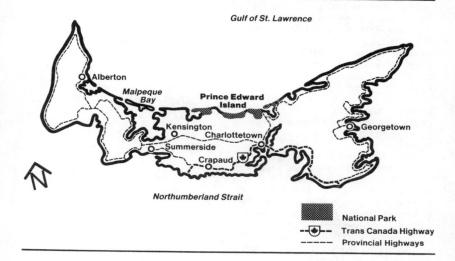

Gulf of St. Lawrence

Prince Edward Island

Alberton

Malpeque Bay

Kensington
Charlottetown
Summerside
Crapaud

Georgetown

Northumberland Strait

■■■ **National Park**
--◆-- **Trans Canada Highway**
----- **Provincial Highways**

Brookvale Ski Park

Location: Central P.E.I. From Crapaud
10 km (6 mi.) north on Hwy. 13.
Length: Three trails totalling 14 km.

This ski resort gave islanders their first real
taste of cross-country skiing when the provincial government put rental equipment into
the ski shop in the early 1970s. Many of
those who tried the sport here liked it well
enough to buy their own outfits and ski both
at Brookvale and elsewhere on the island.
The downhill section is based on a 600 ft.
hill but when the snow is not too packed
cross-country skiers sometimes try their luck
on the same slopes. The skiers also have
trails ranging from 2 to 8 km in length with a
route which climbs beside the ski slopes,
then travels through forest and along the
edge of fields in the area. Rental hut with ski
equipment and toboggans. Lodge with restaurant and club room. Base facilities open
weekends and some weekdays. Map available. For snow information phone Crapaud
109 or Charlottetown 892-2457.

Brudenell Resort

Location: Just south of Pooles Corner, 5
km (3 mi.) west of Georgetown on the east
side of the island.
Length: Three trails totalling 9 km.
This resort is located between the sea and

Hwy. 3 on an arm of land protruding into the
ocean. Three trails start from the rental shop
with a 1300 m circuit along the shore, a
route through bush and across a small inlet
(when it is frozen) and a 5 km trail through
fields and along roadways through the bush
to the west. Shop rents ski equipment and
toboggan and ski accessories. Washrooms
and rest area. Open Wednesday through
Sunday. Map available. For snow information phone Montague 838-2791.

P.E.I. National Park

Location: North shore about 25 km (15 mi.)
from Charlottetown. From Grand Tracadie
west 5.8 km (3.5 mi.) on Hwy. 6 and Gulf
Shore Rd. to Long Pond.
Length: Two loop trails totalling 3.5 km with
plans to extend that to 10 km by start of
1977.

In their search for new terrain, island
skiers adopted some of the summer hiking
trails of the national park and this has
encouraged park officials to plan a trail system for skiers. Now they use the 1.5 km
Bubbling Springs and the 2 km Farmland
trails. Terrain ranges from open fields to
coniferous and mixed woods, with some skiing at the edge of the freshwater Long Pond.
The area is flat and suitable for novices.
Expansion plans call for a loop system

which will allow trips of up to a day and may include benches and a firepit at a stopover area suitable for lunches. A 2 km snowshoe trail is located in the area. Interpretive group tours may be arranged by contacting the park at least two weeks in advance. Maps are available at Dalvay park office on Gulf Shore Rd. just east of the skiing area. For information phone 672-2211 or write: Superintendent, Prince Edward Island National Park, Box 487, Charlottetown, P.E.I.

Mill River Resort
Location: Western P.E.I. Between seashore and Hwy. 162, south 13 km (8 mi.) from Alberton.
Length: Three trails totalling about 8 km.

Trails start from the rental shop along Hwy. 162 and form loops across mostly open land to the shoreline. Trails range in length from 1400 m to about 5 km, with the long trail passing through and along the edge of some woodlands. Mostly flat skiing with some small hills. Ski rentals and sale of accessories weekends and some weekday afternoons. Map available. For snow information phone O'Leary 859-2448.

Woodland Heights Ltd.
Location: Central P.E.I. From Kensington east 8 km (5 mi.) on Hwy 101, then follow signs to resort.

This winter and summer resort has a small downhill operation plus ski trails which follow summer hiking and riding routes and roadways to campgrounds. Skiing on rolling farmland and woods of evergreens and hardwoods. Skating pond, tobogganing. Dining room, bar and dancing. Lodging in area. For information write Woodland Heights Ltd., Kensington P.O., P.E.I.

Newfoundland and Labrador

The wilderness interiors of Newfoundland and Labrador offer many thousands of kilometres of pathways for a skier to explore.

Cross-country skiing in Newfoundland is a relatively new sport generally, though some ski clubs have been around since the 1930s. In the 1970s strong cross-country centres developed at St. John's and Clarenville in the eastern part of the island and Stephenville, Corner Brook and Deer Lake in the west. In Labrador on the mainland skiing is well established at the twin iron ore mining towns of Wabush and Labrador City. The western side of the island, with its longer, more stable snow cover, enjoys a more consistent snow season than the east, where rains drifting in from the Atlantic can wash away the snow.

In Labrador there is plenty of snow from November through to May, but during the middle of winter the temperatures plunge into the very frigid levels and skiing tends to be done in brief trips from heated shelters and lodges. In March, when spring skiing is upon the island, the mainlanders are having the equivalent of an island winter climate and of course the spring skiing season in Labrador continues after islanders have stored their skis for the summer.

With a bit of speculation, subject to archeological proof, one might state that the first skiing in North America probably took place in Newfoundland about 1,000 years ago. In recent years it was established that Norse explorers had a small settlement at l'Anse-aux-Meadows on the northern tip of the island. By that period skiing would have already been established for at least 3,000 years in the Scandinavian countries and we might well think that the first ski tours in the Americas were made along the rugged northern shores as the newcomers to this wild land hunted for food and simply explored the new country.

If they did ski there it was on some of the most spectacularly beautiful land in eastern Canada. Along the western shoreline extend the Long Range Mountains, great black cliffs which rise sharply from the sea and are split by deep river valleys and lakes.

Halfway down the west coast is Gros Morne National Park, encompassing some of the most beautiful part of this wilderness and skiers sometimes follow summer hiking trails into the park interior. On the east coast, north of Clarenville, is Terra Nova National Park where a number of summer hiking trails are used by skiers.

Though there are an estimated 3,000 skiers in the province, there are few marked ski trails. The sport is still in an early stage of development and trail grooming on a permanent basis is still being organized. Many skiers simply follow commonly used routes such as the many logging roads or they explore the endless miles of bog and forest in the interior. Many Newfoundlanders take tackle with them, chop a hole in the ice and try their luck fishing while on a trip across one of the many lakes.

Apart from the Vikings, settlement began in Newfoundland in the 17th century as English and French both tried to claim the island for their respective monarchs. Since those days settlement has tended to concentrate around the many inlets and bays of this rugged piece of terrain where the people would never be far from their staple, the fishing grounds of cod and other species.

Most of the population of about 550,000 is on the mainland, an area of 43,-359 square miles. The rest of the 156,185 square mile province is in that massive triangle of rugged wilderness called Labrador. Until the Second World War there was little settlement in this area save a few coastal villages which depended on supply boats for most necessities. Since then there was the development of the major airport at Goose Bay, then the exploitation first of rich iron ore deposits near the Québec border, then the 7-million h.p. hydro-electric potential of Churchill Falls. To the north Labrador is still virtually uninhabited Precambrian Shield wilderness where boreal forests are pierced by mountain ranges, including the northerly Torngat Mountains with seven massive peaks. An unnamed summit of 5,422 feet is the highest in eastern Canada.

Skiers on both the island and mainland have organized races and marathons in recent years. For example, the Newfoundland Marathon has been run on a 50 km trail through forest and pond land west of Corner Brook, where the snow is consistent. This is usually held in early March. About a month later the Labrador Marathon is run from Fermont in Québec to Labrador City and about the same time a trip is scheduled from Ashuanipi River to Labrador City.

For information about the Newfoundland Marathon and about skiing in the province contact Dr. Jamie Graham, 31 Raymond Hts., Corner Brook, Nfld. In Labrador similar information is available from Alan Trevarthen, Box 405, Wabush, Labrador. General tourist information about the province, including a list of accommodations is produced by the Department of Tourism, Confederation Building, St. John's, Nfld.

		Mean Temperature In Celsius (Fahrenheit)		Snowfall In Mean Centimetres (Inches)	
		Min	Max		
St. John's	Dec	- 3.6 (25.5)	2.8 (37.1)	56.1	(22.1)
	Jan	- 6.6 (20.2)	0.2 (32.4)	82.8	(32.6)
	Feb	- 7.4 (18.7)	- 0.2 (31.7)	74.9	(29.5)
	Mar	- 4.9 (23.1)	1.3 (34.4)	69.9	(27.5)
Corner Brook	Dec	- 5.2 (22.7)	0.4 (32.7)	92.7	(36.5)
	Jan	- 8.6 (16.6)	- 1.9 (28.5)	103.1	(40.6)
	Feb	-10.1 (13.8)	- 2.3 (27.8)	78.7	(31.0)
	Mar	- 6.6 (20.1)	0.8 (33.5)	50.8	(20.0)
Gander	Dec	- 6.7 (20.0)	- 0.2 (31.6)	61.7	(24.3)
	Jan	- 9.8 (14.4)	- 2.4 (27.7)	67.3	(26.5)
	Feb	-10.4 (13.3)	- 2.2 (28.0)	73.7	(29.0)
	Mar	- 7.3 (18.8)	0.2 (32.3)	61.0	(24.0)
Wabush Lake	Dec	-22.4 (- 8.4)	-12.2 (10.0)	76.2	(30.0)
	Jan	-27.5 (-17.5)	-16.2 (2.8)	71.9	(28.3)
	Feb	-27.7 (-17.8)	-13.7 (7.3)	49.3	(19.4)
	Mar	-20.8 (- 5.5)	- 6.3 (20.6)	50.5	(19.9)

Torngat
Mountains

Churchill

Labrador City
Wabush

Goose Bay

Churchill R.

Quebec North
Shore & Labrador
Railroad

Strait of Belle Isle

L'Anse-aux-
Meadows

Long
Range
Mountains

Gros Morne

Deer
Lake

Corner Brook

Stephenville

Gander

Terra Nova

Clarenville *Trinity Bay*

Cabot Strait

St. Pierre and
Miquelon (Fr.)

St.
John's

National Park

Trans Canada Highway

Provincial Highways

Railway

Newfoundland and Labrador Trails

Gros Morne National Park

Location: North of Corner Brook along the west coast of the island. Access via Hwy. 430 northwest from Deer Lake.

Gros Morne, located at the southern end of the Great Northern Peninsula, takes in 700 square miles of the most rugged and beautiful scenery in eastern Canada. It incorporates some of the highest and most impressive peaks of the Long Range Mountains. Along the shoreline there are great cliffs falling to the sea and the occasional beach of sand dunes. The interior is deeply cut by lakes and rivers, surrounded by dense forests. Gros Morne peak at 2,644 ft. towers inland.

There are no designated ski trails but skiers are following some unplowed roads, hiking routes and waterways through the mountainous land. For example, they ski from Rocky Harbour to Eastern Arm Pond or from Hwy. 430 to Western Brook Pond. The latter is an eight-mile-long body of water in the shadow of precipitous cliffs. Park officials will advise skiers about suitable routes and state that they hope to develop ski trails in the future. For more information on trails in the area contact Peter Bowness, c/o G. A. Mercer Jr. High School, Box 458, Corner Brook, Nfld. A2H 6E6.

Terra Nova National Park

Location: Along Bonavista Bay on the east coast, just south of Glovertown.

Length: More than 30 km of trails suitable for skiing.

Since this 153-square-mile park is located on the Atlantic coast, skiing is subject to the vagaries of the weather. There are no formally marked ski trails but at least four hiking trails are suitable for skiing.

– *Dunphy's Pond Trail,* 4 km one way, is the best route for skiing as it leads into the interior. The trail starts about 800 m north of Cobblers Brook on Hwy. 1 and follows a fire access road uphill past small ponds and through burned areas. These allow panoramic views of the landscape and glimpses of Clode Sound behind and Dunphy's Pond ahead. The Pond, largest in the park, is dot-

ted with islands. The trip back is an enjoyable downhill run.

– *Louil Hills Trail.* This 4 km loop trail starts from a gravel pit opposite the Traytown access road on the Eastport Highway and passes through a spruce and fir forest.

– *Blue Hill Fire Road* is another 4 km trip each way. It starts on the opposite side of Hwy. 1 from the Blue Hill Tower Road and follows a fire access road through stands of fir and spruce typical of the park, across bogs, along a stand of birches and across two fast-flowing brooks. The road ends at the park boundary wooden bridge but the trip may be extended about another 2 km by following the boundary north to Square Pond, then taking another old road right to the highway. This route can be wet in spring.

– *Old Eastport Trail* is a 3.5 km partial loop which returns to the highway about 1.5 km from the starting point. Begin at the Alexander Bay Campground and follow old access road toward Eastport. Downhill to small causeway across Southwest Arm, then left through stands of softwoods and mixed hardwoods. Beautiful views of Broad Cove, Malady Head and Alexander Bay.

Park officials keep one section of the campground open for the winter, including washrooms. The park is within an hour's drive of Clarenville and members of the active ski club there use park trails.

Marble Mountain

Location: Just east of Corner Brook on Steady Brook Rd.

Length: About 20 km and under expansion.

An active ski club, dating back to the mid-1950s, operates out of Marble Mountain with both downhill runs and cross-country trips. One logging road leads for about 15 km into barren lands, giving very nice skiing. The ski club plans development of a 5 km trail atop the plateau of 1,800 ft. Marble Mountain in conjunction with the opening of a chairlift up the slopes in the winter of 1976-77. This trail will offer exceptional views over the Corner Brook area.

Corner Brook Area Trails

Skiers in this western coastal section of the province can count on an average of 400 cm (about 150 inches) of snow and in recent years have started exploring the cross-country possibilities.

South of Corner Brook the ski club has marked a 50 km trail for the Newfoundland Marathon with red ribbons, but this is not regularly groomed. The route leads through coniferous areas, many of them logged, over rolling country, past ponds and across several bogs. There are some moose yards in the area where skiers may find the great beasts passing the winter in the shelter of trees. The trail starts about 30 km (20 mi.) southwest of Corner Brook on the Trans-Canada Highway.

About 3 km (2 mi.) southwest of the city there are 5 and 10 km courses marked along old logging trails through rolling, wooded country. In addition, active skiers in the area are exploring and marking numerous other trails on logging roads and across bog areas. For information contact Dr. Jamie Graham, 31 Raymond Hts, Corner Brook, or Peter Bowness, c/o G. A. Mercer Jr. High School, Box 458, Corner Brook, Nfld. A2H 6E6.

Black Duck Trail

Location: From Stephenville Ski Club on outskirts of town to Black Duck siding on CNR line.

Length: About 15 km one way.

This is a popular run with skiers in the western Newfoundland area. Skiers can make the trip in and out in a day and many have lunch at Dhoon Lodge, a private hunting and fishing camp. Some skiers make arrangements to spend the night there. For information about accommodation contact Dhoon Lodge, Black Duck Siding, Nfld.

Maryann Bog

Location: From Deer Lake in western Newfoundland to Main Dam or north from Deer Lake about 5 km (3 mi.) on Hwy. 1 to access road.

This bog area is located between Hwy. 1 and Grand Lake and is traversed by the Maryann Brook. Skiers wait for the snow to settle on the bog, then make trips through the area. When the weather is good they enjoy good ice fishing for trout.

Goose Arm Region

Location: An area north of Corner Brook with access from Deer Lake or Cox's Cove.

Length: Trips possible ranging from 30 to 90 km.

The Goose Arm area, off the Bay of Islands, offers many kilometres of old logging roads for skiers to explore on day trips or overnight camping excursions. One possibility is to drive from Deer Lake to Nicholsville Bridge, then left 5 km (3 mi.) up the Goose Arm Rd., which is about as far as the snowplow goes. From there you can ski a good 30 km one way. This can be extended into a three-day winter camping trip by pushing on for a total of 90 km to Cox's Cove on Middle Arm. Trips can also be made out of Cox's Cove. Also in the Deer Lake area, skiers either travel logging roads from the Nicholsville area or drive Hwy. 430 to ski the Big Bonne Bay Pond area.

Labrador City-Wabush Trails

Location: Trails around the twin cities in western Labrador.

Length: About 40 km of trails.

This iron ore mining centre is a hotbed of skiing, with about 400 members in the Smokey Mountain Ski Club, basically a downhill organization and a smaller number in the Menihek Ski Club. The area boasts one of the greatest vertical drops of any downhill runs in the east, with a 980 ft. rise from the base.

Ski trails for cross-country fan out through the heavy bush in the area. There are about 25 km of trails in the Labrador City vicinity with about another 15 km just to the south at Wabush Lake. The snow season is long in this area. It starts in November and ends in May, but during mid-winter temperatures plunge into the low end of the thermometer and ski trips tend to be brief. The best skiing is in the period from March through May when the sun moves north again. The ski club has a heated ski cabin and waxing room.

The Territories

In the territories skiers are almost literally on top of the world. This region has produced some of Canada's finest racers.

Though population is sparse (about 60,000) in the vast sweep of Canada's northern territories, cross-country skiing is well-established and there is an international ski meet annually. This is the result of what started as a government program in 1964 to find an activity which would keep Indian and Eskimo children from boredom and juvenile delinquency. Rev. Jean Marie Mouchet began with students in the regional educational centre at Inuvik in the Mackenzie Delta. The first efforts proved highly successful and this developed into the now famous Territorial Experimental Ski Training (TEST) Program. Most notable in that group are the Firth twins, Sharon and Shirley, Canada's top female cross-country skiers. Ever since they broke into competition in the past decade they have dominated the races in this country and have been highly successful overseas.

Though that program has been the most noteworthy aspect of skiing in the north, there has been the lasting impact on the residents. They have found a new sport which is being introduced through many of the settlements which dot this land.

The Yukon and Northwest Territories cover 1.5 million miles of northern Canada and that is about one-third of the entire country. The land ranges from the often rugged regions of Baffin I. and some of the north-eastern sections through level tundra, rolling hills, boreal forests and finally great mountains in the west. The Yukon in particular is furrowed with huge peaks including 19,850 ft. Mount Logan, the highest point in the country. There are three major national parks in the north. Wood Buffalo, which crosses the border from Alberta, is the home of bison herds preserved from extinction. Nahanni is famous for the beautiful wild river

		Mean Temperature In Celsius (Fahrenheit)		Snowfall In Mean Centimetres (Inches)
		Min	Max	
Dawson	Dec	-28.9 (-20.0)	-21.8 (- 7.3)	27.9 (11.0)
	Jan	-32.3 (-26.1)	-24.9 (-12.9)	20.6 (8.1)
	Feb	-27.5 (-17.5)	-18.5 (- 1.3)	16.8 (6.6)
	Mar	-21.1 (- 6.0)	- 7.1 (19.2)	13.2 (5.2)
Whitehorse	Dec	-19.7 (- 3.4)	-11.9 (10.6)	20.8 (8.2)
	Jan	-23.1 (- 9.5)	-14.7 (5.6)	20.6 (8.1)
	Feb	-17.9 (- 0.2)	- 8.4 (16.9)	15.0 (5.9)
	Mar	-13.3 (8.1)	- 2.1 (28.2)	16.5 (16.5)
Yellowknife	Dec	-27.8 (-18.1)	-19.7 (- 3.4)	20.1 (7.9)
	Jan	-32.8 (-27.0)	-24.3 (-11.7)	14.7 (5.8)
	Feb	-30.4 (-22.8)	-20.9 (- 5.7)	13.2 (5.2)
	Mar	-24.3 (-11.7)	-12.8 (8.9)	13.0 (5.1)
Inuvik	Dec	-32.1 (-25.7)	-22.1 (- 7.7)	21.6 (9.8)
	Jan	-34.5 (-30.1)	-24.1 (-11.4)	21.6 (8.5)
	Feb	-35.0 (-31.0)	-23.9 (-11.0)	11.9 (4.7)
	Mar	-30.0 (-22.0)	-17.7 (0.2)	18.5 (7.3)
Fort Smith	Dec	-25.9 (-14.7)	-16.8 (18.1)	24.9 (9.8)
	Jan	-32.1 (-25.8)	-21.8 (- 7.2)	19.6 (7.7)
	Feb	-28.7 (-19.6)	-16.6 (2.2)	17.0 (6.7)
	Mar	-21.6 (- 6.8)	- 7.6 (18.4)	15.2 (6.0)

which it is to protect and Kluane encompasses some of the most impressive alpine country in Canada.

Weather is obviously a major consideration for skiers in these latitudes. Though skiing usually starts in October, by December the temperatures are bitter and the 1 ½-month period of almost total darkness has set in. Though many of the ski team members keep working out until temperatures are as low as minus 51 Celsius (minus 60 Fahrenheit), ski touring usually ceases before that time.

When the temperatures are not too low skiers cope with the darkness by lighting short trails near the settlements or by skiing with headlamps like miners or cave explorers wear. At times there is skiing by Northern Lights. Later in the season the lighting situation reverses itself and in the spring skiing that lasts into May, the midnight sun provides all the light a skier can handle.

Northern skiers are proud of their prowess and there are several ski meets every year. The major event is the Top of the World Ski Meet in Inuvik each Easter. This draws an international list of skiers to the most northerly ski club in North America, if not the world. For information write Peggy Curtis, Box 1651, Inuvik, N.W.T., X0E 0T0. General tourist information on the Northwest Territories is available from Travel Arctic, Yellowknife, N.W.T. X1A 2L9.

A party of northern residents follows a trail through the sub-Arctic forest.

A timber wolf howling into the frozen stillness of the Canadian north. The sound alone is an unforgettable experience.

Northwest Territories and Yukon Trails

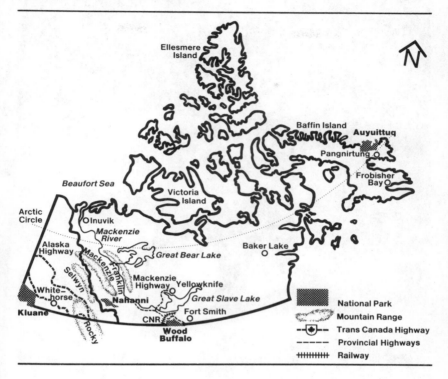

Legend:
- National Park
- Mountain Range
- Trans Canada Highway
- Provincial Highways
- Railway

Fort Smith Ski Club

Location: At Fort Smith on the Alberta Border. Trails located adjacent to eastern subdivision along Slave R. More trails in Wood Buffalo National Park.

Length: Loops totalling 5 km plus many kilometres of touring in the area.

Skiing here is along the 60th parallel at the southern edge of the territories. The active ski club has developed a network of loop trails on the south side of the Slave R. and these are used by recreational skiers and racers. A racer can make the circuit in 16-22 minutes. There are normally one or two scheduled races during the early spring and the main race is in March, drawing racers from Yellowknife, Fort Providence, Rae, Edze and Fort Smith.

In addition to the loop trails, skiers use various paths cut through the rolling, sub-Arctic forest, including old portage trails. The routes are well protected from severe winds by the forests so it is possible to ski even during the cold snaps. Skiers also head to nearby Wood Buffalo National Park for tours, often run by the park naturalist.

This is wilderness skiing in an area with little human settlement, so skiers can frequently pass tracks of such animals as wolf, fox, wolverine and lynx. It is not uncommon to spot rabbit, ptarmigan, ground squirrels and ravens. The ski club has an octangular log ski lodge in a clearing near the Alberta border. The main trail is groomed with a tracksetter and there is a certified ski instructor. A number of skiers make night trips with headlamps. Map available from ski club. Lodging in town.

A Territories skier speeds along a groomed and packed double trail.

Inuvik Ski Club
Location: Trails start in town of Inuvik.
Length: 8 km of racing trails plus endless possibilities for touring.

The title of Canada's most northerly ski area goes, at least until further notice, to the Inuvik Ski Club, north of the Arctic Circle on the MacKenzie Delta. In the mid-1960s skiing was introduced here and the famous Territorial Experimental Ski Program begun. It produced four members of the National Ski Team plus top Canadian junior racers. This is understandable since the ski season is generally six months long: mid-October to mid-May. The ski club has racing trails of 2, 3 and 5 km plus unlimited possibilities for touring on the tundra, river and lakes that dot the region. However skiers must exercise greater than normal caution since the area is remote and there is extreme cold during the winter. This is at the tree line so there is limited shelter. For six weeks during December and January there is virtually no sun. On the other hand there is spring skiing under the midnight sun in early May. Ski club has instruction and limited rentals from club cabin. This is the site of the Top of the World Ski Championships every Easter. Co-ordinator is Peggy Curtis, Box 1651, Inuvik, N.W.T.

Appendix

Wind Chill Factors

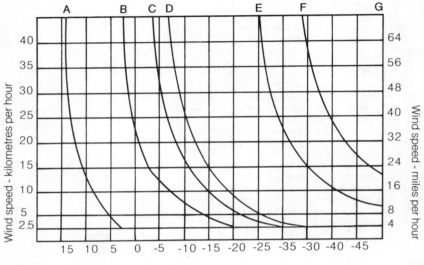

Air temperature - degrees Celsius

(A to B) Conditions considered comfortable when dressed for skiing.
(B to C) Conditions no longer pleasant for outdoor activities on overcast days.
(C to D) Conditions no longer pleasant for outdoor activities on sunny days.
(D to E) Freezing of exposed skin begins for most people depending on the degree of activity and the amount of sunshine.
(E to F) Exposed areas of the face freeze in less than 1 minute.
(F to G) Exposed flesh will freeze within half a minute for the average person.

Time Required to Ski a Given Distance at Different Speeds (hours and minutes)

		speed - miles per hour (kilometres per hour)							
		1.5 (2.4)	2.5 (4)	3.5 (5.6)	4.5 (7.2)	5.5 (8.8)	7.0 (11.2)	8.5 (13.6)	10 (16)
Distance	1 (1.6)	40	24	17	13	11	8	7	6
in miles	2 (3.2)	1.20	48	34	26	21	17	14	12
(kilometres)	3 (4.8)	2.00	1.12	52	40	32	25	21	18
	4 (6.4)	2.40	1.36	1.09	53	43	34	28	24
	5 (8)	3.20	2.00	1.27	1.06	54	44	35	30

Courtesy: Ben Buss

Speed of Travel in Different Activities

MPH	Snowshoeing	Hiking	Cross-Country Skiing	Running
10.00			Trained cross-country racer on a variety of trails and snow conditions.	Running hard.
8.50			Trained cross-country racer on a variety of trails and snow conditions.	Running hard.
7.00			Trained cross-country racer on a variety of trails and snow conditions.	Running.
5.50	Snowshoe jogging on packed or crusty snow by well-trained individual.		Pronounced kick and glide by touring skier on tracked trail. A racer working hard in unbroken snow.	Jogging.
4.50	Snowshoe jogging on packed or crusty snow by well-trained individual.	Stepping out vigorously on level, firm trail.	A touring skier showing gliding movements on tracked trail.	Light jogging.
3.50	Fast, well-trained individual travelling in deep snow.	Brisk walk on any trail.	Walking on skis with some gliding movements.	
2.50	An individual of average ability moving on hard trail or who has good technique in deep snow.	Slow walk.	Walking on skis in unbroken snow.	
1.50	Average or less ability in deep snow.	Ambling with young children.	Walking on skis with very young children.	

Courtesy: Ben Buss

Canadian Ski Association – Offices and Awards

One of the interesting things about cross-country skiing in Canada is the speed with which it has recently become so developed on a national basis. Clubs which had carried on for years with a hard core of devotees, often of Nordic extraction, suddenly started drawing members from the general public. New clubs have sprung up as skiers moved into areas where there was no organization, and many newcomers to the sport simply ski alone or with friends but are not affiliated with any organized body.

The nearest thing to an umbrella group for the sport is the cross-country section of the Canadian Ski Association. For many years this was a relatively small branch of the CSA and dealt mainly with competition. Now that the sport is gaining popular acceptance this branch is expanding and is taking an interest in the development of touring and events which attract a wide range of skiers.

The association is based in Ottawa but has representatives scattered across the country. In some areas there are permanent or semi-permanent offices, while in others CSA is represented by volunteers. A large number of ski clubs are affiliated with CSA.

The head office address is:

Canadian Ski Association
333 River Rd., Tower A
Ottawa, Ont. K1L 8B9

The latest list of division and zone offices is as follows:

Western Division Office
1606 West Broadway
Vancouver, B.C.

Alberta Division Office
Box 610
Calgary, Alberta

Saskatchewan Division Office
106 Wilson Cres.
Saskatoon, Sask.

Northern Ontario Zone
1353 Gemmell St.
Sudbury, Ont.

National Capital Zone
c/o Ottawa Ski Club
Old Chelsea, Que.

Southern Ontario Zone
2 Bloor St. W., 31st Floor
Toronto, Ont.

Local contacts where available can be obtained from the central or the regional offices.

Among its activities the CSA awards emblems and plaques for ordinary skiers who are active enough in the sport to ski certain distances each year or fit enough to pass certain time trials. Detailed information on how to register for the events is available from the central or regional offices. Following is a summary of the distances and times for the awards.

Trail Signs

Markings for cross-country trails can vary widely. Sometimes there is just a path cut through the bush and the skier follows it relying on map and compass if the route is long or complicated. On organized trails there is often a splash of paint or a piece of orange surveyor's tape tied around a tree every so often along the route. Some trail developers have taken time to put name signs on pathways and even attempted to mark trails for the degree of difficulty.

Under a recently introduced program a commercial ski equipment distributor, Fisher Marker Humanic Canada Ltd., is supplying the Canadian Ski Association with signs to indicate the difficulty of trails. The signs, based on an international code, are as follows:

green beginner

blue ◆ intermediate

red ▲ expert

Signs are free to organizations which provide free trails to the public and there is a small charge to those which have trail fees. The markers are available through the CSA, 333 River Rd., Tower A, Ottawa, Ont. K1L 8B9.

Touring Distances for a Ski Season

Adults (17 and over)	Bronze	Silver	Gold
Men	200 km	400 km	750 km
Women	150 km	300 km	500 km

Juniors			
Age 7-9	40 km	100 km	150 km
Age 10-13	60 km	150 km	250 km
Age 14-16	100 km	200 km	400 km

Time Trial Awards

Men 10 km	Bronze	Silver	Gold
Age 17-34	65 min.	56 min.	48 min.
Age 35-49	70 min.	62 min.	56 min.
Age 50 and over	100 min.	72 min.	64 min.

Women 5 km			
Age 17-34	40 min.	35 min.	27 min.
Age 35-49	45 min.	40 min.	35 min.
Age 50 and over	55 min.	50 min.	45 min.

Boys	Bronze	Silver	Gold
Age 7-9 (2.5 km)	30 min.	27 min.	25 min.
Age 10-13 (2.5 km)	23 min.	20 min.	17 min.
Age 14-16 (5 km)	34 min.	26 min.	23 min.

Girls			
Age 7-9 (2.5 km)	33 min.	30 min.	28 min.
Age 10-13 (2.5 km)	26 min.	22 min.	19:30 min.
Age 14-16 (5 km)	39 min.	33 min.	30 min.

Photograph Acknowledgments
Michael Keating   vi, 7, 11, 12, 13, 14,
15, 22, 23, 28, 31, 35, 38, 41, 49, 53,
97, 102, 103
Shelia Hirsch   33, 123, 128
Wilfried D. Schurig   56, 92, 204
British Columbia Government
Photograph   59, 62, 69, 72, 75
Simon Hoyle   77
Alberta Public Affairs   86
J. Omholt-Jensen   89, 203, 206, 207
Alberta Government Photo   x, 94
Manitoba Department of Tourism and
Recreation   97, 105, 195
David Aston   107
Parks and Recreation, City of
Thunder Bay   110
Svein Dhauge   111
Ontario Ministry of Industry and
Tourism   113, 117, 138, 144, 146
The Hamilton Spectator   126
Ontario Department of Lands and
Forests, photo by R. Johnson   133
Gouvernement du Québec
gracieuseté de la direction Générale
du Tourisme   153, 157, 165, 167,
171, 172, 175, 195
New Brunswick Department of
Tourism   177, 183, 187, 189, 191
Island Information Service   191